LONDON
bodies

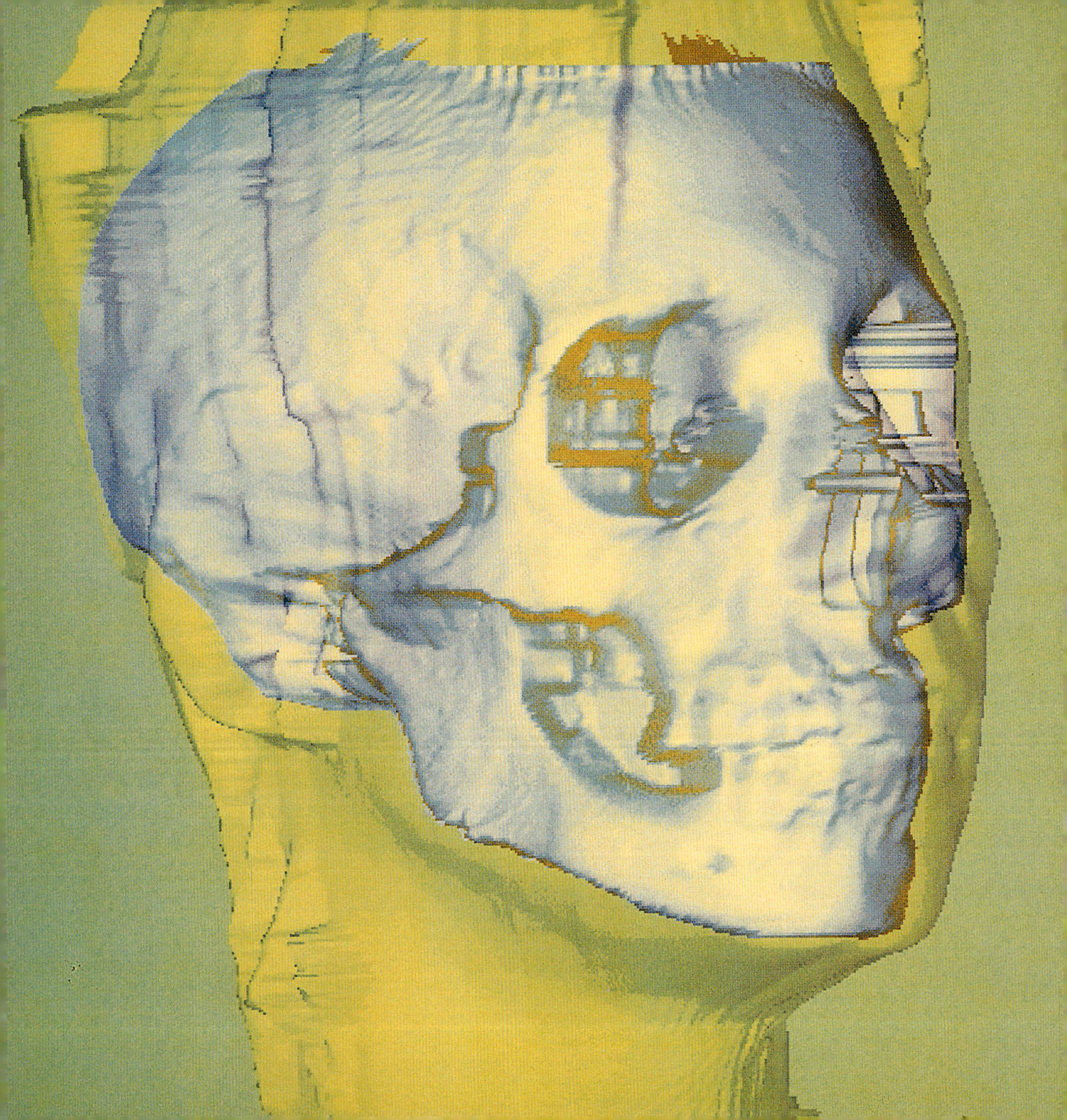

LONDON bodies

THE CHANGING SHAPE OF LONDONERS
FROM PREHISTORIC TIMES
TO THE PRESENT DAY

Compiled by Alex Werner
Introduction by Professor Roy Porter

MUSEUM OF LONDON

Cover: Xeroradiograph of a 17th-century bathrocranic skull. One of the great mysteries is the occurrence of skulls with a pronounced bump at the back of the head – a trait known as bathrocrany. One in ten 17th-century Londoners had it. Today the figure is one in a million. The reasons for the sudden appearance and disappearance of this skull shape are unknown. Perhaps these people were migrants to London from the same rural area, or perhaps there was some environmental cause.

Frontispiece: Computerised facial reconstruction of bathrocranic skull, showing the layers of muscle and skin.

First published in Great Britain in 1998 by the Museum of London, 150 London Wall, London EC2Y 5HN

British Library Cataloguing in Publication Data. A catalogue record for this book is available from the British Library

ISBN 0-904818-90-X

Project leader: Alex Werner; Editorial: Tony Dyson, John Schofield, Julie Targett, Jane Elstone, Nina Behrman and Mandi Gomez; Design: Kirsten Laqua; Photography: Torla Evans, John Chase, Richard Stroud and Jeff Hopson; Index: David Lee

Printed and bound in Belgium by Snoeck-Ducaju and Zoon

A complete catalogue of Museum of London publications is available on request.

This book is published to coincide with the exhibition of the same name at the Museum of London

CONTENTS

LIST OF ILLUSTRATION CREDITS

Archbishop of Canterbury and the Trustees of Lambeth Palace Library, p53, Fig. 3

The British Library: by permission of the British Library (Harl. 4866 f.88), p71, Fig. 6

The British Museum, Department of Prehistoric and Romano-British Antiquities, photograph by Stuart Needham; courtesy of the British Museum, p30, Fig. 8

Viscount De L'Isle, from his private collection, reproduced with his kind permission, p81, Fig. 5

City of Bayeux, Musée de la Tapisserie, Bayeux/Giraudon/Bridgeman Art Library, London, p56, Fig. 7

Lucas, Derek, p36, Fig. 2

City of London Record Office, p62, Fig. 2

Guildhall Library, p70, Fig. 2

Hatfield House, Hertfordshire/Bridgeman Art Library, London, p76, Fig. 5

London and Middlesex Archaeology Service, p17, Fig. 4

Mercers' Company: reproduced by courtesy of the Mercers' Company, p63, Fig. 3

The Morley Collection, Saltram Park (National Trust), photograph: The Photographic Survey, Witt Library, Courtauld Institute of Art, p58, Fig. 1

Museum of London Archaeology Service, Andy Chopping and Maggie Cox, pp16, Fig. 2; 19, Fig. 6; 20, Fig. 7; 30, Fig. 8; 31, Fig. 9; 35, Fig. 1; 37, Fig. 3; 48, Figs. 1, 2, 3; 49, Figs. 4, 5, 6; 54, Fig. 4; 66, Fig. 6; 67, Fig. 7

National Portrait Gallery, London, by courtesy of the National Portrait Gallery, pp75, Fig. 4; 81, Fig. 3, 6

The Royal Collection © Her Majesty the Queen, p58, Fig. 3

St Bartholomew's Hospital, Archives and Museum, pp86, Fig. 5; 90, Fig. 10; 97, Fig. 19

St Helen's Church, Bishopsgate, p71, Fig. 5

The Scottish National Portrait Gallery, p73, Fig. 1

Singh, Kikar for MoLAS, p64, Fig. 4

Surrey County Archaeological Unit, p26, Fig. 4

Tate Gallery, London, p80, Figs. 2

University College London, Department of Medical Physics and Bioengineering, pp2, 18, Figs. 5b, 5c

University College London, Galton papers Library, p101, Figs. 4a, 4b

Victoria and Albert Museum, London/Bridgeman Art Library, London, pp80, Fig. 1; 81, Fig. 7

The Board of Trustees of the National Museums and Galleries on Merseyside (Walker Art Gallery), p81, Fig 4

West Stow Anglo-Saxon Village Trust, St Edmundsbury Borough Council, p59, Fig. 5

Westminster Abbey, Malcolm Crowthers/Dean and Chapter of Westminster Abbey, pp70, Fig. 1; 71, Fig. 4

ACKNOWLEDGEMENTS

The authors would like to thank all those who gave freely of their time and information in the preparation of this book. They are particularly indebted to Professor Roy Porter for writing the introduction; to Benjamin Zephaniah for allowing us to reproduce his poem, 'The London Breed'; to Dr Stuart Needham of the British Museum; to Dr Robin Richards, Medical Physics and Bioengineering Department, University College London; to Dr Barry Knight (for producing the xeroradiographs) and Glynis Edwards of the English Heritage Ancient Monuments Laboratory; to Reg Davis, formerly of the Physics Department, Royal Marsden Hospital; to Annabel Gregory of Birkbeck College; and to Phyllis Jackson, Penelope Rogers, Andy Tyrell and Dr Heinrich Härbe.

We would also like to extend our thanks to all our colleagues in the Museum of London who have helped: to Simon Thurley and Kate Starling; to those in the Early Department, particularly Nikola Burdon, Francis Grew and Hedley Swain; to those in the Later Department, Edwina Ehrman, Rory O'Connell, Cathy Ross and Jill Spanner; in the Conservation Department, especially Jill Barnard, Rose Johnson, Renée Waltham, Johan Hermans, Barbara Heiberger and Robert Payton, who have conserved items reproduced in this book; to those who administer the object collection and the archaeological archive, Robert Howell, Alan Thompson, John Shepherd and Raoul Bull, who managed to locate and extract objects, some whilst the store was in the process of being moved; to the editorial team, Tony Dyson, John Schofield, Mandi Gomez, Julie Targett, Jane Elstone, Matthew Hodson and Nina Behrman; and finally to those in the Design and Exhibitions Department, to Torla Evans, John Chase and Richard Stroud in photography, to Kirsten Laqua, our designer, who has valiantly coped with last minute text and image changes but still managed to come up with a fabulous design, and to Moira Gemmill for her support and creative input.

DIRECTOR'S FOREWORD

Part of London's magic is that its history survives in brick and stone all around us. We see it every day in the medieval masonry of our oldest churches, the brick-built terraces of the eighteenth century and the tube stations of the 1930s. But the buildings and streets are only the stage set; those who acted out their lives in our city have long departed. What did our ancestors in London really look like? This book tries to repopulate the empty stage set of history and make it come alive.

Thanks to 25 years of research into London's archaeology and social history we now know, more than ever before, what past Londoners really looked like, how tall they were, what their health was like and for how long they lived. We understand better what diseases they suffered from and how these affected their bodies. We know more about their attitudes to their own bodies and how people changed themselves to fit contemporary fashions.

In the search for the appearance of our ancestors one crucial message comes through. Londoners of the past, given a healthy and prosperous lifestyle, were remarkably like us. Given the chance, Londoners have always had the potential to live long lives and grow to a good height. Yet although a greater proportion of Londoners today live in adequate housing and have a balanced diet, many others do not. Those who live in the poorest boroughs now, as in history, are on average shorter, less fit and die earlier than those who live in the wealthier parts.

This book, and the research that it encapsulates, also makes a contribution to people's lives today. Intensive research by the Museum of London into skeletal remains has begun to make a contribution to modern medicine. The 6500 skeletons in the Museum's stores hold important information about the spread and development of a number of diseases of the bone such as rheumatoid arthritis. This historical enquiry therefore provides us with a lesson not only in social science but also in medical science. Like all good history it is as much about the present as the past.

Dr Simon Thurley, Director

INTRODUCTION

by Professor Roy Porter

The distinguished historian G. M. Young once said that a historian should keep reading 'till you can hear people talking'. He was dead right. But he should have added that historians should also soak themselves in the sources so that they can actually see and hear the people they study.

In some ways that's a taller order, because far more verbal than visual evidence has come down to us from the past. More books, diaries, letters and other documents survive than drawings, illustrations, suits of clothes and other artefacts – and that becomes all the truer when you go back before the age of photography. Governments have systematically kept written files for official purposes, and individuals have used pen and paper to take stock of their lives. Vast diaries have come down from all sorts of folk from whom not a single artefact survives. Even very famous Londoners – for instance Robert Hooke, founder member of the Royal Society, the name behind 'Hooke's Law' and the architect of the Bethlem Royal Hospital building erected in Moorfields in the 1670s – seem to have left no portrait behind them.

In trying to envisage Londoners' bodies from earlier centuries, historians' tastes or prejudices have also to be taken into account. Scholars have been brought up to value the written word but have tended to be somewhat snooty about pictures. There's that notorious phrase, 'coffee-table book', used as a put-down against academics who illustrate their works heavily – and who, as a consequence, are judged by their peers as less 'serious'.

There's a further problem, moreover, when you try to discover what people of the past looked like. Those who have kept written accounts have often been doing so for their own personal benefit, for private purposes – most diarists are like that. In reading such writings, be they from the Middle Ages or the Victorian period, we are eavesdropping on impromptu records, gaining access to the intimate secrets of yesteryear.

Rarely, however, do we have such good fortune with the visual record. Far fewer ordinary people drew, painted or doodled for purely private purposes – certainly relatively few such artefacts survive. What we possess of the visual archive of the past is what artists rather than Joe Soap produced, and hence it is largely a record created for public presentation and consumption.

And however much artists have proclaimed that they are 'realists', what they have produced, far from being realistic, has tended to be the cultivated and studied creation of images and stereotypes with certain ends in mind. Sometimes – think of townscapes – these images have been promotional, attempts to present the great city or its inhabitants in a good light: triumphal, grand or just clean and healthy. Or they might be grotesques, satirical, or critical and reformist – think of all those Victorian images of the huddled poor, produced to move the hearts and minds of reformers and politicians and get them to create the city beautiful with a population that is moral, respectable and salubrious. When we survey the celebrated Hogarth images of Londoners going about their business – *Beer Street*, *Gin Lane* – what we see is not a documentary record of Londoners as they really were, but Georgian London as interpreted by one of the great moral agitators of the metropolitan stage. Or take the *Marriage à la mode* sequence. In the final print of that series, the suicide of Countess Squanderfield in her father's old-fashioned City house, the artist has obligingly opened a casement window, affording us a view down onto London Bridge, where the houses lean vertiginously. Hogarth's houses perhaps tell us less about London Bridge itself than about his views of modern marriage.

The fact that we see historical London through the eyes of artists with a mission, visionaries with designs on their audience, may at first sight be regarded as a difficulty: we are seeing the past through tinted spectacles. But it may be a privilege rather than a problem. For those promotional or reforming images enable us to peer into the minds of Londoners in the past, to grasp their own preferred ways of exhibiting themselves, showing off their own identities – as aldermen or apprentice boys, as East- or West-Enders. We catch Georgian or Victorian Londoners in their favourite guise, that is, dressing up.

Historians' eyes have been opened of late to the languages of the city. They have been devoting attention to the customs, rites and conventions shaping popular culture and out-of-doors activities in the 'world we have lost'. In face-to-face local communities, comradeship and conflict, loyalties and distinctions – of rank, occupation, politics, religion – were acted out through time-honoured and highly legible systems of conventional signs publicly displayed. Clothing, finery, gestures, banners, songs, slogans, parades, pickets and protests – all these constituted eloquent public cultural rites. Recurrent annual events, such as festivals, celebrations, holidays and fairs, punctuated and preserved the rhythms of the ceremonial year: the King's Birthday, the anniversary of William of Orange's landing, Guy Fawkes Night. City spaces provided arenas for a multitude of convivial diversions, public spectacles, entertainments, political parades, mayoral shows, civic pageantry and apprentices' rallies.

Such festive activities often carried political messages. Our attention has been drawn to the expression in Georgian times of economic, judicial and political grievances through highly orchestrated, well-structured public behaviour, notably by means of protests and crowd activities, sometimes culminating in riots. These might typically involve a limited and restrained use of force with a view to securing redress of grievances, justice, fair prices, traditional wages and other moral demands. Here was a politics that gloried in highly public, visible appeals to fundamental moral, social and political values and verities, articulated and upheld by what E. P. Thompson dubbed 'the moral economy of the crowd'.

This eye-opening book draws upon the images of Londoners left by artists like Hogarth, as well as the verbal descriptions of journalists and writers like Henry Mayhew. Alongside these, it also makes use of the most first-hand evidence we possess about Londoners' bodies – the bodies themselves, or their remains from burial sites and graves, as they have been carefully reconstructed by archaeologists. Bone evidence in particular tells us much about the changing physique and health of the inhabitants of a city which, with perhaps a population of 30,000, was one of the larger towns in the northern part of the Roman Empire, and which then shrank, had grown again to around 140,000 people by the death of Elizabeth I, and thereafter became easily the largest city in the western world with over a million people by the early nineteenth century. Later expansion was quite staggering: between 1890 and 1940, Greater London grew by three million, from 5,638,000 to 8,700,000. Such an astonishing increase inevitably had an impact upon the physical bodies of Londoners, affecting their nutritional status and their susceptibility to illness, as chapters in this book investigate. But it also reflected the changing composition of the citizenry, including a diversification which followed massive immigration – from Scotland, Ireland and Wales, from the Continent, and later from the Commonwealth and the world at large. Anthropometrists – experts in the study of the human physique – are still in the thick of often fierce controversies about the data which we possess regarding the bodies of Londoners of three hundred, two hundred or a hundred years ago. The best sources suggest a general improvement in height and health over the long haul – with perhaps a dip around the middle of the nineteenth century, indicating the poor sanitation and public health of the early Victorian city. But it is obvious that there were huge differentials between classes, and until much more work has been done – exhuming bodies, or examining school medical records for instance – the jury will remain out.

This splendid book, and the glorious exhibition on which it was based, straddles various traditions of archaeology and history – the history of material remains, the history of culture and representations. It insists that we can get at a 'real' London as it were, a London of plague pits and bones, of grime and crime. But it also displays London in fancy dress, Londoners as they liked to be seen. A city's image is at least as important as its institutions, its representations as crucial as its realities. The London of the citizens' imagination is just as authentic as the London of everyday life. Both aspects are captured in this book. It is crucial that, as we move into the new millennium, we do not lose sight of London as a city of the imagination.

Roy Porter
London, 1998

EXCAVATING BODIES

EXCAVATING AND ANALYSING HUMAN SKELETONS

by Bill White and Helen Ganiaris

FINDING SKELETONS

In a large city continuously occupied for so long it is not surprising that human skeletons are frequently uncovered. Archaeologists, such as those at the Museum of London, can confirm that the remains are human, and also advise on whether they are of recent or more ancient date, to help the police decide whether to investigate a 'suspicious death'. Skeletons are more usually found during building works which affect graveyards of Roman, medieval or later date. When the cemetery is not to be totally excavated, or the burials disturbed, efforts will be made to preserve the remains in situ. If human remains are to be disturbed, a Home Office licence must be obtained, and on the sites of consecrated churches or their cemeteries, permission is required from the church authorities. The Home Office licence will probably state that the remains must eventually be reburied but usually allows a period for scientific research on them.

With permission granted to disinter the bodies, and local health and safety regulations complied with, excavation of the cemetery commences. Each burial is first partially uncovered in order to reveal its extent, the skeletal margins and grave cuts being ascertained by careful use of trowel and brush (Figure 2). The skeleton is then revealed, ready for recording, before any of the individual bones are lifted.

The skeleton is recorded in three dimensions and photographed. Details such as orientation and disposition of the body, bone elements present and any associated finds are entered on a pro forma recording sheet. It is then safe for individual bones to be lifted carefully. It may be worthwhile to raise the hands and feet in the blocks of soil surrounding them, ensuring that subsequent wet-sieving will retain all the small bones of the wrist and digits that otherwise might be overlooked.

Further cleaning of the bone is required before analysis. Adherent soil is washed

1 Xeroradiograph of the bathrocranic skull in Fig. 5a, showing features such as internal blood vessels in greater detail than seen with conventional X-radiography (see page 18).

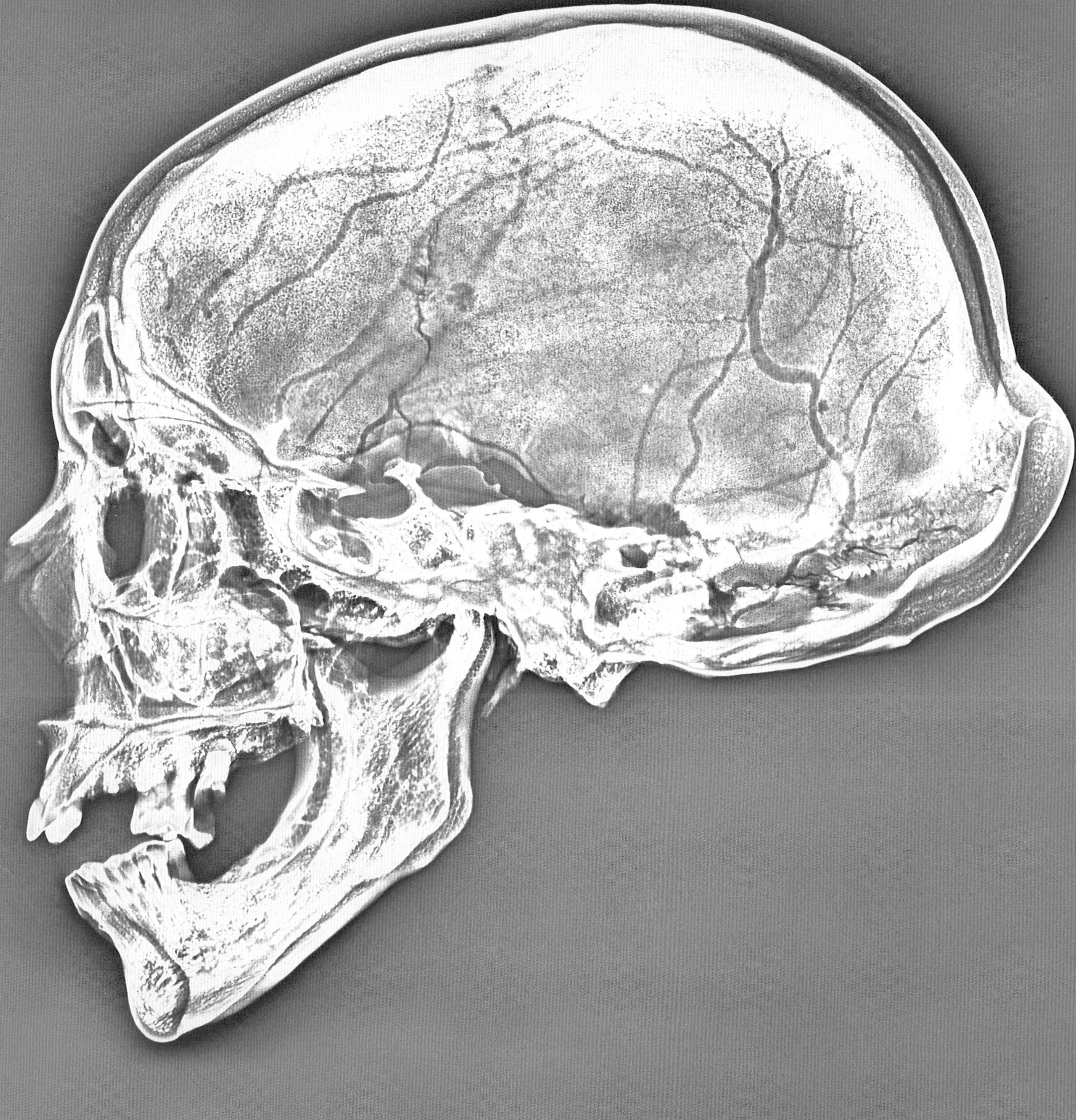

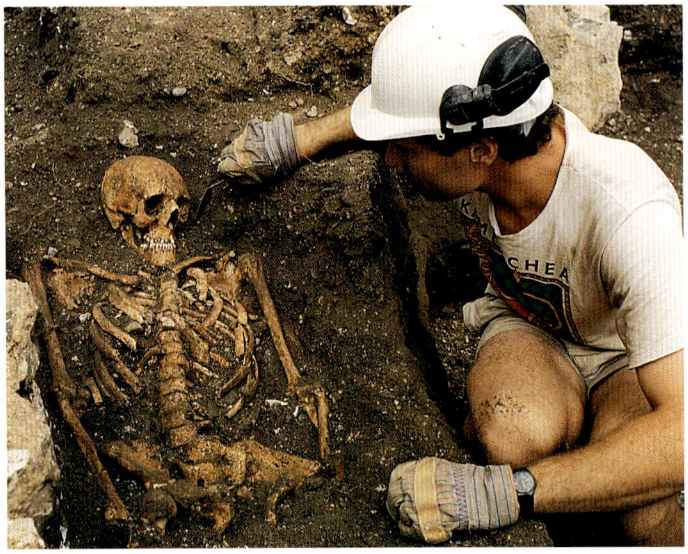

2

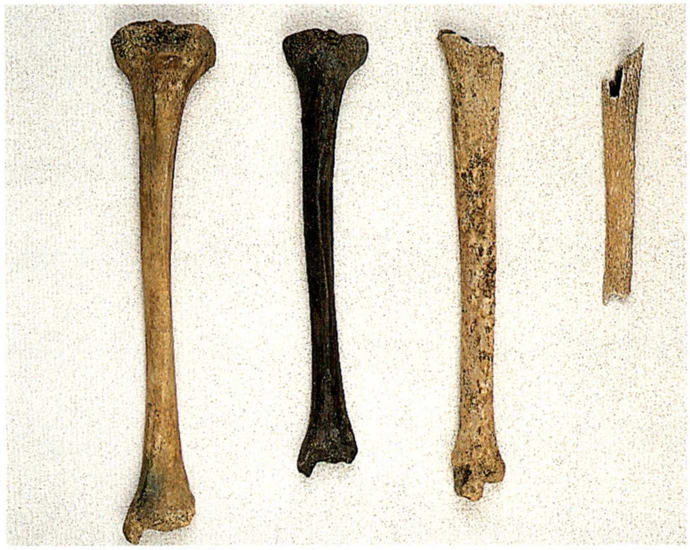

3

free with soft brushes and a supply of gently running water. Particular care is exercised when dislodging extraneous material from delicate areas of the skull such as the orbits (eye-sockets), nasal passages and exterior meatus of the ear. The teeth should not be cleaned thoroughly lest information be lost to subsequent osteological analysis. The bones are laid out carefully on trays and allowed to dry out thoroughly. Finally they are bagged in polythene, labelled inside and out, and stored in boxes made of cardboard of a standard specified for archives.

2 Cleaning a skeleton on site before photography, using small tools and brushes. The bone is allowed to dry before it is removed; adhesives and consolidants are avoided on site as they could affect future analysis.

3 Excavated human bones (left tibiae) showing several states of preservation. The varience in colour of these bones was caused by different burial conditions.

WHAT SKELETONS CAN TELL US

The scope for the study of human skeletal remains is governed by the state of preservation of the bones themselves. There is the question of whether the condition of the individual bones is adequate for detailed study. Ideally the bone should show an undamaged cortex and any joint surfaces should be complete, though in practice the information obtainable is limited by erosion of the bone surface and extremities after burial (Figure 3). Generally, damage is the result of human activity such as the cutting of a grave for a subsequent inhumation, or the erection of a building on that part of the cemetery. Even when the skeleton is incomplete, it can give up its secrets.

Human osteologists routinely seek demographic information from the study of skeletons. The determination of age at death depends on identifying stages in development of the individual (from knowledge of how the teeth develop or how bone

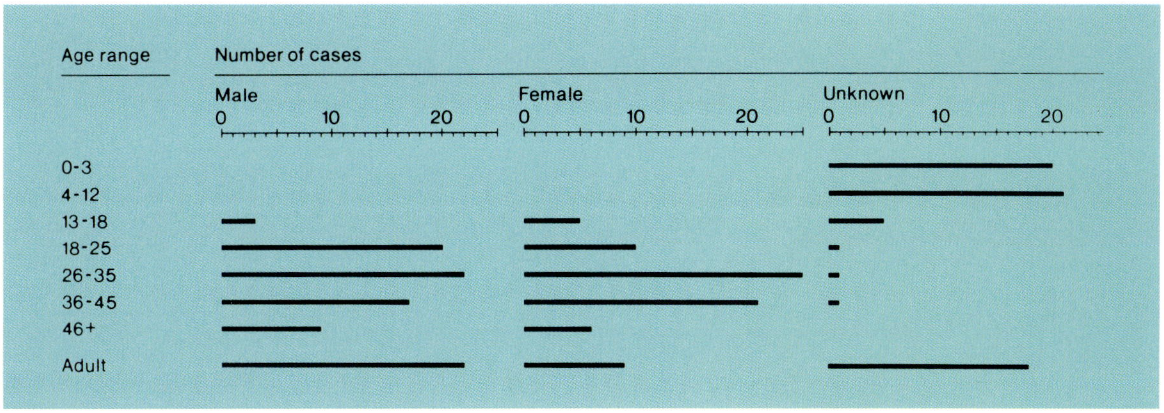

4

growth proceeds) or, in the adult individual, from studies of the degenerative changes in the skeleton that can occur with ageing (such as tooth-wear and -loss, changes in the skull, the symphysis pubis, the spinal vertebrae and ribs). It will be seen that damage to such key areas of the skeleton could interfere with age estimation. Likewise, diagnosis of sex can be made with great accuracy provided that the pelvis and skull are preserved. However, the determination of the sex of child skeletons still presents difficulties and remains a topic for further research. Where appropriate, skeletal morphology may be used to give an indication of racial affiliations. Again, the skeleton ideally needs to be intact, and information may be lost if the bone is not well preserved. Conversely, demographic information may be obtained from the study of cremations (when the body is burned and the ashes put in a container, either a pot or a box, to be laid in the grave).

Different types of cemetery will provide different demographic results. A parochial cemetery may yield female and male skeletons in roughly equal numbers, and a high proportion may be children (Figure 4). On the other hand, a monastic cemetery will show a high preponderance of male interments, and very few children, whereas a 'catastrophe cemetery', such as a plague pit, ought to present a broad cross-section of the population at the time when the pestilence carried them off. Puzzlingly, a Romano-British cemetery may also have both a low female-to-male ratio and few children, but we do not know why. Intensive research continues in all these areas.

Measurements made on the long bones can provide information on the range of heights and the average height of people on the site. This depends upon substituting the measured bone-lengths into mathematical equations developed for the purpose. Different equations apply for different sexes and races so these last two must be known before we

4 **Histogram: age at death from the medieval cemetery at St Nicholas Shambles.**

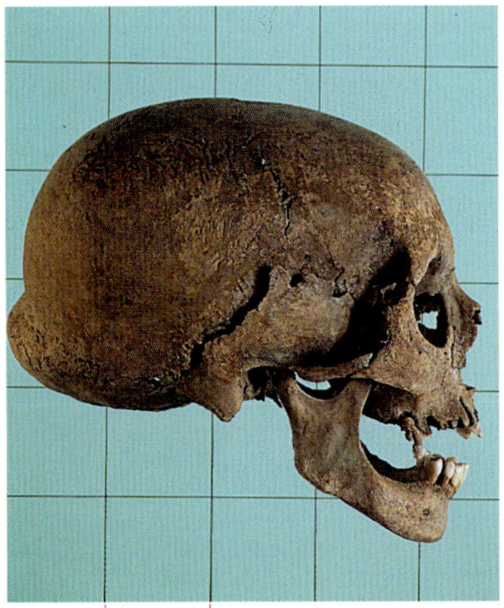

5a 5CM

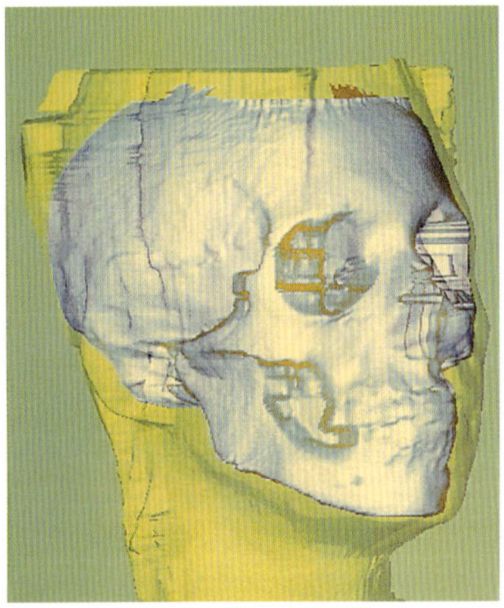

5b

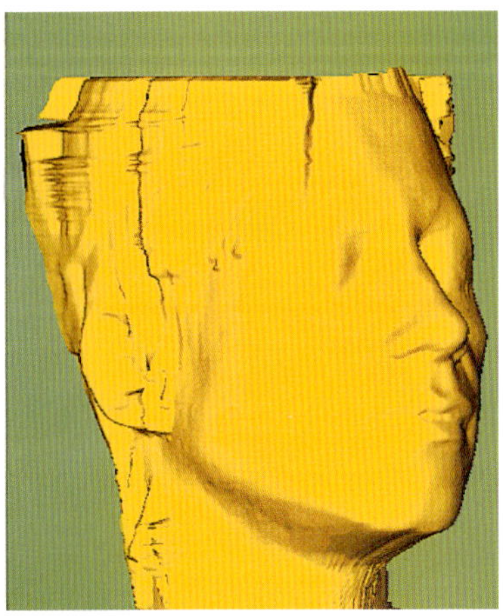

5c

can make a calculation of stature. Other measurements made upon the bones will give an indication of the relative robustness of the population and the physique of its individuals.

Beyond these vital statistics, human skeletons provide the raw material for the study of society and environment. Their study can shed light on a society's beliefs and organisation and on family grouping and relationships. Human bones may bear the marks of bad health, bad hygiene, poor nutrition and, through patterns of repetitive stress, of customs (such as kneeling) or of certain types of work. Although not all diseases leave traces in bone (determining cause of death is usually impossible), the bones nonetheless reveal evidence of infectious and degenerative disease, cancers and accidental or deliberately inflicted trauma. Examples of all these cases are noted throughout this book.

NEW TECHNIQUES

In recent years new techniques have become available for extending the potential of the study of human bone. Advances in radiocarbon dating now mean that relatively small samples can provide accurate dates for burials. This has proved invaluable in assigning the rare Saxon skeletons from the London area to different phases of occupation. The co-operation between forensic science and archaeology has even encompassed the reconstruction of the living face on the dead skull. Various techniques had previously been used in this exciting area but the one noted here involves a computer-based plot of the various landmarks of the skull, followed by the generation of an approximation of the face of the deceased based upon the known thickness of facial muscle and skin (Figure 5). Furthermore, the successful extraction and multiplication of DNA from ancient bone is paving the way for genetic studies in such topics as the affinities of geographically separate societies, the human colonisation of the continents, the demonstration of close family relationships, the investigation of ancient disease and – at the simplest level – the sex of immature skeletons.

Further information about the past environment or way of life may result from chemical analysis of the bones. Thus a high level of heavy metals in the bone may point to industrial pollution of the locality, although other factors need to be excluded (eg a high lead content ought to be disregarded if the skeleton was in a coffin made of lead). The pattern of chemical elements present in bone may shed light on the type of diet enjoyed, whether high in meat, in seafood or wholly vegetarian. As for the last of these, analysis of stable carbon isotopes may indicate the types of plant consumed.

ETHICS

There is a wide feeling that buried human remains ought not to be disturbed at all, but it is rarely the archaeologist who seeks their disinterment. The disturbance of burials and the clearance of graveyards is usually a consequence of property development, and in fact the involvement of archaeologists is normally the best assurance that exposed skeletons will be treated with the maximum respect and care possible under the circumstances. It is relatively simple to perform a scientific examination of the remains before they are reburied. The benefits of the latter study are manifold. Knowledge of previous human societies is enhanced (for the prehistoric period, human remains are a major source of information since other material evidence is lacking) and in particular the increasing knowledge of how human diseases evolved in the past supports the research that could lead to their eradication in the future.

CONSERVATION OF OBJECTS BURIED WITH THE DEAD

While conditions in London are generally favourable for the preservation of buried bone, and excavation and cleaning are largely carried out by the excavators and environmental scientists, the artefacts that often accompany burials call for attention from archaeological conservators. Their task is to ensure that such finds survive the transition from the burial environment to archive storage or display. On many sites, burials have included grave

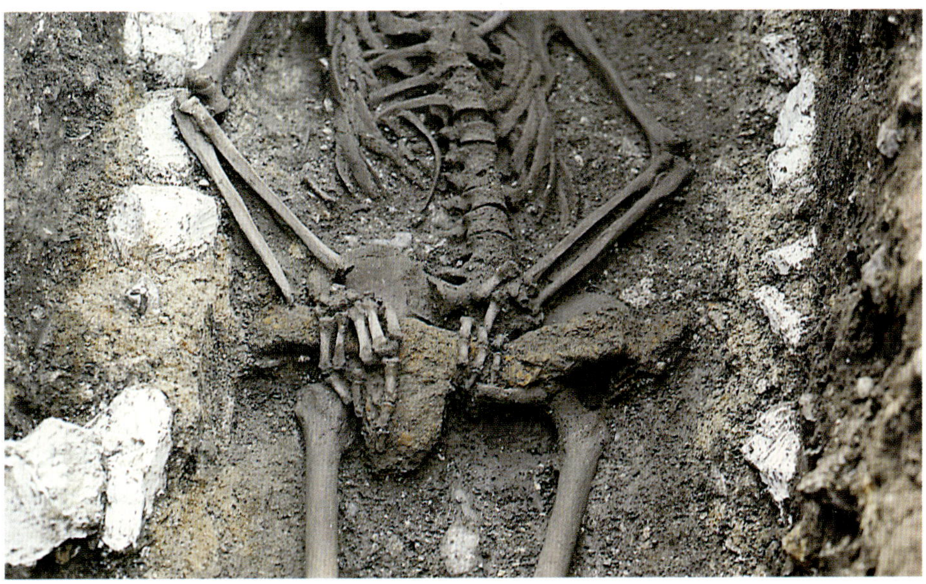

6

5 Stages in facial reconstruction of the bathrocranic skull: (5a) the dry skull shown in Fig. 1: (5b) building up the layers of muscle and skin using laser scanning and computer imaging: (5c) applying facial features to the computer model.

6 Skeleton of a young medieval man from a monastic site (Merton Priory) with a leather strap placed over his pelvis. The leather has been preserved by iron corrosion. The strap does not seem to be a belt since it does not go around the waist. Its function is mysterious and there seem to be no parallels for it.

ANCIENT BODIES

THE LIVES OF PREHISTORIC LONDONERS

by Jonathan Cotton and Bill White

There are a number of problems surrounding the study of the earliest Londoners. The first and most obvious is that 'London', at least as an urban place, simply did not exist in prehistory: it was a Roman foundation of the mid-first century AD (though the name Londinium is a latinised British one). The evidence considered here therefore relates to the prehistoric people who lived in the middle and lower Thames valley, in the area now covered by Greater London and its surrounds. Secondly, prehistory is an awfully long time, and covers everything from the earliest hominids to members of sophisticated tribal communities of the late Iron Age; climate and landscape changed out of all recognition too. Thirdly, and crucially, until the island of Britain attracted the passing and invariably biased attentions of classical writers in the last few centuries BC, we have no names, dates or events to which we can refer, nor any contemporary manuscripts or paintings with which to document population levels, ages at death, physique, diet, health or the appearance of these ancient peoples. Instead, we must rely solely on the evidence provided for us by archaeology.

Despite the occasional spectacular discovery, such as the preserved bodies of the Italian Iceman, Ötzi, and the Lindow Moss bogman from Cheshire, which quite literally puts flesh on prehistoric bones, for direct evidence of the people themselves we usually have to rely on the discovery of burials, very few of which have survived to be discovered anyway. Furthermore, for much of prehistory, formal burials in the modern sense were never made. The dead were simply exposed to the elements, a custom widely used by, amongst others, tribes of Plains Amerindians (such as the Sioux and Cheyenne) and by the Parsees of the Indian sub-continent. All this being so, what then can we say about the thousands of human generations who lived in the area now called London in the time before the Romans?

1 The classic 'power grip'. But were hand axes held and used in this way? Modern experiments suggest that it was the edge rather than the point which was the key feature, and that the axes were more likely to have been used in a series of shorter, more dextrous strokes, to skin and butcher animal carcasses.

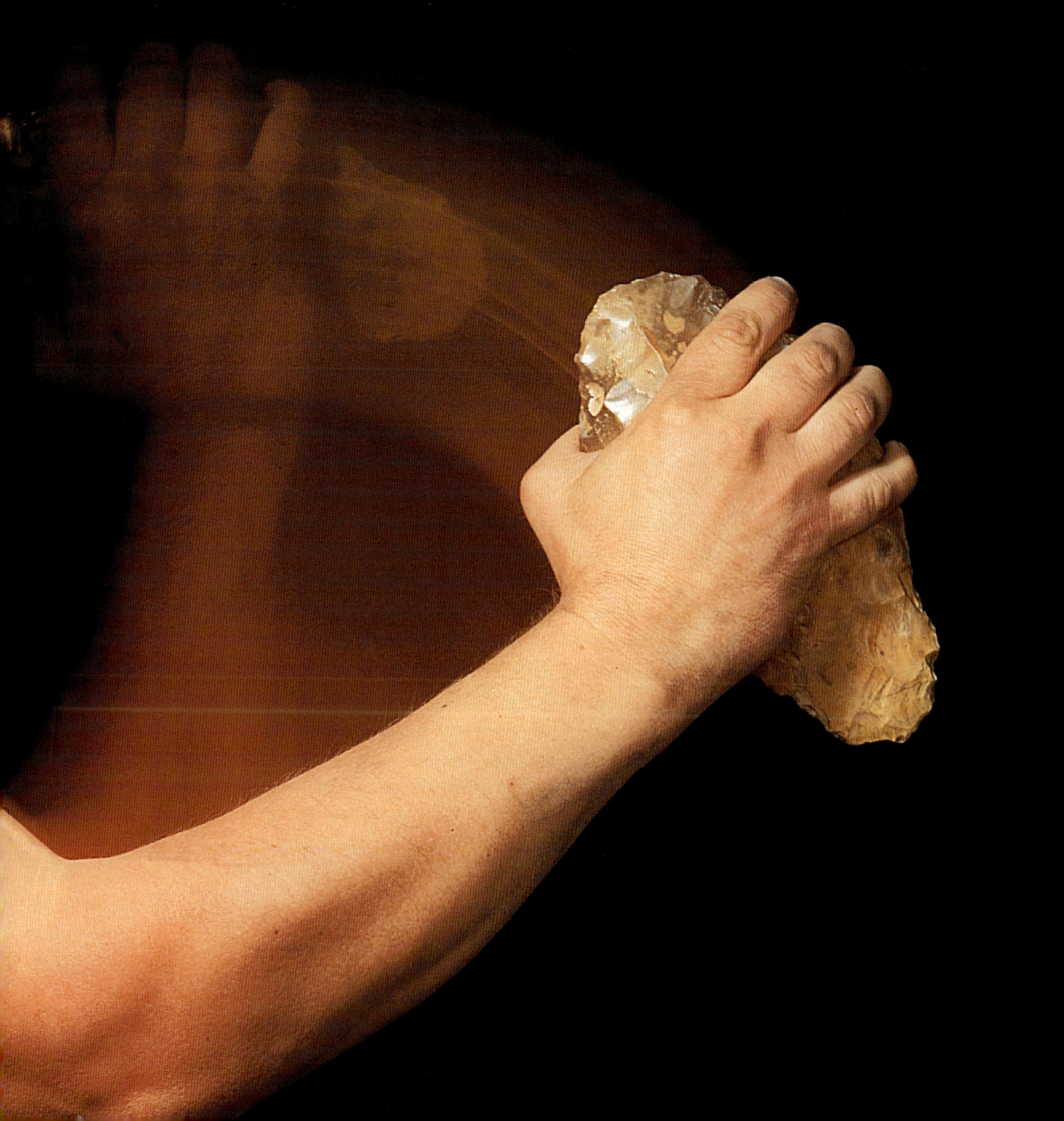

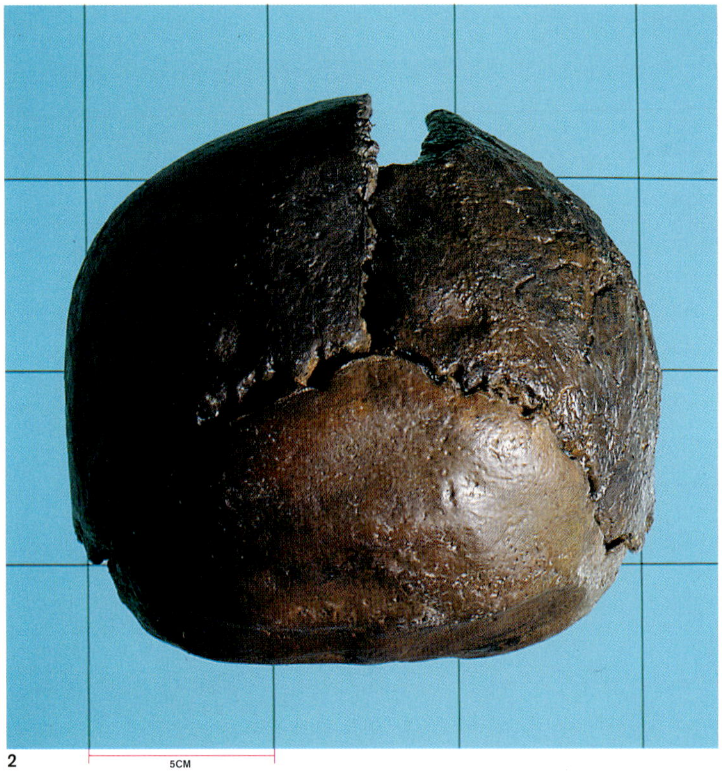

2

2 The Swanscombe skull, found in three pieces between 1935 and 1955 and dated to around 400,000BC. Belonging to an 'Archaic Homo sapiens' female in her early twenties, this was for many years the only early fossil hominid known from Britain. More recently, however, other remains have turned up at Boxgrove in West Sussex (500,000BC) and Pontnewydd Cave, North Wales (230,000BC).

SWANSCOMBE, BOXGROVE AND EARLY HOMINIDS

In the very earliest periods, several tens of thousands of generations ago, a number of different hominid species competed against nature (and probably each other) along the margins of the River Thames. At this time Britain was still linked to the Continent (the English Channel was only finally flooded by the sea around 8000 years ago), and lay at the furthest north-western corner of the European land mass. Fragments of a skull found deep within gravel laid down by the Thames at Swanscombe provide our earliest local evidence, currently dated to around 400,000 years ago (Figure 2). Found on three separate occasions between 1935 and 1955, they belong to a female in her early twenties whose brain capacity, estimated at 1325ml, lies well within the modern range. However, a number of anatomical details indicate that she belonged to a species of Homo ancestral to our own. For nearly forty years, until the discovery near Boxgrove, West Sussex in 1993 of a robust leg bone and two teeth which are 100,000 years older, the Swanscombe woman was the oldest fossil hominid known from Britain.

Early humans like those found at Swanscombe and Boxgrove appear to have developed first in Africa, and spread from there around one million years ago, reaching northern Europe up to half a million years later. The physical appearance of these hominids remains quite unknown, though we might reasonably imagine them to have had a generally dark 'Mediterranean' colouring. With an estimated height of nearly six feet, the Boxgrove hominid (probably a male and also in his early twenties) certainly betrays a 'warm-adapted' African origin, as tall thin bodies are better able to cope with hot climates. Both individuals are likely to have been meat-eaters, and, if the evidence from Boxgrove can be relied on, this meat was hunted rather than scavenged. The two teeth found in a slightly lower level at Boxgrove betray some evidence of the way in which the meat might have been eaten. They show signs not only of dental plaque (indicating poor oral hygiene) but also of distinctive transverse scratches: these suggest that the teeth were used like a vice in which food was gripped, before being cut or sliced by a right-handed individual using a sharp flint edge which occasionally nicked the tooth enamel. While their spoken vocabulary was probably limited to just a few words, early hominids were quite capable of co-operative action in the hunt, and were able to solve problems and plan ahead. These latter characteristics are particularly evident in their flint tools known as hand axes, the manufacture of which has been likened to playing chess, as the individual knapping the flint has to have a clear mental picture of the end product and to think five or six moves ahead. Many hand axes (Figure 3) are also of large size and perfect proportions, underlining the strength and manual dexterity of their makers.

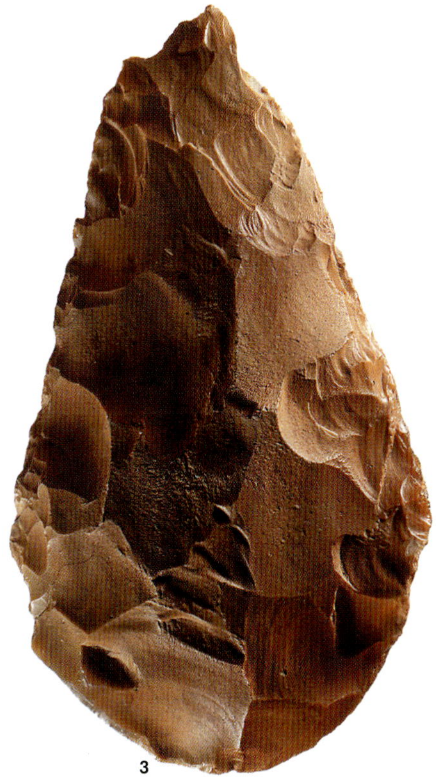

3

FROM AFRICA TO UXBRIDGE...

A second wave of migration out of Africa occurred around 100,000 years ago, as fully modern humans, Homo sapiens sapiens, spread across Europe. They gradually marginalised the chunky, cold-adapted Neanderthals who preceded them but who appear to have died out by around 30,000 years ago. Homo sapiens sapiens set about exploiting the new ecological niches created by quickening climate changes at the end of the Ice Age. They coped with the extinction of the more easily hunted 'big game', such as mammoth, by switching to smaller migratory prey like reindeer and horse. As temperatures rose and trees colonised the landscape they switched again to hunting woodland species including red and roe deer. We are able to document this moment of transition on a site dated to the very end of the Ice Age at Uxbridge, in the valley of the River Colne in north-west London.

Here a series of butchery sites of around 9000–7000BC have been examined, where small mobile groups of hunters sat round hearths skinning game and repairing tool kits. We can say little about their physical appearance, though it seems likely that they would have relied on their prey animals to furnish them not only with protein-rich meat and bone marrow, but also with leather for clothing, pouches and bags, sinew for bow strings and thread, and bone and antler for needles and harpoons. Remains of beaver, fox and swan in one area suggest an interest in costume elaboration too, though swan feathers could equally well have been used for fletching arrows. While there is no evidence on this site for gathered foodstuffs, such groups are known to have exploited seasonally available sources of protein such as hazelnuts, together with other wild plants. This 'hunter-gatherer' lifestyle was tremendously successful, though it could support relatively few people in any one area at a time.

3 **A large flint axe from Glasshouse Street, Piccadilly, c.300,000 years old. Modern experiments have confirmed how effective such hand-held tools were for butchering animal carcasses.**

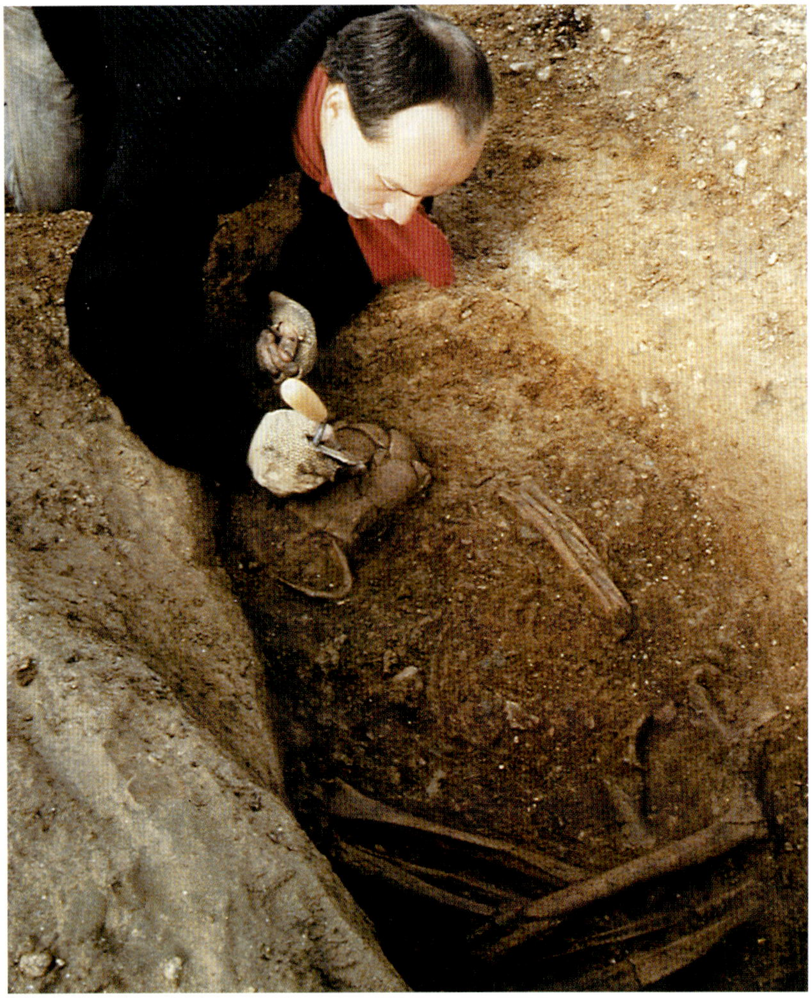

4

4 The tightly flexed skeleton of a woman dated 3640-3100BC emerges from the ditch of a small earthen enclosure at Staines Road Farm, Shepperton. The wear of her teeth indicates that she was between 30 and 40 years of age at death, while examination of her bones shows that she suffered from a bad back.

Gradually, however, increasing numbers of such groups outgrew the land's ability to sustain them, leading them to adopt a more efficient but more sedentary way of life. Instead of roaming the landscape exploiting seasonal resources, people began to settle down and experiment with the domestication and herding of animals and the cultivation of previously wild plants. They developed new technologies, such as making pottery and the polishing of stone tools, and different communities may have begun to express their identities through dress, ornaments and weapons, and by the construction of territorial markers such as earthen tombs and enclosures.

THE FIRST 'MODERN' LONDONERS

In the centuries after 4000BC (around 200 generations ago), we catch our first glimpse of 'modern' Londoners – or at least, parts of them. For these early farmers appear to have exposed their dead to the elements to rot, perhaps in trees or on elevated wooden platforms. Once picked clean by birds and other scavengers, the larger parts of the skeleton such as skulls and long bones were then collected up for use in rites enacted within the confines of settlements, tombs and along the riverbank. As a result fragmentary human remains have been found on a number of sites and in the Thames, but there are few complete bodies. It could well be that the Thames itself functioned as the final repository for the majority of the local population.

Remains scattered within the ditches of earthen enclosures at Staines and Shepperton (Figure 4) are typical. At Staines, parts of two skulls, one male and one female, a lower jaw and several long bones from a slender right arm (probably also female) were found. All belonged to seemingly well-nourished young adults aged between around 17 and 30, whose teeth, while worn, showed little or no sign of decay (indicating a sugar-free diet), but some light dental plaque. Perhaps most interesting is the pathology of the male skull: forensic examination showed that the cause of death was 'four blows delivered at close range by a blunt object from the right side of the neck' (two old head wounds were also present in the same area). This is a somewhat novel death for the period: elsewhere in lowland Britain, for example at Fengate near Peterborough and Hambledon Hill, Dorset, adult males were killed by flint-tipped arrows. The remains at Shepperton are much better preserved, which allows us to say more about the individuals concerned and the ailments that afflicted them. They comprise two individuals: the incomplete remains of a possible male aged 25–35, and a female aged 30–40, buried in a tightly flexed posture and radiocarbon dated to the period 3640–3100BC. While we have no estimates of height for either individual, evidence from other sites of the period such as the West Kennet long barrow in Wiltshire suggests that men averaged between 157cm and 173cm (5ft 2in. and 5ft 8in.) and that women tended to be shorter, between 147cm and 163cm (4ft 10in. and 5ft 4in.). Both of the Shepperton people suffered from back problems which were clearly endemic within early farming communities, and presumably brought about by strenuous living. The woman also had a significant flattening of her lower limb bones which could indicate either repetitive stress through habitual squatting or a nutritional deficiency.

Information relating to the diet of these people has been recovered from a third site at Runnymede Bridge, near Egham. In addition to the butchered remains of cattle and, particularly, pig (an animal much favoured for feasting purposes), burnt food residues on the insides of broken pottery vessels show that their contents included fruit and malt, pork dripping, fish and honey-based products. The last named is particularly interesting, as a fragmentary human jaw found elsewhere on the site bore traces of tooth decay. Other seasonally gathered foods included hazelnuts, crab apples and sloes, while emmer, bread wheat and barley were grown and ground into flour using stone querns.

We have a little evidence for the appearance of people of the period, provided principally by the Italian Iceman, Ötzi (dated to around 3300BC), who was dressed, admittedly for freezing alpine conditions, in a probably smoke-tanned knee-length upper garment or 'poncho' of deerskin, with a fur cap, leggings, a leather loincloth, one-piece leather shoes stuffed with grass, and a plaited grass cape. He was tattooed, but whether for decorative, magical or medical reasons (eg 'acupuncture' to alleviate rheumatism) is unclear. He had also suffered a number of broken ribs in life, all of which had healed successfully. Arms and collar bones appear to have been more commonly fractured in

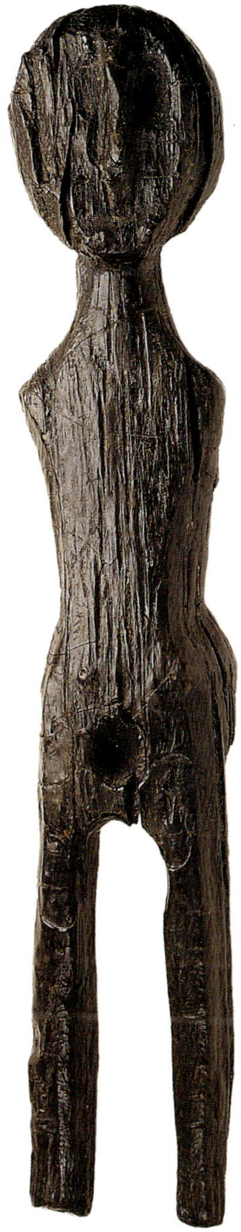

5

5 The so-called Dagenham Idol is the earliest representation of a human figure from the London area. Made of Scots pine, it is dated to between 2351 and 2139BC.

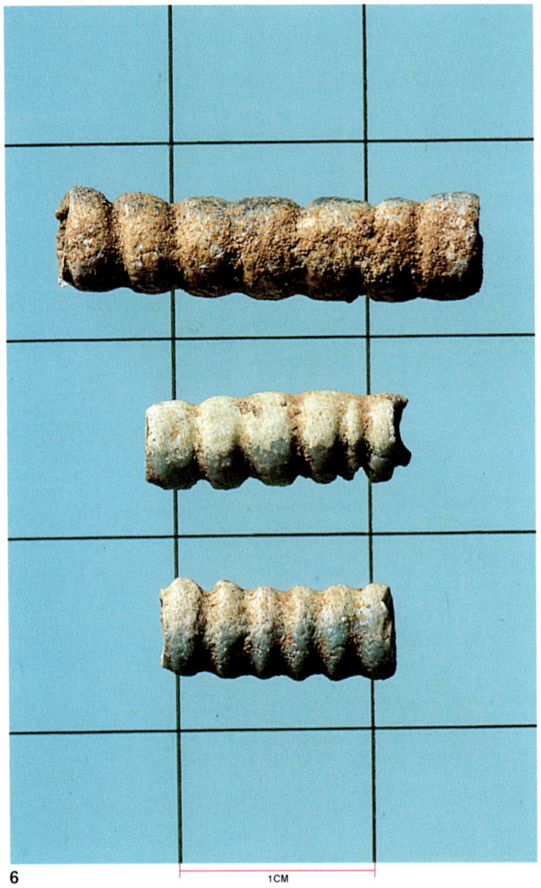

6

British farmer communities, and at Isbister in Orkney had afflicted some two per cent of the community.

CULTIVATING AN IMAGE...

Ötzi apart, it is difficult to see these early farmers as individuals because of the way in which parts of the same body were dispersed in different tombs and settlements across the landscape. Individuals, however, come more into focus in the centuries after 2500BC, as does a new burial rite – that of cremation. Such developments may mark a fundamental shift in the way society operated, as reverence for anonymous communal ancestors gave way to the commemoration of members of powerful elites, whose appearance and status in both life and death were underpinned by the possession, display and disposal of fine objects of stone, pottery and, increasingly, metal. The local evidence suggests that London communities of this time retained much of their former egalitarian outlook, though they were numerous and well organised enough to undertake major projects like the construction of a two-and-a-half-mile-long embanked earthen avenue near Heathrow. While many fine objects were deposited in the Thames, the few burials of the period eschew overt displays of finery such as those found in certain Wessex graves. An inhumation burial placed in a grave at Mucking in Essex was accompanied by a pottery drinking vessel and a quiverful of eleven flint-tipped arrows, for instance, while cremations placed beneath two circular earthen burial mounds at East Molesey and Teddington were simply accompanied by faience (a kind of glass) beads and a bronze dagger (Figure 6).

The East Molesey burial, contained within a large pottery urn, was a double one comprising the mixed remains of two adults, one certainly female. More interesting from a pathological point of view, however, were the cremated remains of an 'older mature adult' lying just beyond the confines of the earthen barrow, who had clearly suffered from painful abscesses in the sockets of three teeth (Figure 7). The three blue faience beads which accompanied the double burial could have been worn around the neck, on the clothing or in the hair of either of the individuals in life. The presence of beads in the grave also points to a growing concern with personal appearance, which manifests itself in the form of jet, amber, faience and metal beads and pendants, pairs of bone tweezers and bronze razors placed with the dead. There is evidence from several graves that the razors were used to

6 **Three segmented beads of blue faience found with a double cremation burial beneath a round earthen barrow at Hurst Park, East Molesey. They signify a growing interest in personal appearance in the centuries after 2000BC.**

shave off the eyebrows of the mourners – presumably as a mark of respect for the departed.

In the centuries after 1500BC we can begin to see the first full use of true mixed farming as field systems were laid out on areas of good soil. Pressure on the land increased steadily and people appear to have used seasonal feasting and competitive display as a means of maintaining their positions in society. At first the dead continued to be cremated and placed in pottery urns buried in cemetery plots close to the settlements, rather than beneath barrows. Whether these local cemeteries were originally arranged in kinship or family groups, as might be supposed, remains unclear. So far, examination of their contents has revealed little more than further examples of double burials in single pots, and the presence of age-related wear and tear on the bones of several older females. Later, in the centuries after 1000BC, formal burial ceased. Instead, token deposits of cremated and unburned bone were placed in prominent positions close to the entrances of settlements, and in the Thames. Skulls were clearly especially significant, and may even have been displayed, as at Runnymede (Figure 8), though whether the individuals represented were ancestors or enemies is unknown. Social rivalries could certainly break out into physical violence on occasion, however, and several skulls from the river bear traces of healed and unhealed wounds inflicted by swords and spears; there are also instances, from Dorchester, further up the Thames valley, and from Tormarton in Gloucestershire, of the broken-off tips of bronze spears found firmly embedded in the spines and pelvic regions of unfortunate young warriors.

Though females were generally more slightly built than the often muscular males, both sexes appear to have been well nourished on the products of the mixed-farming regime: cattle and sheep were herded and wheat and barley grown, though there was now less reliance placed on wild resources. Pork retained its popularity for feasting purposes and was either boiled, or roasted in wood-lined troughs or large bronze cauldrons; additional flavour was provided by salt, extracted from seawater around the Thames estuary. Horse meat may also have been eaten, although horses were probably more important as moving platforms from which mounted warriors could display their finery to best effect. Spinning and weaving were certainly carried on in the settlements, suggesting that the flowing lines

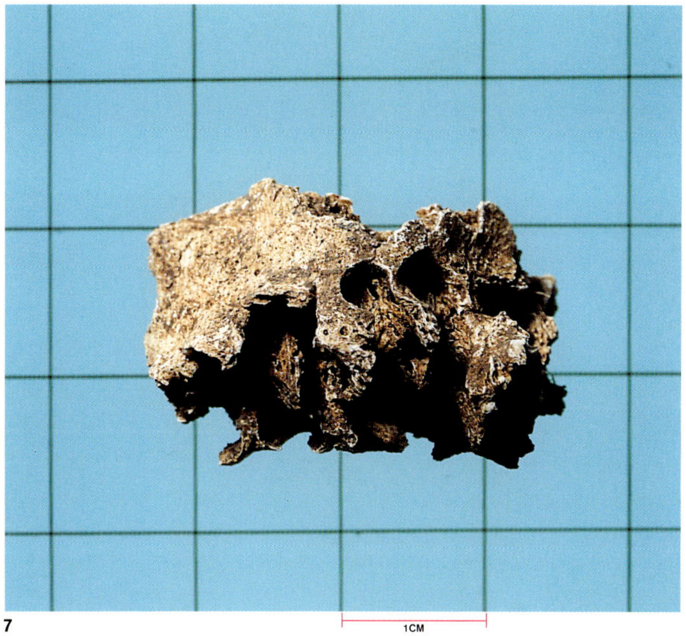

7

7 Part of the jaw of an 'older mature adult' from Hurst Park, East Molesey, dated sometime after 2000BC, with painful dental abscesses in three right maxillary sockets (premolar and molar).

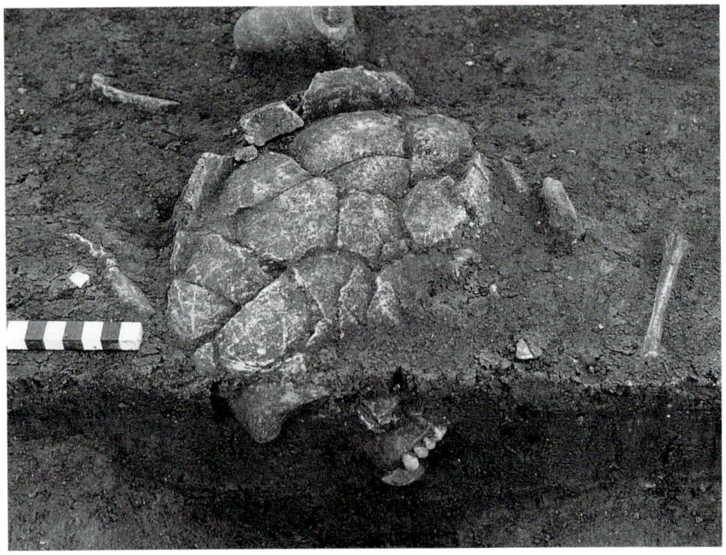

8

of warm woollen garments had been adopted, fastened by long wooden and metal pins. Beautifully preserved sets of woven woollen clothing have been found on a number of Danish bog bodies of both sexes, several of whom also sported intricately plaited hair styles. It is extremely likely that Bronze Age Londoners would have dressed their hair in similarly elaborate ways, and perhaps secured it using long metal pins like those found in the river.

PREHISTORY INTO HISTORY

Unfortunately, we have virtually no direct physical evidence of the people themselves in the centuries between about 700 and 100BC, despite the existence of various burial rites in other parts of the country. For this period we are therefore forced to rely on secondary information such as the presence of animal and plant remains on settlements (for diet) and the weapons, tools and trinkets such as brooches and pins found mainly in the Thames (for appearance). The situation improves after about 100BC, however, with the re-emergence of the cremation rite, perhaps imported from the Continent, and the local adoption of an inhumation burial rite. There is also evidence of a renewed interest in skulls, particularly those of young males, many of which were deposited in the waters of the Walbrook stream within the outline of the later city, presumably as part of some cult practice. This information can be supplemented by the evidence provided by the Lindow Moss bogman from Cheshire, and by the eye-witness account of Julius Caesar.

8 **Friend or foe? This skull was probably displayed on a pole set up inside the island settlement at Runnymede Bridge in the 9th-8th centuries BC. A number of other skulls of similar date have been recovered from the Thames, though whether their disposal in the river indicates reverence or revulsion remains unclear.**

Writing in the 50s BC, Caesar records that male Britons wore their hair long, shaving the rest of their bodies except their upper lips, and dyed themselves blue with woad to terrify their enemies in battle. The Lindow Moss man, however, had a full beard and sideburns neatly trimmed with a pair of shears. He was well-built, in his mid-twenties and around 168cm (5ft 6in) tall. Although otherwise healthy, he suffered from worms: we know too that he had eaten a flat unleavened griddle cake of finely ground wheat and flour shortly before he met his violent death in the Moss. The few burials of the period from the London area paint no such dramatic picture. They include two male inhumations, from the Tower of London and Borough High Street, Southwark. The individual from the Tower was aged between 13 and 16 at death and 163cm (5ft 4in.) tall; he had tooth decay and traces of plaque. He also wore a simple bronze ring on the finger of one hand. The Southwark man was older, about 30, but shorter at 160cm (5ft 3in.) tall.

A further inhumation burial from Harper Road in Southwark – a site lying in the fork between two Roman roads a kilometre south of the Thames – is worthy of particular note. For here were found the remains of a woman 157cm (5ft 2in.) tall in her early twenties, buried in a simple nailed wooden coffin. She was accompanied by a pottery flagon datable to the middle of the first century AD, placed at her head, together with a decorated bronze neck collar and a tinned bronze mirror at her feet (Figure 9). The significance of this otherwise unremarkable grave is that the occupant is probably the nearest we will ever come to someone who was alive at the founding of Londinium across the Thames to the north. Not only may she have been present at a defining moment in British history, she also effectively closes the door on the silent 20,000 and more generations of prehistoric people who went before her.

CONCLUSION

This brief survey has attempted to summarise what little we know about the actual physical remains of the prehistoric people who lived and died in the half a million years or so before the Romans came. Because of the obvious limitations of the evidence, no population figures have been attempted here, though it is likely that there was an incremental rise in population once people settled down to herd and farm in the centuries after 4000BC. Before then, numbers would undoubtedly have fluctuated from season to season as small hunter-gatherer bands moved in and out of the area on the trail of migrating game.

Despite a punishingly high infant mortality rate (which one estimate for pre-industrial communities puts at between 100 and 400 per 1000 births, compared to the modern figure of just over 6 per 1000), and the inevitable if invisible bouts of crop failure, famine, warfare and disease, the local population was probably at its greatest extent in the period between about 1500BC and 300BC. Thereafter, while the Thames continued to act as the focus for ritual offerings of fine metalwork in the years down to the Roman Conquest, many people seem to have congregated in distant tribal centres like St Albans (Verulamium) and Silchester. London, however, was a new frontier town just eighteen years after the Conquest and on the eve of the great British tribal uprising of AD60–61, the Roman historian Tacitus could speak of it as 'an important centre for businessmen and merchandise' – a position it has held virtually ever since.

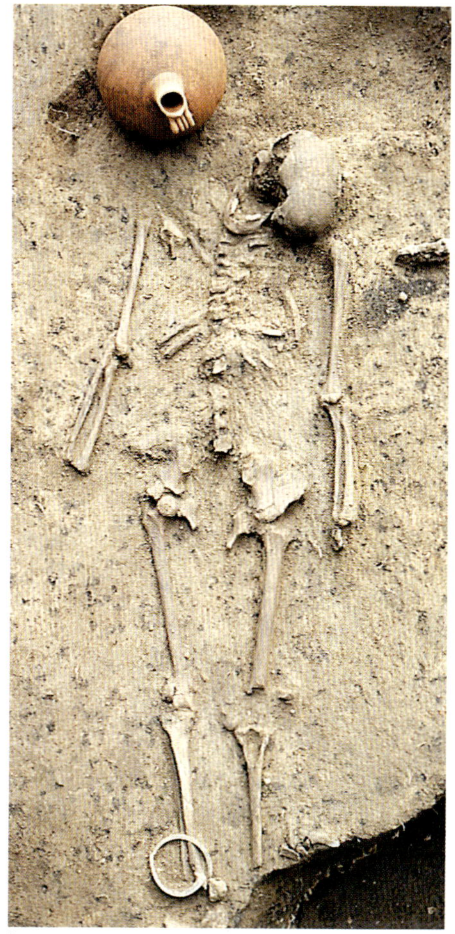

9

9 **One of the first true Londoners? This woman in her early twenties, found in Harper Road, Southwark, was buried in a wooden coffin in the middle of the 1st century AD. She was accompanied by a decorated neck-ring and a mirror (the latter made in a north Italian workshop), together with a pottery flagon probably containing wine for her journey into the next world.**

VICTORIAN BODY HUNTERS

Victorian antiquaries recorded human remains uncovered during building works or dredged from the Thames, though they were unable to date their finds accurately. More often than not, for example, skulls recovered from the river were assumed to be the remains of British tribesmen killed while opposing Caesar in 54BC. Indeed the discovery at Chelsea of skulls of apparently two types associated with bronze and iron weapons led H. Syer Cuming to believe that he had discovered the very site of the fortified ford itself. Similar claims were entertained for Kingston, and Dr William Roots even suggested that a cremation burial found with a bronze dagger in Teddington (actually a much earlier Bronze Age grave) was that of a British tribal leader killed in the skirmish.

Discoveries of fossil hominids in Germany also prompted local antiquarians to mount a patriotic search for British contenders for the title of the 'earliest European'. Remains found at Galley Hill near Northfleet in 1888, and at Baker's Hole in the same locality a few years later, put England on a par with its European super-power rival for a while. Unfortunately, tests carried out after their sale at auction in 1948 showed conclusively that neither find was truly ancient.

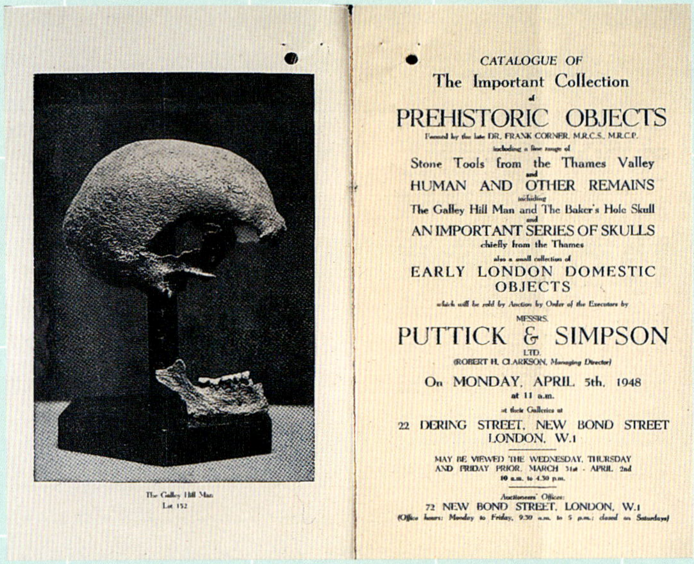
The Galley Hill Man
Lot 152

CATALOGUE OF
The Important Collection
of
PREHISTORIC OBJECTS
Formed by the late DR. FRANK CORNER, M.R.C.S., M.R.C.P.
including a fine range of
Stone Tools from the Thames Valley
and
HUMAN AND OTHER REMAINS
including
The Galley Hill Man and The Baker's Hole Skull
and
AN IMPORTANT SERIES OF SKULLS
chiefly from the Thames
also a small collection of
EARLY LONDON DOMESTIC OBJECTS
which will be sold by Auction by Order of the Executors by
MESSRS.
PUTTICK & SIMPSON
LTD.
(ROBERT H. CLARKSON, Managing Director)
On MONDAY, APRIL 5th, 1948
at 11 a.m.
at their Galleries at
22 DERING STREET, NEW BOND STREET
LONDON, W.1
MAY BE VIEWED THE WEDNESDAY, THURSDAY AND FRIDAY PRIOR, MARCH 31st - APRIL 2nd
10 a.m. to 4.30 p.m.
Auctioneers' Offices:
72 NEW BOND STREET, LONDON, W.1
(Office hours: Monday to Friday, 9.30 a.m. to 5 p.m.; closed on Saturdays)

1

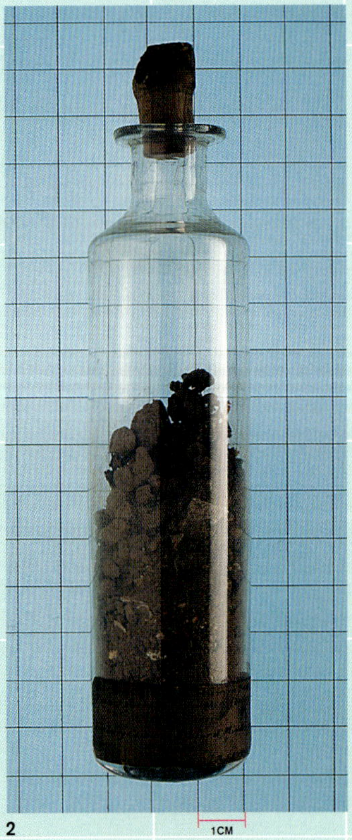

2

1 **Puttick & Simpson Auction Catalogue, April 1948. The sale of the collection belonging to the late Dr Frank Corner of Poplar contained a number of important human remains then thought to be as old as any found in Europe, such as the Galley Hill Man and the Baker's Hole skull. Recent scientific analysis has shown that neither of these finds is older than the Bronze Age.**

2 **Small glass phial containing earth and cremated bone from a Bronze Age cremation cemetery. The original hand-written label reads:**

'Earth & Calcined Human Bones
From a bucket-shaped Urn of baked Clay
Stone Period
Sunbury Common Ashford Middlesex
1871'.

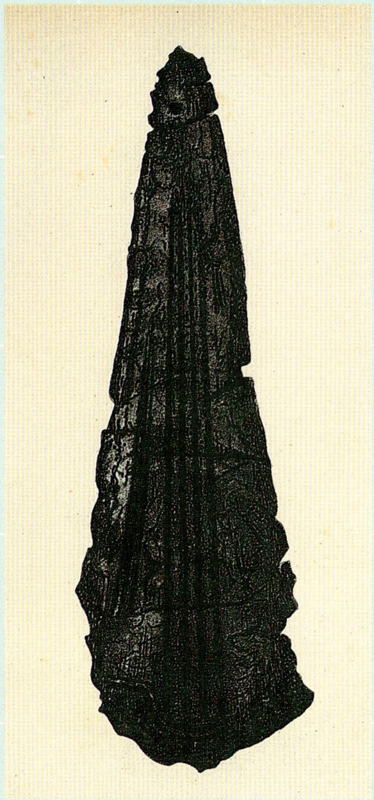

3a

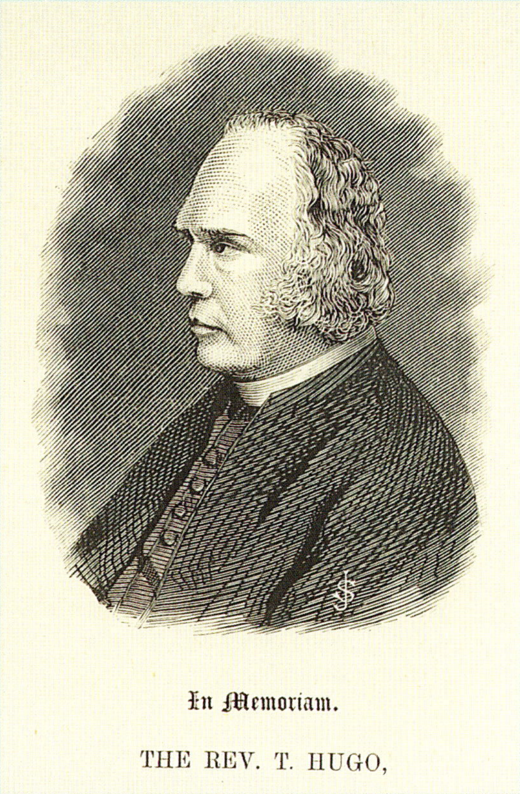

3b

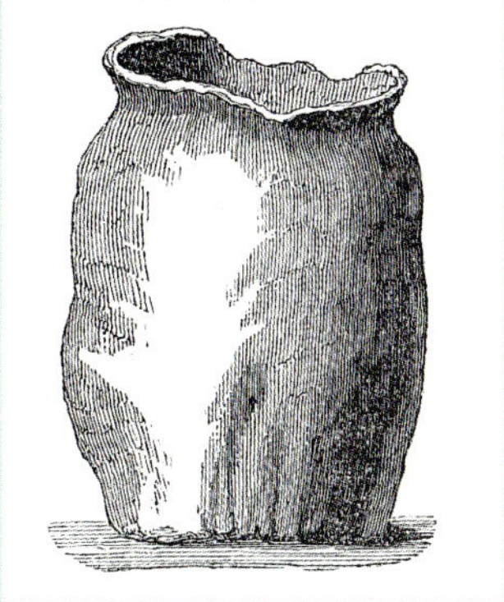

4a

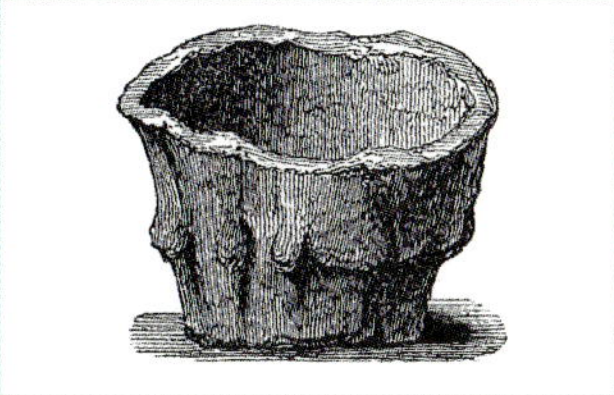

4b

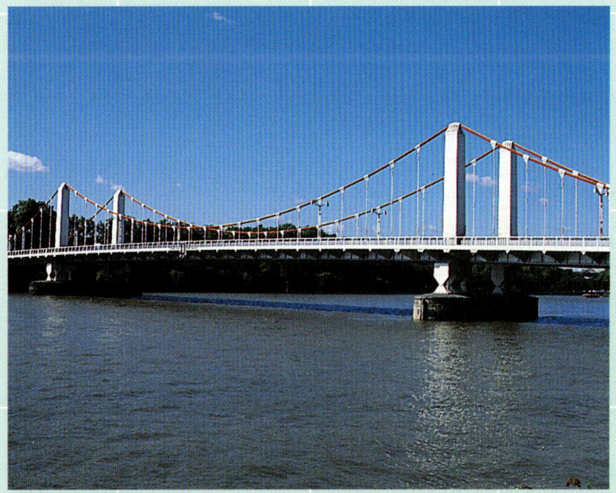

5

3 Engraving of the bronze dagger found with a cremation burial placed beneath a large earthen barrow in Sandy Lane Teddington (3a). This engraving, made by the Reverend Thomas Hugo (3b) shortly after the discovery of the dagger in June 1854, is doubly valuable as the dagger itself has not been seen since 1860!

4 'Sepulchral urn' (4a) half full of ashes dug up on Kingston Hill in November 1844. The smaller 'lachrymatory' or *Thuringium* (4b) was placed near the rim of the larger vessel. Originally thought to be Roman, both are likely to date to around 1000BC, and are now in the collection of the Society of Antiquaries of London. (The engraving is taken from Biden's *History of Kingston,* 1852.)

5 The Thames at Chelsea, a locality described by the London antiquary Henry Syer Cuming in 1857 as 'our Celtic Golgotha' because of human skulls found there.

ROMAN BODIES

THE STRESSES AND STRAINS OF LIFE IN ROMAN LONDON

by Jenny Hall and Janice Conheeney

The population of Britain was to change rapidly with the advent of a formidable Roman army of more than 40,000 men which invaded Britain in AD43. Their purpose was to annex Britain and enhance the reputation of the emperor Claudius. Thus Britain became the most northerly province of the Roman Empire. The army created the infrastructure of the province with a network of roads for the rapid deployment of troops and supplies. In around AD50, about seven years after the initial invasion, the Romans created Londinium. It was a new town on a green-field site, ideally situated on the banks of the Thames, accessible to the largest sea-going ships and an excellent centre for trade and communications with the rest of the Roman Empire. Although the army was probably responsible for its inception, the town's growth and affluence were most likely due to merchants and traders anxious to increase their sales outlets, and to land speculators with an eye to the development potential of such a new site. It has also been suggested that many of the slaves, refugees and economic migrants who made up the early population of London were native Britons.

The Roman Empire, few of whose citizens were Romans by birth, was the first true European community, uniting many races and tribes which normally lived in peace within one imperial organisation. Latin was therefore used as a necessary common language, along with a common currency. Citizens were expected to follow the ways of Rome irrespective of the province in which they lived. One of these ways was the disposal of the dead. Roman cemeteries were, by law, situated outside the town boundaries, and Londinium was no exception. Cemeteries were laid out beyond the city gates of Aldgate, Bishopsgate, Aldersgate, Newgate and Ludgate on the northern side of the river and to the south, beyond the settlement in Southwark.

1 The cremated bones of a Roman Londoner deposited in a ceramic container. Roman Londoners were laid to rest in designated cemetery areas outside the city wall. Cremation and inhumation were both practised during the 400 years of Roman occupation of London.

The burial practices found in London are well paralleled elsewhere, the dead being either cremated or buried according to Roman custom. The two rites of

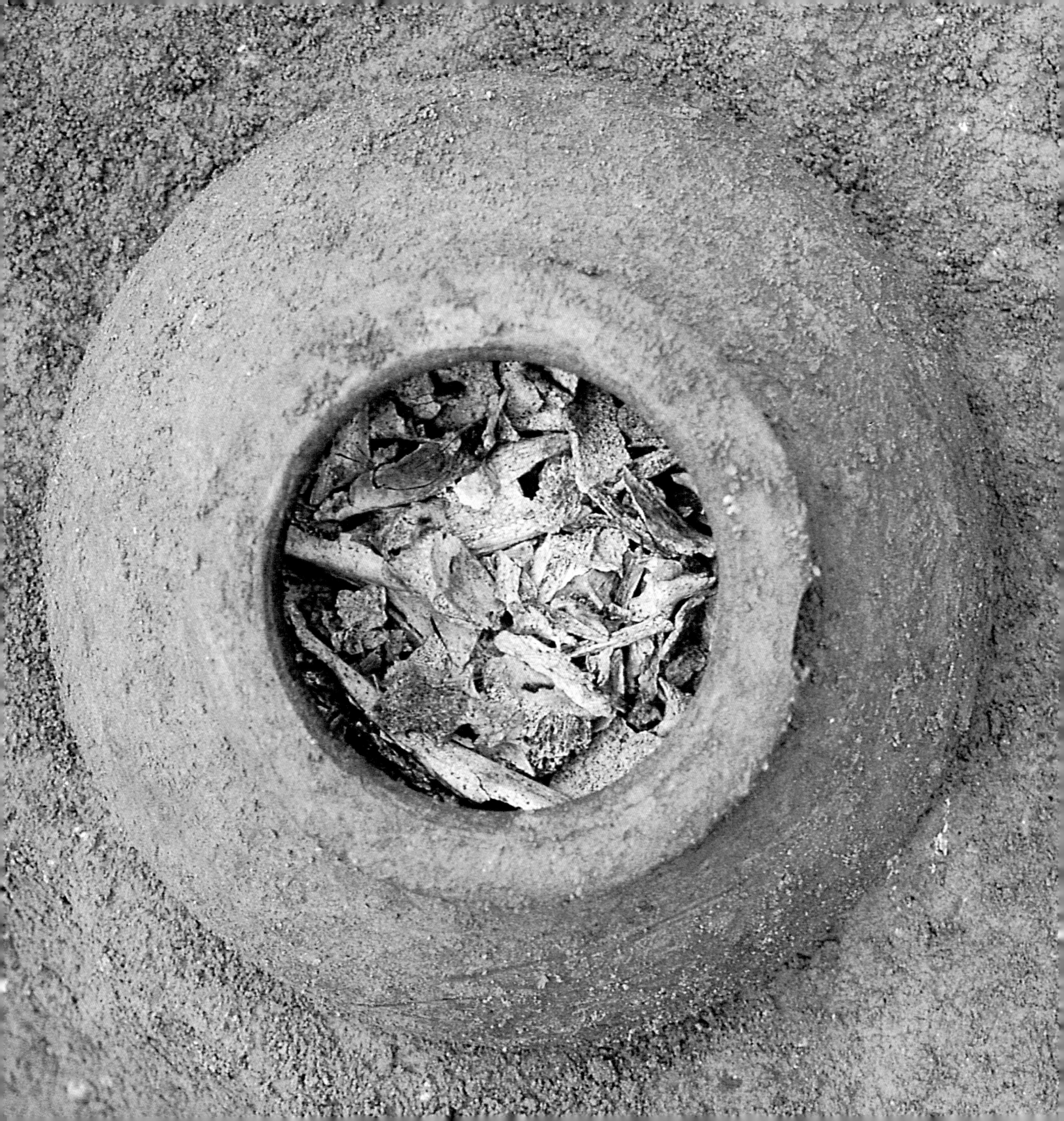

cremation and inhumation were practised contemporaneously but preference for one over the other varied over time and was sometimes restricted to particular age groups (Figure 1). The cemeteries were organised into family plots, other areas being reserved for burial clubs or special groups.

The discovery of cremation urns, coffins and skeletons from Roman London is recorded from the sixteenth century onwards. The early discoveries have no osteological record, and the skeletons were often reburied. Grave goods that were buried with the deceased have in many cases survived, and account for a number of complete pots, glass and jewellery held in museum collections today.

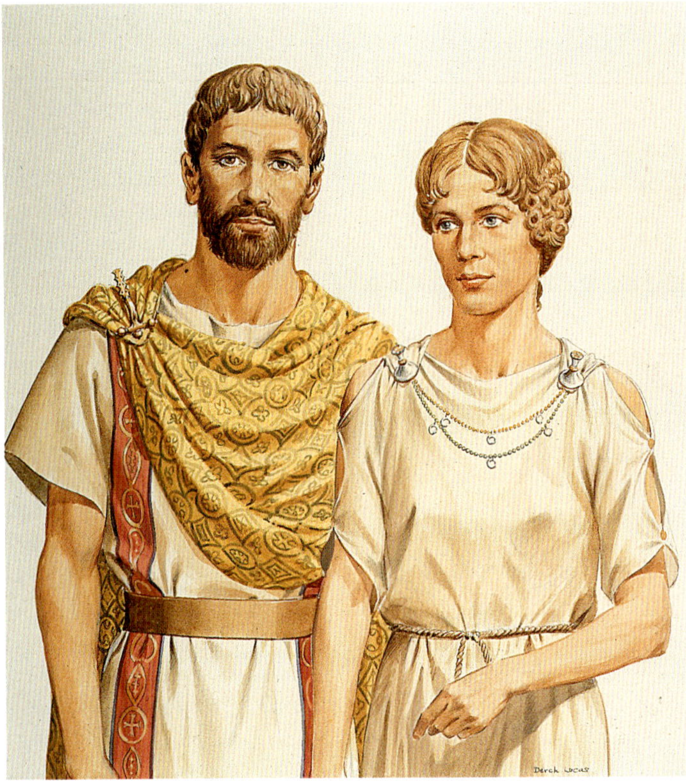

2

WHERE DID ROMAN LONDONERS COME FROM?

Written evidence for Roman London's inhabitants comes from stone inscriptions, both building and funereal, and from graffiti. The names of more than one hundred Roman Londoners are recorded, although only rarely is there information about their origins. Evidence from surviving tombstone inscriptions, for example, reveals that a soldier named Lucius Pompeius Licetus was born in Arretium (modern-day Arezzo in Italy), and that Aulus Alfidius Olussa, possibly a wealthy merchant or financier, was born in Athens and died in London at the advanced age of 70.

We are able to gather only a limited amount of information about the origins of Roman Londoners from the written evidence. Analysis of skeletal evidence has attempted to provide more information by comparing visible characteristics of the skeletons collected in London with those from Roman sites elsewhere in England where indigenous British people are thought to be represented. From this it has been possible to show that most Roman Londoners were native to Britain. Future research should compare samples from London's cemeteries (particularly the eastern cemetery at Aldgate) with large cemetery samples from Gaul, Germany and elsewhere in the Empire with a view to detecting any differences. It may be that Britons were too closely related to their European cousins for any significant differences to show up in their skeletal remains (Figure 2).

2 The excavation of two skeletons in the eastern cemetery showed that they had been buried with Germanic-style grave goods. Their bones indicated that there were no obvious racial differences from the other skeletons in the cemetery but the grave goods, being either German in style or actually made in Germany, indicated that the owners may have hailed from Germany. (Reconstruction by Derek Lucas.)

ARE WE ABLE TO DISTINGUISH SOCIAL STATUS OR CLASS IN SKELETONS?

Status or social class is not distinguishable in a single skeleton, but there are several indicators which appear to vary between burials of differing social or economic status. Thus those with a better diet may grow taller than those on a deprived diet; and while certain diseases, such as tuberculosis, are widespread among the poor and those living in overcrowded quarters, other conditions, such as gout, may reflect relative affluence. Overall, however, the burials from Roman London represent a community in which most people had adequate nutrition and only a few displayed evidence of either an exceptionally rich and ample diet on the one hand or nutritional deficiency and environmental stress on the other.

The eastern cemetery (that around Aldgate) may have been organised according to a social hierarchy. There appear to have been 29 separate groups of burials, described as plots. Throughout these plots the burials were orientated in two principal directions, roughly north–south and east–west. The physique, skeletal data and dental pathology do not suggest any difference in status between individuals buried in different orientations, and although those laid on the north–south alignment had eaten a less coarse and more processed fare than the other group, there are many possible reasons for this, other than status. The explanation for the differing burial alignments may also have been the influence of previous land-boundaries and the enclosure round the cemetery (a feature also of Christian graveyards later).

Different areas of the cemetery could have been segregated by age, sex or occupation, whether or not related to social status. For example, the bone evidence from the cremations in one of the plots included a high proportion of immature individuals, which may indicate a lower-status area, although in the same plot there were no infant burials amongst the inhumations. This plot and another were also unusual in that they had more males than in other plots. Generally, the low numbers of infants and babies in the excavated sample support the view that they lacked the same status as juveniles and adults. As for the wealthier section of the population of Roman London, finds of stone sarcophagi, lead coffins (two of them found in the eastern cemetery excavations) and ornate cremation vessels may represent higher-status burials. In the eastern cemetery the richer graves seemed to be concentrated towards the western side, where there were possible mausolea structures, and lead and stone coffins. Grave goods were not found to

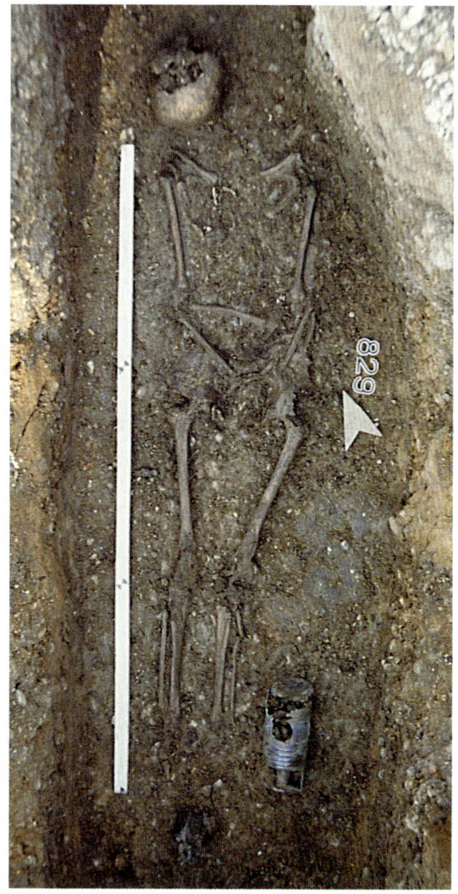

3

3 A Roman Londoner laid to rest with possessions. Two glass bottles lie at the feet of the skeleton. A number of bodies were buried with grave goods, deliberately chosen to ease their journey to the underworld and to protect them in the afterlife.

be indicative of the social status of individuals, and there were few indications that status was commonly expressed in this way. Indeed, the practice of including grave goods with the body was the exception rather than the rule (Figure 3).

MEN AND WOMEN, YOUNG AND OLD

The London cemetery evidence would suggest that London had a 'normal' urban population balance with no excessive numbers of men, and so was not primarily military in character (Figure 4). The eastern cemetery revealed a male-to-female ratio of 1.7:1. The ratio from burials recorded at Giltspur Street, part of the western cemetery immediately outside Newgate, was similar at 1.5:1, as was that at Lankhills near Winchester, an indigenous town cemetery (1.6:1). However, Cirencester, an urban centre, varied slightly at 2.2:1 and was matched by Poundbury in Dorset, an indigenous rural cemetery. At Trentholme Drive, York, interpreted as a garrison town, the ratio was 3.6:1. The sex ratio remained constant in all age groups in the London inhumations, except at Giltspur Street in the western cemetery, where there were more females aged between 17 and 25 years present, perhaps due to death in childbirth. The ratio differed, however, for cremation burials. Of 92 of these, only 33 could be determined as female and 16 as male, a reversed ratio of almost 2.1:1, but the sample was very limited and the sex of half of the bodies cremated could not be determined.

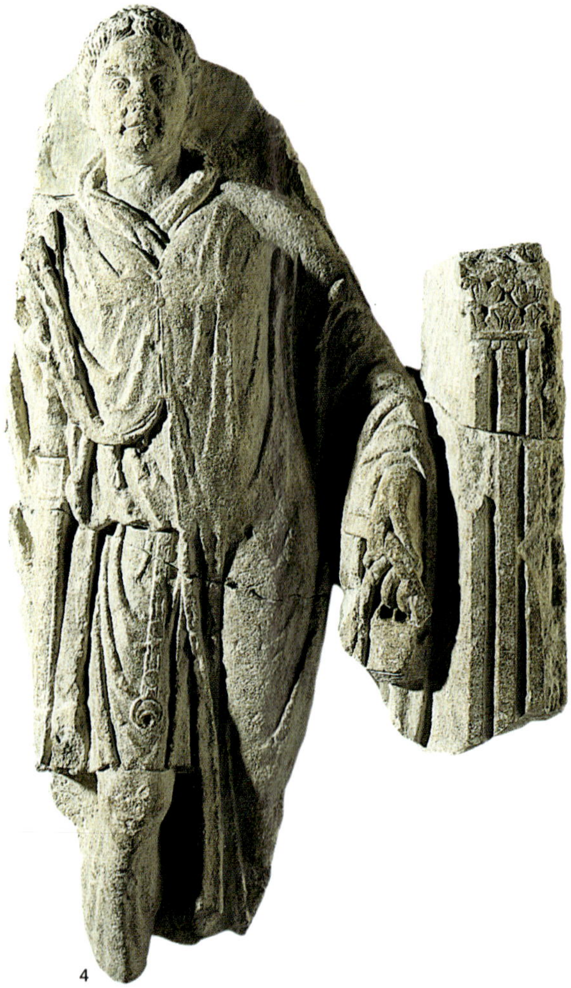

4

4 The portrayal of a male inhabitant of Londinium shows him as clean-shaven with his hair cut short and neatly tonsured. This soldier's tombstone was found re-used in a tower of the city wall at Camomile Street but he is likely to have been buried in the Bishopsgate area of the northern cemetery.

If, as suggested above, London had a normal urban population one would also expect a normal age mix. In the eastern cemetery, three-quarters of the inhumation skeletons were adult (19 years or older), and the remaining quarter 18 or under, 15.5 per cent being classed as children or teenagers (6–18 years) and 9.5 per cent as infants (under 5). The greatest number of deaths (31 per cent) occurred in mature adulthood, between the ages of 26 and 45. Only 10.5 per cent survived beyond the age of 45. The evidence that Olussa died at the age of 70 marks him out as an exceptionally old man. At the other end of the age range, very young individuals were largely missing from the sample. It has been calculated that the ratio of those under one year of age to those aged under 20 years in a sample from a normal population should be in the region of 4:1 to 4:3. For the eastern cemetery, however, this figure was 1:16.8. This is very unlikely to be a true representation of the living population, and the most likely explanation is that a proportion of young individuals, especially infants, were buried in areas of the cemetery which were not excavated. There is also evidence that young babies may not have been buried in the cemetery at all: Roman law allowed dead perinatal and neonatal babies to be buried at their parents' homes, and the skeleton of a baby up to two months old was found buried under the floor of a workshop on the Roman waterfront at Regis House, Lower Thames Street.

Classical writers described British women as being as tall and well-built as their husbands. Boudica, Queen of the Iceni, was described as 'very tall in stature, in appearance most terrifying, in the glance of her eye most fierce, harsh in voice . . . and with a great mass of bright red hair falling to her hips'. Average Roman Londoners would have been slightly shorter than their modern-day counterparts, who are taller and healthier thanks to better living conditions and diet. In the eastern cemetery, the average male height was 169cm (5ft 6in.), with a range of 158 to 180cm (5ft 2in. to 5ft 11in.), while the average female was 158cm (5ft 2in.) tall, with a range of 145 to 172cm (4ft 9in. to 5ft 8in.): not as tall on average as the classical writers believed. This does not of course mean that there were no tall men and women in the population. Tall individuals have been discovered at other sites, such as a man at Giltspur Street who was 188cm (6ft 2in.) tall, and a woman from St Bartholomew's Hospital who was 172cm (5ft 8in.) tall. Comparable heights have also been recorded at Cirencester and Trentholme Drive, York.

The overall build tended towards the robust. The majority of skeletons were strikingly uniform in their skull shape and type, many of the females even having characteristics generally accepted as male around the jawline. Metrical indices for the shape of the skull and facial bones match those frequently quoted for Romano-British populations. Skulls were of a form midway between rounded, and a long oval from front to back when viewed from above. When viewed from the side they were of average width across the forehead and with broad palates. A small proportion of males had very emphatic angles to their jaw, flaring outwards (Figure 5). This was a characteristic also noted at Poundbury Roman cemetery in Dorset, a rural cemetery which contained people local to that area and not dissimilar in looks to the area's inhabitants today.

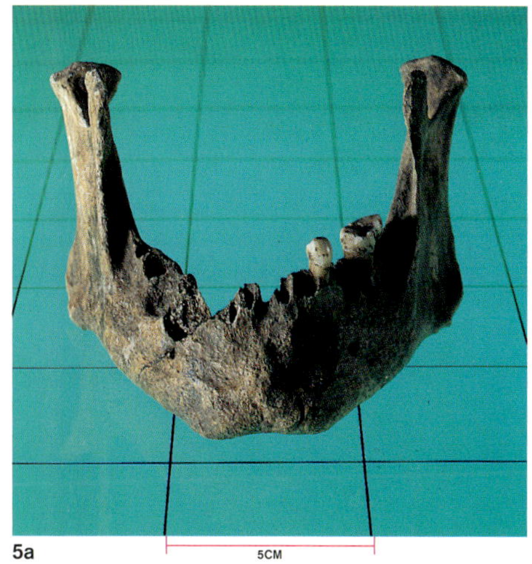

5a

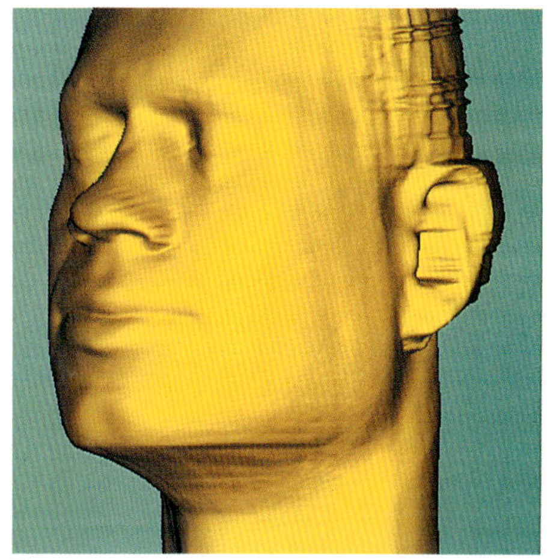

5b

5 **(5a) The jawbone of one of several males who must have had very pronounced jawlines. (5b) Facial reconstruction of a Roman Londoner with a flared jawline.**

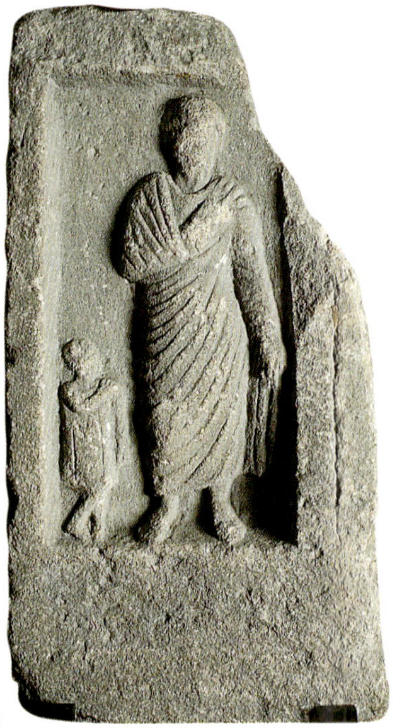

6

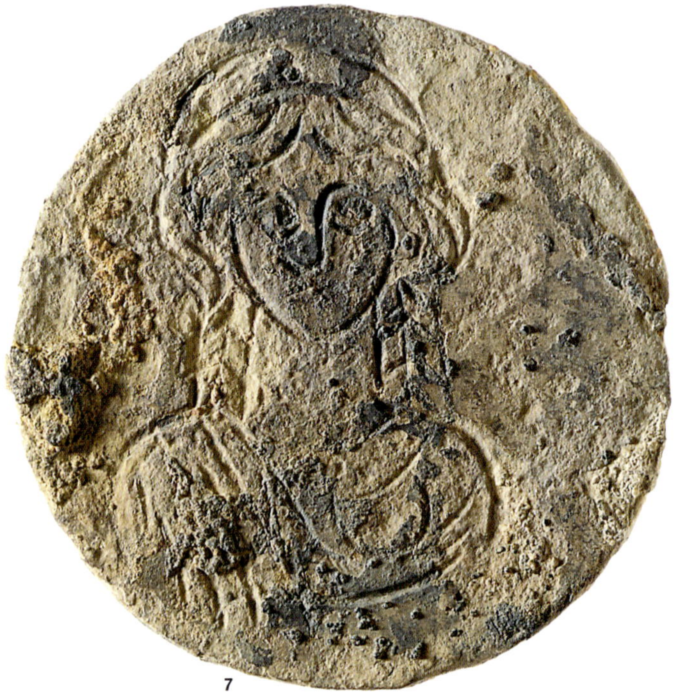

7

HOW ROMAN LONDONERS LOOKED

To flesh out the skeletal information we need to look elsewhere for clues to the appearance of Roman Londoners. The reconstructed head from a skull of a middle-aged male from St Albans was the first attempt at creating the likeness of a Romano-British person, followed by one of a woman from Colchester. Surviving sculptures and tombstones depicting the deceased, together with wall paintings, all presumably show how people may have looked (Figure 6).

Roman Londoners would, no doubt, have followed the fashion of emperors and empresses as portrayed on coins. Women's hair was always grown long, and was either left loose or fixed up in a bun, coils or other elaborate styles held in place by hairpins (Figure 7). An ornate bone hairpin depicts a style favoured by late first-century empresses in which the hair was built up on a wire frame and secured by long pins. Fashions changed, and two hundred years later female hair was crimped in waves while shorter pins held a bun at the nape of the neck. Unfortunately there are no examples of hair surviving from Roman London to indicate hair colour. The Roman writer, Cassius Dio, noted the preponderance of red hair among the southern tribes of Britain, and this has been confirmed by traces of hair found in graves. Brown and blonde hair was also found

6 A tombstone depicting two male figures. The adult wears a toga, a semi-circle of cloth draped around the body over a tunic, and the boy wears a simple tunic and cloak. Both are examples of styles of clothing which were worn in Roman London.

7 This portrayal of a young girl shows her wearing her shoulder-length hair loose in ringlets with a centre-parting and a possible band over the forehead. The copper-alloy disc is thought to be a brothel token.

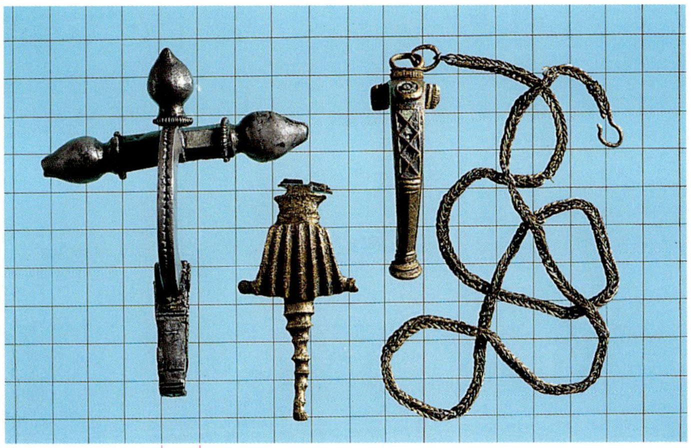
8

1CM

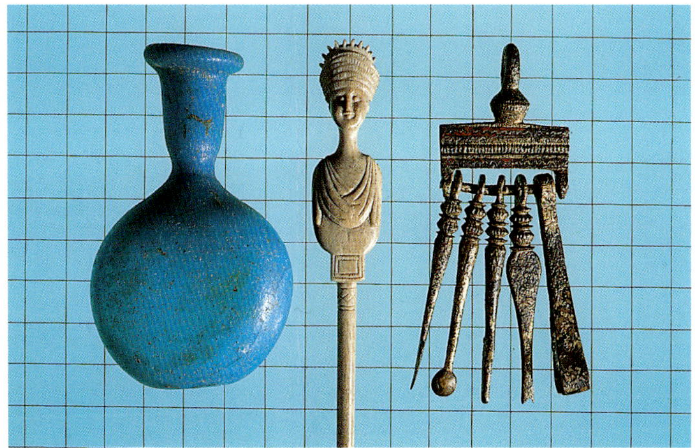
9

1CM

at Poundbury. However, dyed and false hair were not unknown in the Roman world, saffron or henna being used as dyes, and wigs and hair-pieces being made with sought-after blonde German hair or black Indian hair. It is likely that within only a few generations every hair colour and skin tone would have been commonplace in London.

The application of make-up must have been a time-consuming business, confined to the wealthier women with the leisure time available and the maidservants to help. Mineral-based pellets and powders were ground in special cosmetic grinders to produce a fine powder, and the face and arms could be whitened using chalk or white lead. Cheeks and lips were reddened with the lees from red wine or ochre. Eyelids and brows were blackened with mascara made of charcoal or powdered antimony, and unwanted hair was plucked with tweezers or removed with pumice or depilatories containing such ingredients as resin and pitch (Figure 9).

Little evidence survives from London of the type and style of dress the Roman Londoner might have worn. Textile fragments indicate that the most popular material for clothing was wool made in a variety of weaves: plain, herringbone and diamond twill. Most people would have worn tunics tied at the waist: under the bust with tablet-woven braid bands for women and with buckled leather belts for men. Men would have worn short cloaks, usually with hoods that could be pulled over the head in bad weather and fastened at the shoulder by a brooch. The toga, a symbol of Roman civilisation, must have been worn only on formal occasions (see Figure 6).

Women wore long tunics with brooches fixing the garments at each shoulder.

8 **A selection of brooches used to pin clothes together. Brooches were made in many designs, their style dependent on fashion trends.**

9 **Items for personal grooming: a glass phial for expensive perfumed oils, a hairpin decorated with an elaborately coiffured female bust and a set of implements for plucking hair and manicuring nails.**

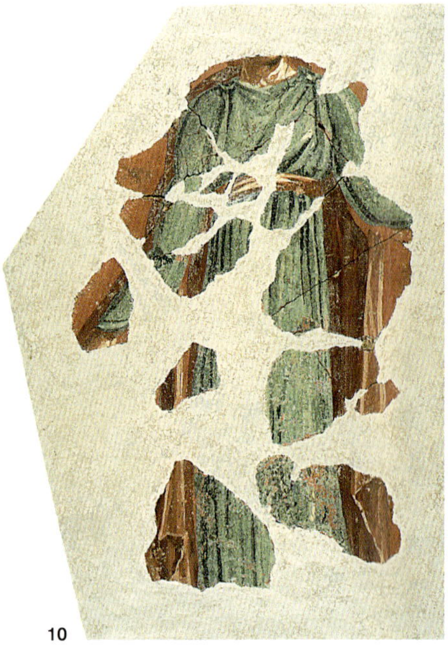
10

Depending on their age, they would then wear a type of shawl around the shoulders which could also be pulled up around the head as a hood. Literary evidence and surviving materials provide an idea of the colours used in clothing, dye-stuffs being available which created blue, black, yellow, green, brown, bright red and purple (Figure 10).

Individual preference and taste are reflected in the variety and amount of jewellery recovered from Roman London. Most brooches were functional rather than ornamental, and of a ubiquitous 'safety-pin' type used to hold the clothing together (Figure 8). Women also wore necklaces of glass, amber and emerald beads. Excavated burials in London indicate that women often wore several bracelets at the same time. Jet would appear to have been worn only by women, as were earrings which were made for pierced ears: one Roman writer commented that girls had their ears pierced while still babies. Both sexes wore finger-rings both as ornament and for use in sealing business documents and letters.

The only examples of dress to survive from London are those made from leather, which remains in good condition when waterlogged (Figure 11). Shoes recovered from waterfront sites at Billingsgate Buildings and New Fresh Wharf had clearly been discarded when worn out. The wear indicated that some must have been too tight, causing the feet to distort with bunions. The sizes varied from those of small children to adult, the largest adult examples being British sizes 8 to 11. Styles varied between nailed shoes, sandals and one-piece shoes. Some shoes had uppers with openwork decoration allowing the wearer's coloured stockings to show through the design. Stout boots were also worn by both sexes, the upper a separate piece of leather stitched and nailed with iron hobnails to the sole of the shoe. Burials in the cemeteries included pairs of shoes showing the hobnails in matching patterns. Like textile clothing, leather was likely to have been brightly coloured.

10 A typical example of a female tunic, fastened at the shoulders and gathered in under the bust. This woman in a light green tunic, depicted on fragments of a wall painting from Fenchurch Street, is possibly a goddess or a muse.

DIET, TEETH AND NUTRITION

Life for the majority of those living in the Empire must often have been a struggle for survival. The dietary complaints of the poor would have been malnutrition, vitamin deficiency and food poisoning. In Pliny's *Natural History*, for instance, stomach ache is the most frequently mentioned ailment, and was due to intestinal parasites. Overall, most of the available diet contained adequate protein from fish, meat, dairy produce and pulses, adequate vitamin C from fresh fruit and vegetables, and adequate vitamin D from fish oils, liver, eggs and exposure to sunlight. The skeletal evidence for the Roman Londoners' diet indicates that most people had access to an adequate diet, only a small proportion suffering from parasitic infestation or chronic upsets that hindered efficient uptake from the diet. Such instances revealed evidence of either possible deficiencies of iron, or of vitamins C or D, or both, and a general overall inadequacy of diet. An even smaller proportion enjoyed an excessively rich or plentiful diet.

In periods of nutritional stress, physical growth is affected before tooth development. Fewer than five per cent of children from the eastern cemetery showed any evidence of stunted growth relative to their dental development age, and as only a small proportion was affected it may be that the population at large was not subject to a severely inadequate diet. Low male stature, another symptom of protein deficiency, was absent from the eastern cemetery, suggesting that, overall, diet would appear to have been adequate.

Developmental defects in the enamel of teeth (enamel hypoplasia) can reflect nutritional stress during childhood, but other causal factors can be psychological and physical stress as at periods of severe illness. Hypoplasia affected nearly 12 per cent of teeth. Many cases in the living person would not have been apparent to the naked eye. Female teeth were slightly more affected than male. Of 2031 teeth inspected, only seven per cent had cavities due to caries. This is comparable to proportions from other Romano-British sites, and suggests a relatively sugar-free diet or high standards of oral hygiene. Where caries was present, the third molars were the most affected, which might indicate that hygiene (or lack of it) was of more account than diet, for this is the most difficult part of the mouth to keep clean. Men, then as now, were less successful than women. The most frequently affected part of the tooth was the surface adjacent to another tooth, showing that trapped food was a major cause of caries. In children's milk teeth the cavities were confined to the molars. While caries was not widespread, most teeth were affected by calcified plaque and gum disease. A number of teeth were missing before death, and periodontal disease and the resulting tooth loss may have become a serious problem for Roman Londoners in later life.

Wear on the teeth, however, was often severe, particularly among older individuals, and this suggests a coarse diet, such as cereal baked into bread, which required prolonged mastication. The wear also accounts for the lack of caries on the chewing surfaces of the teeth, for the surfaces were worn smooth. The combination of caries and

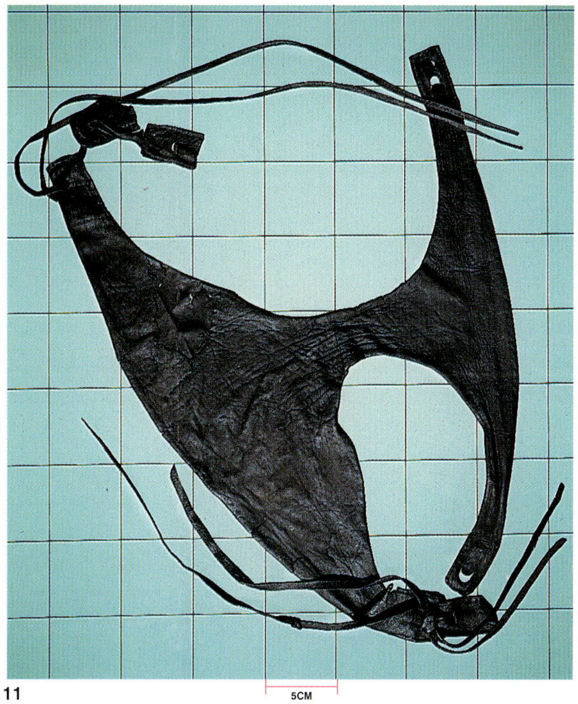

11

11 **A pair of leather briefs, of a size to be worn by women and young girls. Their exact pupose is uncertain but it would seem that they were worn by young female acrobats in Roman London.**

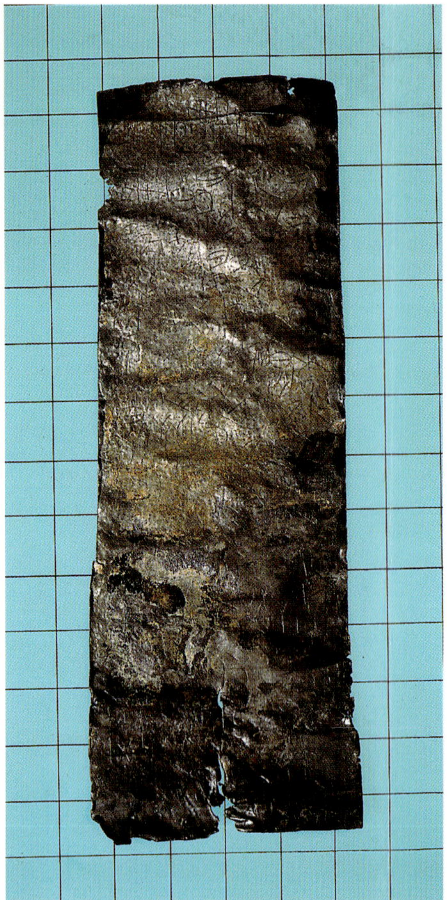

12 1CM

severe wear meant that there were frequent cases of dental abscesses on the sides of the jaws. The affected people may have had swollen faces and perhaps halitosis.

Vitamin deficiencies were not uncommon in the Roman world. The ancient writers Hippocrates, Pliny and Galen recognised that scurvy was caused by insufficient fresh fruit and vegetables and that 'night blindness' was due to the lack of animal fats and oils in the diet (and therefore vitamin A). There is some indication of vitamin C deficiencies in the diet of Roman Londoners, perhaps resulting from insufficient fruit and vegetables, or from overcooking. This could have been responsible for the pathology (periostitis) observed. In the eastern cemetery 10 per cent of skeletons were affected and the condition has also been observed in other skeletons from London, as in the ulcerous lesion on the tibia of an older individual from the Courage Brewery site in Southwark. There is one possible case of infantile scurvy in the eastern cemetery sample, and this would have been visible in the living person as slightly reddened, swollen gums. It is possible that scurvy was widely present in the population but was not well advanced enough to be evident in the majority of skeletons.

Skeletal evidence suggests that a small proportion of individuals may have suffered from a vitamin D deficiency which can reveal itself as rickets in children or as osteomalacia in adults. This could be the result of a dietary deficiency or lack of exposure to sunlight. There were classic examples of bowed long bones and splayed ends of ribs, and the bowed legs would of course have been apparent in the living person. Gallstones are formed as a result of dietary, genetic and hormonal factors, and one was found among the cremated bones of an older adult from the eastern cemetery.

For a few, the diet may have been excessively rich. There are two possible cases of gout, a metabolic disorder which results in an inflammatory reaction in the joints. Affected individuals tend to be older, overweight men. Ingestion of lead can produce similar symptoms, the resultant kidney damage triggering the same increased levels of uric acid in the blood. High lead levels in the bone of individuals from other Roman sites such as Poundbury, the existence of lead water pipes, the preparation of food and drink in lead-lined vessels, and the use of pewter tableware all suggest the possibility of food contamination in London. At West Tenter Street the lead levels were found to be twice those of the modern adult population elsewhere. At the eastern cemetery a few possible instances of Paget's disease were identified, which may also support the likelihood of lead poisoning, a contributing factor in the onset of the disease.

12 **Demetrius, the wearer of this rolled piece of lead alloy containing an inscribed prayer, must have been worried by the fear of plague and other contagious diseases. In the prayer he asks the god Apollo to protect him from such calamities.**

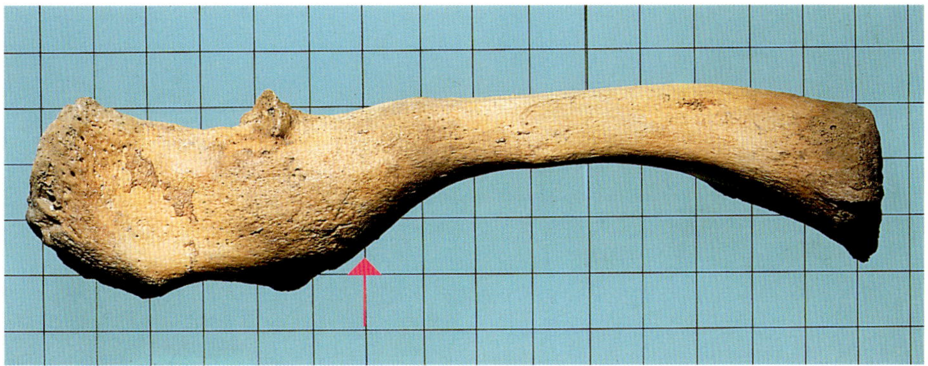

13

13 Many fractures were well aligned, implying a knowledge of setting techniques. In the eastern cemetery the most frequent breaks suffered were to the ribs, hand and feet bones and less commonly to the collar bone. This example from Southwark shows a left clavicle collar bone which had been well aligned in the setting process and had healed correctly.

DISEASES, THE EFFECTS OF REPETITIVE ACTIVITIES AND FRACTURES

Ill health was ever present and difficult to avoid. It stemmed from overcrowding and contagion, aided by indifferent waste disposal, limited access to running water and minimal medical knowledge. Tuberculosis is an indicator of overcrowded living conditions, poverty and poor hygiene, and though few of those suffering from it would have undergone any skeletal changes, there were at least two cases in the eastern cemetery where the bones were affected. It is likely therefore that a much larger sample may have suffered from the disease. The parts of the skeleton affected made tuberculosis a more likely diagnosis than brucellosis, a similar malady caused by contaminated milk or meat products.

The mobility of both the military and civilians increased the chances of widespread contagion. Plague in Rome in AD166, for example, was one of the many epidemics brought back from the east by the army and the fear of plague troubled at least one inhabitant of Roman London (Figure 12). Roman Londoners could also be expected to have suffered from such respiratory infections as bronchitis or sinusitis brought on by the cold, damp climate, but of these there is no surviving evidence.

Diseases of old age shown by the skeletons include diffuse idiopathic skeletal hyperostosis (DISH) and Paget's disease, which tend to affect men over 45 years and 65 years respectively. There was also a case of possible psoriatic arthritis which also tends to affect individuals in later life, and would have been visible as a chronic skin condition. Some post-menopausal women were probably present, as there was evidence of the characteristic effects of hormonal changes on the frontal bone of the skull. A more common disorder, affecting five adults in the sample, was osteoporosis, which involves

14

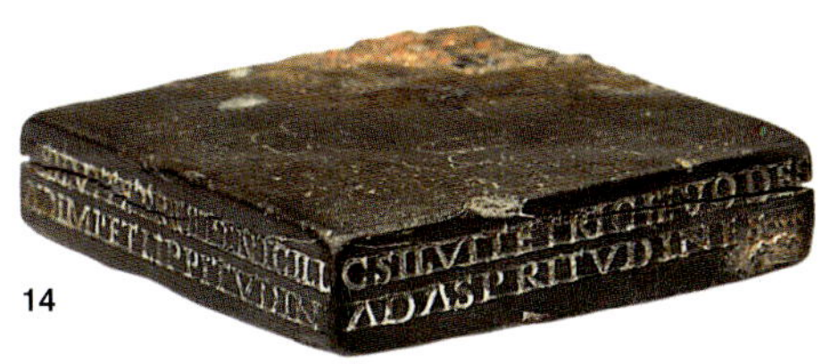

14 A stone stamp belonging to an oculist of Gaulish origin, Gaius Silvius Tetricus, who probably travelled the country with his medical preparations for various eye complaints. His stamp is labelled with prescriptions for ointments for eye inflammation.

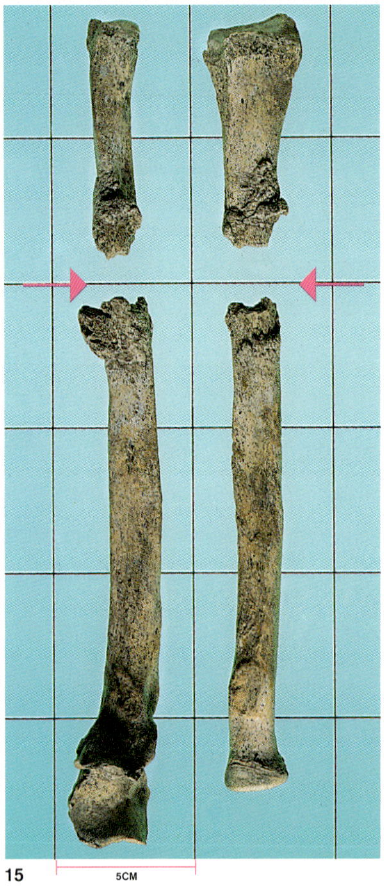

15

the loss of bone mass and a tendency to stress fractures in persons over 50 years of age.

Osteoarthritis is an age-related wear-and-tear disease more likely to affect those already affected by disease, injury or obesity. It can occur in different bones, the most common locations in the London sample appearing in the spine, hip and shoulder; a similar pattern is recorded at Cirencester but not in Poundbury. It has been suggested that the presence of osteoarthritis can also indicate stress on particular joints as a result of repeated postures, and differences in male and female patterns may indicate different working roles. Common throughout the sample were 'Schmorl's nodes', lesions on the vertebral bodies sometimes attributed to lifting excessive weight in an immature individual: both men and women were affected. Another similar condition, spondylolysis, or the separation of the neural arch from the vertebral body, has been attributed to trauma or excessive strain on the lower back in adolescence. This was not common, however, and found to be present in only five cases.

Changes to the bone at the sites of muscle and ligament insertions can suggest activities of a repetitive nature. In the eastern cemetery, differences in the distribution of these changes were apparent between individuals of different plots and on different orientations, raising the possibility that the groups had been involved in distinct activities. Some individuals from one of the orientation groups revealed a combination of changes suggestive of the erect posture and controlled leg movements required in an activity such as horse riding, and there were similar examples at Poundbury. Members of the other orientation group had undergone changes to the legs and feet consistent with habitual movement over rough ground. Both kinds of changes were observed amongst the members of one of the plots, whereas those in another plot exhibited changes consistent with both erect posture and stress to the elbow, very similar to modern repetitive strain injury and associated with a controlled sweeping movement such as that employed in scything. Because of problems with dating, it is not possible to attribute any of the burials showing these characteristics to a particular period. It is interesting to note, however, that they are present in one group.

The people of Roman London suffered various fractures and injuries as a result of physical activity and manual labour, and the distribution and types of fracture can be used to suggest distinct patterns of activity. The skeletons of the eastern cemetery had more frequently suffered breaks to the ribs, hand and feet bones, and only to a lesser extent to the collar bone. These injuries are typical of bad falls and everyday accidents to the hands

15 **Although the cemetery evidence showed that it was a relatively law-abiding society, there are some examples of 'parry' fractures where the individuals had protected their heads from blows.**

and feet. Some arm fractures were indicative of putting out the arm to break a fall. There were also a few cases of parry fracture which suggest that the forearm had protected the body by warding off a blow (Figure 15). In addition, there are a couple of examples of depression fractures to the skull, perhaps also indicative of violence. One individual had cuts to three of the lumbar vertebrae which showed no sign of healing and could have been the cause of death. Such small numbers of injuries attributable to assault suggest that London was not an unduly violent place.

The surgeons' ability to set bones is well documented: trained and untrained practitioners of medicine were to be found throughout the Roman world (Figure 14). Many fractures were well aligned and free from secondary infection, suggesting some level of competent care and an understanding of splints and setting (Figure 13). Equally, some fractures were very badly aligned and had become chronically infected. Those with fractured arms and legs would have needed temporary assistance with daily life. There are no examples from London of severe congenital defects that would have required prolonged care of the infant, although there are several cases of spina bifida occulta which would not have caused disability. There was one possible case of advanced ankylosing spondylitis, a form of arthritis that can fuse the spine and sometimes other joints, and this individual may have been incapacitated and needed long-term care.

CONCLUSIONS

The majority of Roman Londoners appear to have been native Britons. On average, they were a little shorter than modern Londoners and quite robust in stature. Their bones reflect the usual degenerative complaints of old age, although they did not live as long as Londoners today. They enjoyed an adequate diet and suffered little from dental problems, though tooth loss may have been a serious problem in later life.

And when all else failed, the Romans resorted to prayer. Healing deities flourished alongside medical knowledge, and the patron of physicians was the god Aesculapius. His symbol was the caduceus, a staff entwined with snakes, still used in medical contexts today. The gods were petitioned at shrines where supplicants would seek help with ailments of particular parts of the body, or thank the gods in the event of a cure. Anatomical votive miniatures of legs, feet, arms, hands and genitalia have been found throughout what was the Roman Empire, but seem to have been particularly popular in Gaul and Britain (Figure 16).

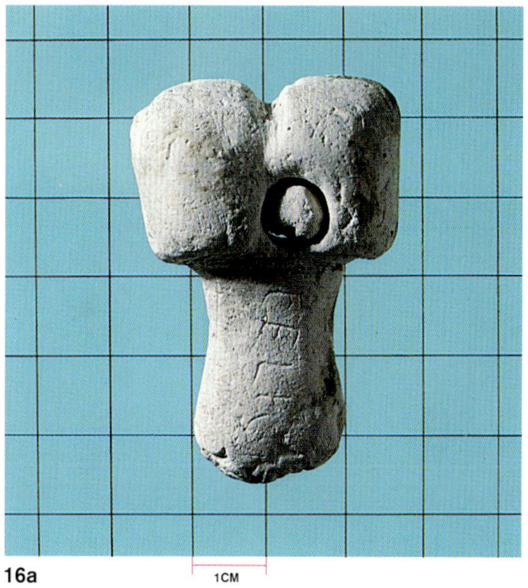

16a

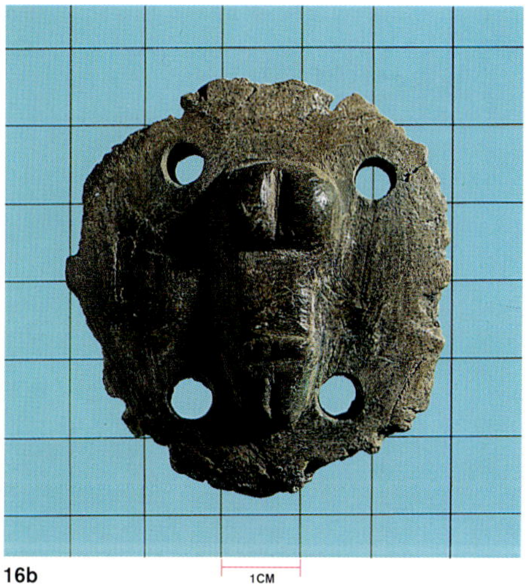

16b

16 A number of anatomical votive offerings that portray male genitalia have been found from Londinium. Men must have sought help from the gods for impotence, infertility and sexually transmitted diseases. One offering shown (16a) has 'Good Luck' scratched on it.

ROMAN CEMETERIES

RECENT DISCOVERIES

Just as each person differs from the next on the surface, so each skeleton differs from all others, increasing the importance of large samples. Excavations in recent years have revealed an extensive Roman cemetery area to the east of Londinium in the Aldgate area. Altogether, 550 skeletons and over 100 cremated individuals were recovered. In the western cemetery at Giltspur Street, 128 inhumation burials were similarly excavated, and earlier investigations at St Bartholomew's Hospital recovered 20 burials. It is these two main cemetery areas, and especially the extensive research on the skeletal material from the eastern cemetery, which have provided the first real opportunity for the controlled gathering of data on a large scale. Although it represents only a small proportion of the entire populace of London throughout the 400 years of Roman occupation, this invaluable material forms the basis of this analysis of Roman Londoners.

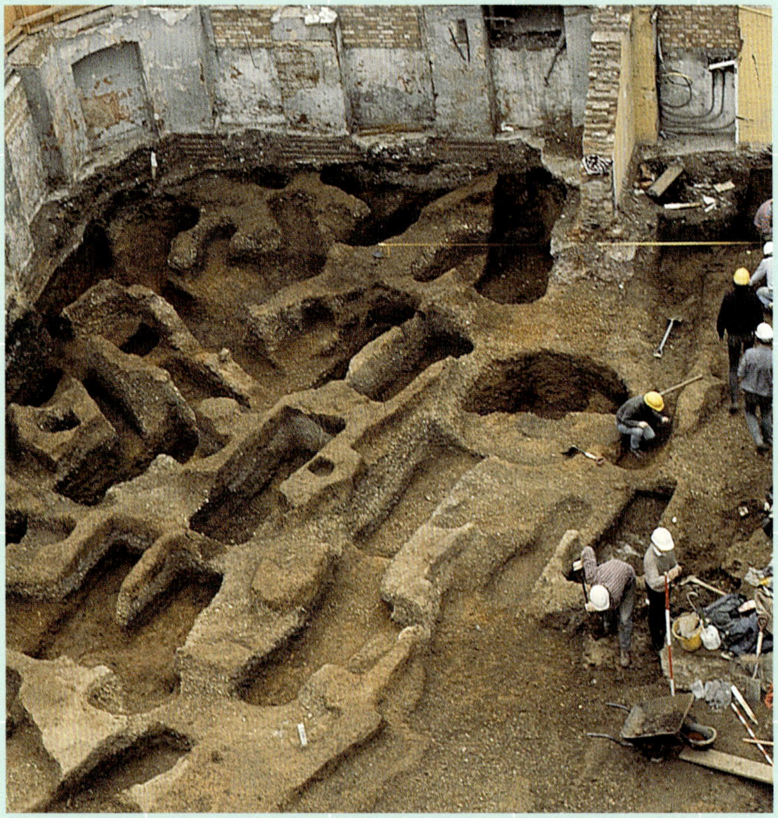

2

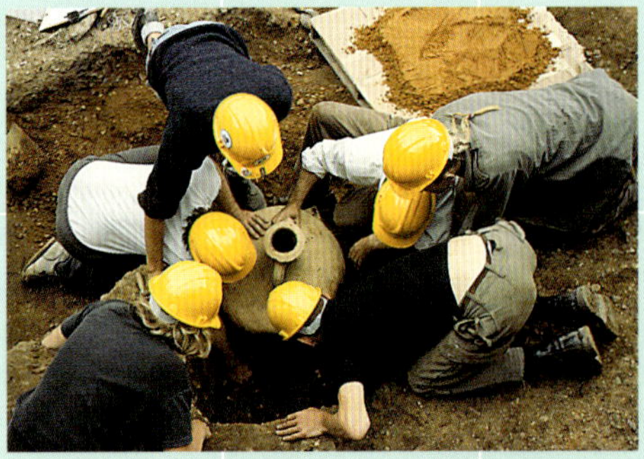

1

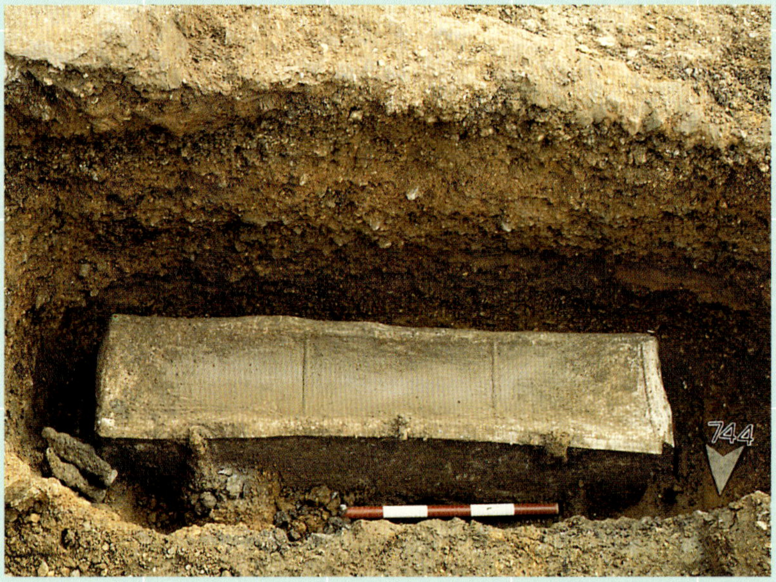

3

1 Archaeologists excavating a cremation that had been deposited in an amphora, more usually used for transporting foodstuffs. A total of 234 cremation burials have been found from Roman London.

2 Part of the Roman eastern cemetery during excavations. The skeletons have been removed but the empty grave cuts indicate the crowded nature of the cemetery.

3 A lead coffin indicated a more wealthy burial. The skeleton of the young child inside showed evidence of possible rickets, temporary arrested growth and some physical or environmental stress.This was probably the burial of a sickly but much loved child.

4 Excavation of a skeleton in the Roman eastern cemetery. An archaeologist carefully cleans the bones before the skeleton is recorded, photographed and removed for research. A total of 1092 inhumation burials have been recorded from Roman London.

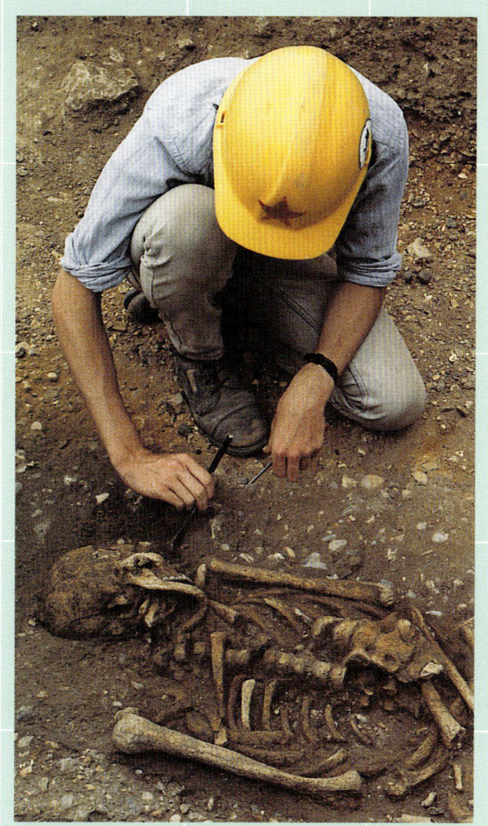

4

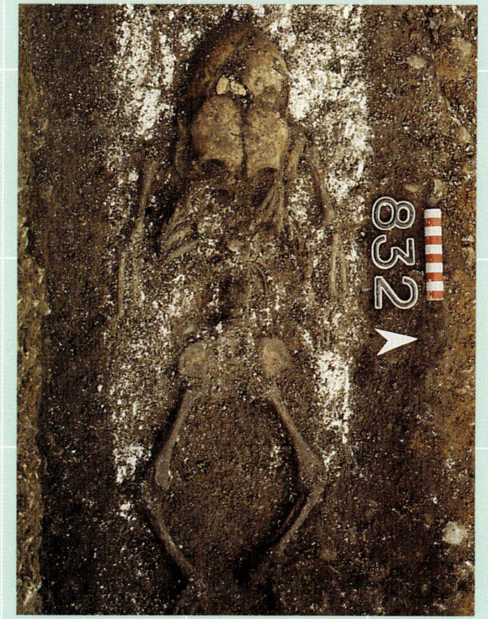

5

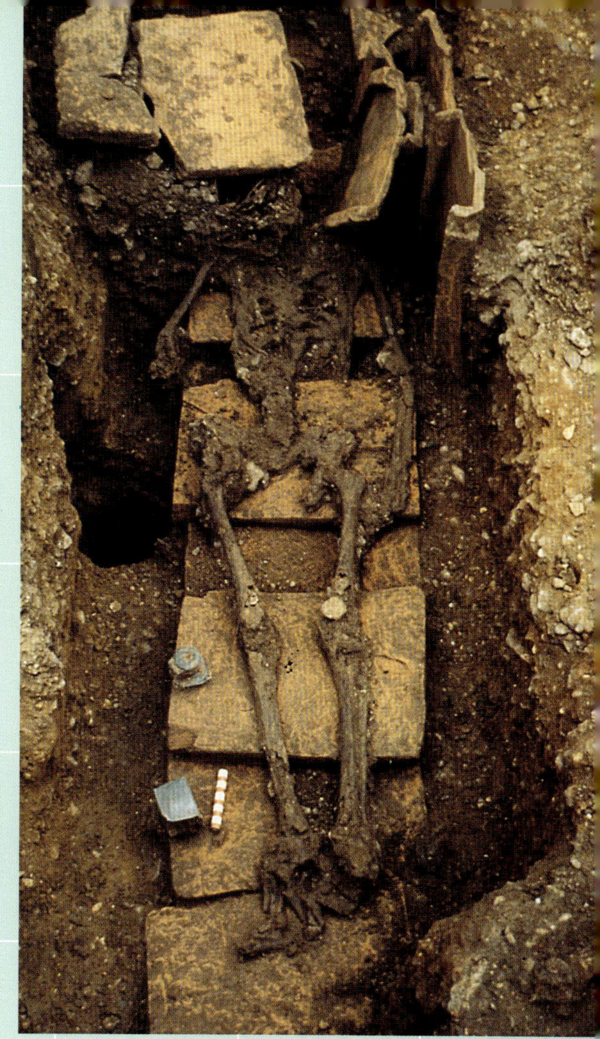

6

5 Excavation of an infant from a chalk-packed wooden coffin.

6 There can be problems in identifying a skeleton's gender. This skeleton, buried in a tile cist, was sexed as a probable male but the grave goods, a bead anklet, two mirrors and two glass perfume bottles, indicated a female burial.

SAXON BODIES

A GREAT MELTING POT?

by Judith Stevenson

The years between AD400 and AD1100 represent one of the most complicated periods in European and British history. This was a time of political, economic and social change, when different peoples migrated around Europe in response to invasion, expansion and settlement. British history is littered with the names of such ethnic groups as Britons, Picts, Scots, Angles, Saxons, Jutes, Frisians, Vikings, Danes, Norsemen and Normans. In England the level of immigration and intermixing remains unclear, as does the extent to which changes in lifestyle and culture, shown by archaeological finds, reflect the adoption of new ways by the people already here and by the newcomers.

The origin myths of the migration period, from historians like Bede, plus past and present-day ethnic labelling, make it difficult to sift through and separate the strands of accurate record from constructed history. It is clear that history and archaeology must be viewed together, since history emphasises movements of people, invading, fighting, and settling, while archaeology suggests cultural change, with people adopting and adapting different ways of living. This is shown in their buildings, ornaments and clothing.

Archaeologists have found four successive phases in the development of settlement in the London area during these centuries. In the Early Saxon period (fifth to sixth centuries), the population was totally rural, and included both a native and probably an immigrant element. There was a gradual urbanisation in the Middle Saxon period (seventh to ninth centuries) through the establishment of a port town called Lundenwic. Thirdly, at the start of the Late Saxon period (late ninth to mid-eleventh centuries) in the face of Viking raids, King Alfred developed a new town, Lundenburg, within the walls of the old Roman city. Finally this town became the most important in England and was conquered by the Normans in the winter of 1066.

1 The size of feet in Saxon and Norman London was as wide-ranging as today. This woman's feet would fit a modern size 6 1/2 shoe. She was buried in the Norman cemetery of St Nicholas Shambles (11th–12th century). Her toes have visible nodules or bony outgrowths, called arthrosis, probably from repeated bruising and badly fitting shoes. The bones of two toes are also fused.

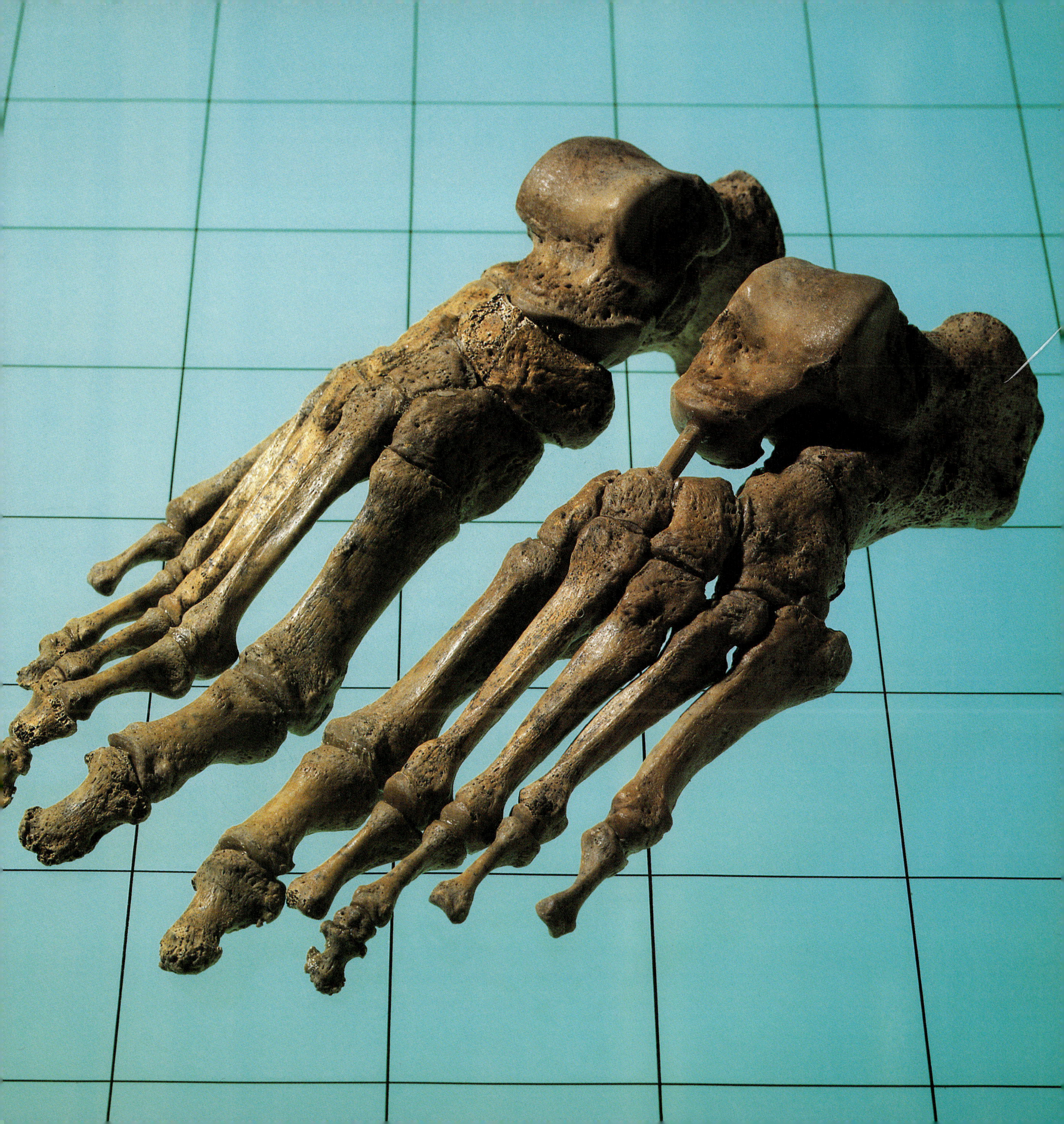

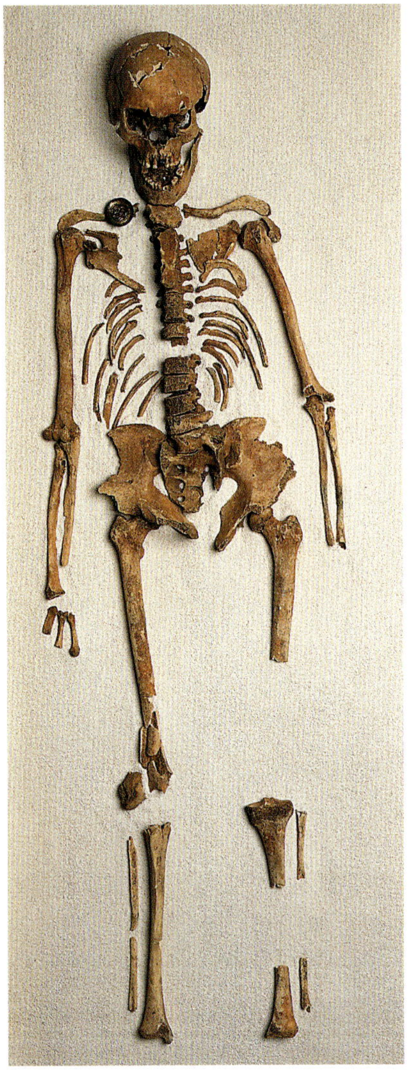

2

2 A woman who died in her thirties, who had a congenital lower back disorder – the lowest vertebra is fused to the sacrum. A fracture on her left collar bone and caries in her teeth are also evident. She was buried at Ewell in Surrey in the 5th–6th century in an overgown fastened by a brooch.

A PERIOD OF CONSTANT CHANGE, BUT FEW BODIES

Though there is a scarcity of skeletal material for the Saxon period as a whole in the London area, it is still possible to piece together evidence from the scant human remains, artefacts and ecofacts recovered from settlement and burial sites in Greater London and elsewhere, and to consider these in the light of historical records. The fifth to sixth centuries are characterised by scattered farming communities whose pagan (non-Christian) beliefs are reflected in their burial practices. Burials were accompanied by food supplied for the journey into the afterlife and the material requirements of the deceased person – clothing, weapons, tools and other personal possessions, perhaps their finest. Cemeteries from this period have been found scattered over the London region, mostly away from the modern-day centre. The largest concentrations of cemeteries and settlements lie to the south in the area between Croydon, Mitcham and Ewell, in the south-east around Farningham and Orpington, and to the west, scattered along the Thames and its tributaries. A large Early Saxon cemetery at Mitcham produced some 230 burials, of which only a few complete skeletons and some 30 skulls were retained for study.

Grave deposits provide many clues to the appearance of the people, whether native British or Germanic settlers. In one of the graves excavated at Ewell in the early 1930s a woman was buried in an overgown fastened at the right shoulder by a gilded bronze saucer brooch (Figure 2). The textiles have long vanished but contact of the brooch with the right collar-bone and lower jaw has stained them green. A similar staining on the bones of the left wrist indicates the wearing of a bronze bracelet or sleeve clasp, now lost. The woman was around 157cm (5ft 2in.) tall, and died in her thirties. She had been born with a deformation of the pelvis, her lumbarised first sacral vertebra possibly compounding the arthritis in her lower back and neck vertebrae. These may have caused her to stand awkwardly, and would have caused her pain at times, limiting her ability to undertake daily chores, particularly the carrying, bending, lifting and pounding involved in most domestic work. A well-healed fracture on her left collar bone indicates that the bone was treated soon after the fracture occurred by an experienced medical hand. She also suffered from dental disease, the crowns of her lower first molars having been destroyed by caries which left only the infected roots and an abscess on the right side. This level of caries is symptomatic of a sweet diet including such foodstuffs as honey or alcohol, probably ale.

Interest in personal appearance is suggested by the presence of tweezers, used for hair removal, and found particularly in male graves. Female graves commonly have a 'toilet set' of picks, scoops and tweezers, and occasionally cosmetic brushes, perhaps for the application of powders or paints. Grooming the hair was important to both men and women, as shown by the number of combs found on settlements and in burials, and by written sources. Combs carried a significance beyond the practical purpose of controlling head-lice, combing the hair and possibly the beard. In the Frankish kingdom, long hair was considered a sign of nobility and perhaps had magical significance. Anglo-Saxon men, unlike some of their Frankish counterparts, may have kept their hair short and their faces clean-shaven, perhaps occasionally sporting a moustache. A fifth-century poet, Sidonius, in describing Saxon seamen, gives us the first description of a 'crew cut':

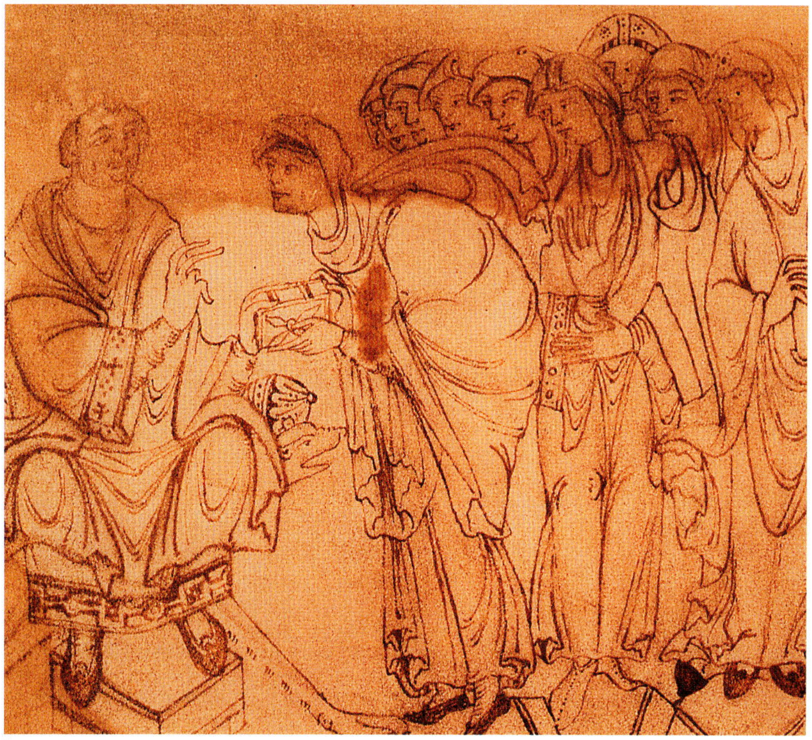

3

> Here in Bordeaux we see the blue-eyed Saxon . . . along the extreme edges of his pate the razor, refusing to restrain its bite, pushes back the frontier of his hair and, with the growth thus clipped to the skin, his head is reduced and his face enlarged.

At the same time as the adoption of Christianity during the seventh century, a Saxon settlement called Lundenwic grew in the modern 'West End' of London around Covent Garden and the Strand. Grave goods were forbidden by the Christian church so burials no longer provide clues about body adornment and clothing. The church was keen to discourage elaborate dress amongst religious orders of both sexes, and to exclude the sporting of weapons by the male monastic and clerical orders. In the early eighth-century treatise written for the nuns of nearby Barking Abbey, Aldhelm criticised such fineries of dress as the use of linen, scarlet and violet tunics, sleeves edged in silk, hair curled at the front and the temples with a curling-iron, finger-nails sharpened like falcons' or hawks' talons, and coloured wimples worn beneath the veil which hung down to the ankles (Figure 3). Such fashions as these were evidently adopted by the wealthier members of society, though the ordinary Londoner was probably more simply and practically attired for daily life.

3 **St Aldhelm presents his book, *De Virginitate*, to the nuns of Barking Abbey. Like most women of the time, their bodies and heads are fully covered. The elaborate draping robes ornamented around the sleeve are rather finer than most daily wear. This picture is from a 10th-century copy of a book written for the nuns in the 8th century.**

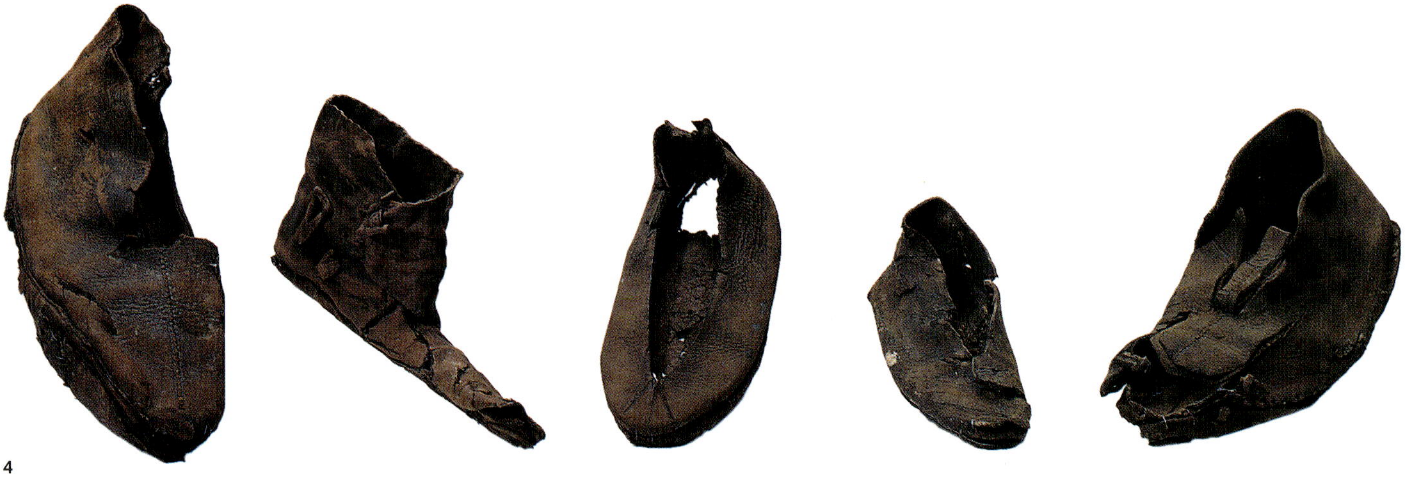

4

In Lundenwic, environmental archaeological evidence such as seeds and animal bones reveals the staple diet to have consisted of: bread, wheat and barley for making bread and soups; possibly lentils; beef, pork, mutton, lamb and goat products; fish and shellfish, particularly from the Thames; and berry and tree fruits including nuts, grapes and figs. The nuns and monks of Barking Abbey were better-off still, eating a greater variety of meat, particularly venison and water-fowl.

The earliest inhabitants of Lundenwic, from the seventh century, were buried in a scattered cemetery between Long Acre and Covent Garden. Whilst the population of Lundenwic is estimated at around 4000 by the year 800, the remains of people of this later date have so far not been located. From the old Roman city, however, come two different but fascinating burials. Each burial was of two women. One of these, on the bank of the Thames at Bull Wharf close to Southwark Bridge, has been radiocarbon-dated to 670–880 (probably 850–880); the other was found at Rangoon Street (a street which no longer exists), near Fenchurch Street Station, and was dated 680–945. At Bull Wharf, the older woman was buried in a shallow grave, while the younger was interred in a sandwich of birch bark, held at the head and at the knees with a stake or marker. The elder was a robust, middle-aged woman who stood around 157cm (5ft 2in.) tall, and had met a violent end: a large circular hole in her skull almost certainly represents a fatal wound from a blunt instrument. She had suffered an illness or upset during childhood and, like other Saxon skeletons studied in the London area, had severe dental disease. The general appearance of the younger woman in the birch bark burial is easy to visualise from her skeletal remains: she was small, only about 145cm (4ft 9in.) tall, and lightly built, and she had three teeth

4 These workaday shoes excavated from an 11th-century pit include two shoes of about English sizes 7 and 8. The smaller (far right) has several cuts on the upper, probably made to relieve a badly swollen foot or toe. A thong was then needed to hold the shoe together. Wear on the shoe sole shows that the person was unable to flex their foot and had to rock from heel to toe to walk around. The ankle boot is an English size 2–3, and the slipper-shoe (centre) a size 3–4. Worn holes on heel and ball, frequently mended, are a common feature of this footwear.

missing, along with a damaged finger on her left hand. She also had a congenital lumbar disorder similar to that of the fifth-to-sixth-century woman found in Ewell, and which was exacerbated by osteoarthritis of the lower spine.

The Rangoon Street burial features two women who died in their mid-twenties. The larger of the two was laid out supine; on her lap rested the head of the smaller, younger, woman, who was curled up next to her with her knees drawn up to fit into the grave. Both women were sturdily built; the larger was around 167cm (5ft 6in.) tall, and had noticeably strong legs and feet, the equivalent of today's English size 7–8. Evidence of 'squatting facets' on both leg bones (tibiae) was the result of extreme flexion of the knees and ankles probably from an habitual squatting posture. The bones of her feet suggest intense pressure and weight-bearing during the course of her life, which may be the result of pregnancy or routine work such as lifting and placing heavy loads.

The old Roman walled city was largely reoccupied in the late ninth century, no doubt in response to increasingly regular attacks on Lundenwic, and nearby establishments, by Vikings from Denmark. Lundenburg, as it was called, was developed by King Alfred, and took over from Lundenwic as the main trading port and town. Though few burials of this period have been excavated, there are finds of everyday life including items of dress and footwear. A group of shoes found in an early eleventh-century pit in the City of London is probably typical (Figure 4). They include two men's shoes of about sizes 7 and 8, a size 5 boot and a slipper-shoe size 5½. Still in remarkably good condition after nearly a thousand years, they show the strenuous wear in the various mends at the balls and heels. One shoe has even been cut at the front to relieve a badly swollen toe that was probably dressed or bandaged (Figure 4).

Ever since the first Viking raids in the early ninth century there had been a strong Scandinavian influence on the English population, culture and language. This was greatly reinforced through trade, the presence of the 'Danelaw' in east and north-east England in the late ninth to early tenth centuries, and probable Viking settlement in the London area. Renewed Danish attacks in the late tenth century culminated in the crowning of King Cnut in 1016 and subsequent Danish rule of England for 25 years. Viking influence can be seen in styles of ornamentation on clothing accessories and other artefacts. In St Paul's churchyard a tombstone to mark the grave of an important Scandinavian was found in 1852. Church names with Norse and Danish associations, such as St Clement Danes and those dedicated to the Norwegian saint Olaf or Olave, suggest the existence of a sizeable

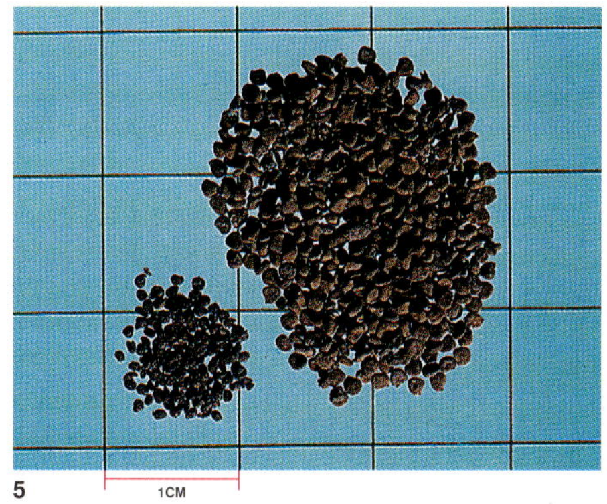

5

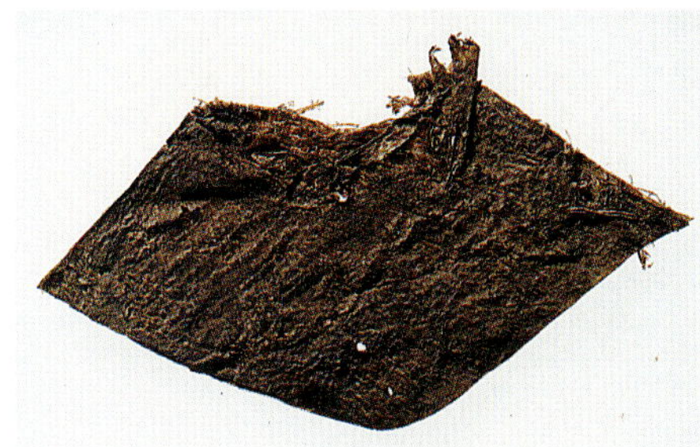

6

5 Opium poppy and henbane may have been used as sedatives and painkillers. These seeds were found in a pit dating from the late 10th to early 11th centuries.

6 'Dane's skin' from the door of Southwark Cathedral. Popular tradition claims that Vikings who were caught pillaging churches were flayed alive and their skins nailed to the church door. Several of these skins have been found on church doors in Essex and elsewhere, but their origins are unclear. The skin is almost certainly human.

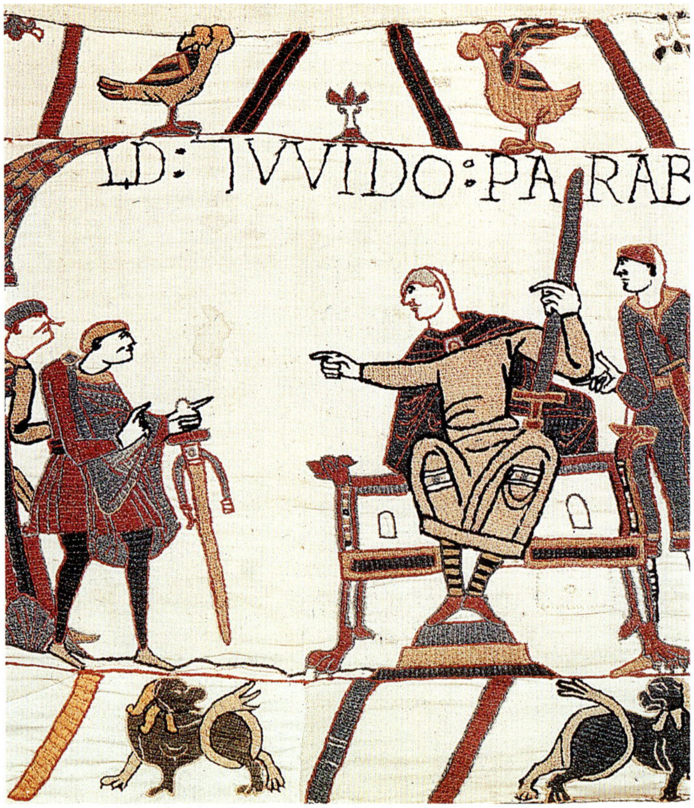

7

number of Scandinavians in London; but no distinctively Scandinavian features have been identified in human skeletons

Women's bodies would probably have been totally covered in Late Saxon London, with little bare flesh on view. Long, flowing, usually unbelted, gowns, with many folds and drapes, and a veil to cover the head, are often depicted in contemporary imagery. Men may have worn a knee-length full-skirted tunic with trousers or hose, as depicted on the late eleventh-century Bayeux Tapestry which illustrates the events leading up to the Norman conquest of 1066 (Figure 7).

By this date, London was the largest and most important town in England, and was becoming a royal centre. Its inhabitants may have numbered around 10,000–12,000. The Normans brought with them new ways, legislation and language. Their fashions and language became hallmarks of the ruling classes, though the everyday appearance of Londoners as a whole remained little changed.

From this period, the eleventh and twelfth centuries, comes our best group of medieval skeletons from a parish churchyard in London. Excavations between 1975 and 1979 at the cemetery of St Nicholas Shambles on Newgate Street produced over 200 burials. The average heights of the people buried in the cemetery were 173cm (5ft 8in.) for men and 157cm (5ft 2in.) for women. Most of the people died before the age of 45 and many showed the signs of poverty – a poor diet and a hard-working life. One of them, a woman who was of the average height, died before the age of 40, having lost five teeth during life and with evidence of osteoarthritis on her spine. For such Londoners, the majority, the diet would have been simple: daily pottage (a vegetable and cereal thickened soup) with some meat and fish added when available, and bread, hard cheese, fruits and nuts, and ale or sweet wine.

7 **In the Bayeux Tapestry of the 11th century many Normans are depicted with their hair shaved up the back of the head. In some cases the top of their hair is also brushed forward. Harold and other English men are shown with long moustaches. Here Guy, Count of Ponthieu (enthroned) discusses a ransom with Harold (left) whom he has captured.**

LOOKING FOR ETHNIC DIFFERENCES

How different did people look? Were there clear racial differences or any visible differences due to styles of dress? Immigrants may have worn features of clothing that stood out from the crowd. They may have had different skin tone, hair colour or style, a different body language, perhaps a distinctive 'look'. Some traditions suggest that Danes were red-headed, that freckles were a sign of Danish blood, and that Anglo-Saxons were fair-headed. From the evidence left to us today it is difficult to ascertain the extent to which such differences existed and how visible they were at the time.

From before the time of Roman rule, links between the different cultures of Europe were well established, and through them small-scale movements of people were possible from one region to another. The Romanisation of Britain involved the adoption of Roman ways by the native British, and an increase of new foreign settlers in the form of military personnel, merchants, traders and skilled professionals. During the breakdown of Roman rule in Britain in the late fourth and early fifth centuries, mercenary soldiers or 'foederati' from Germany and elsewhere were given land in eastern Britain in return for military service, and are believed to have initiated the waves of immigration from northern Germany in the mid-fifth to sixth centuries.

Osteologists have tried to distinguish Germanic immigrants from native British, and the later Viking and Norman immigrants from native 'Anglo-Saxon' populations, but despite linguistic and cultural differences, these peoples may all derive from the same basic gene pool, so that racial variations as evident in the skeleton are insignificant. A nineteenth-century theory that the Saxons were long-headed (dolichocephalic) and the Normans were round-headed (brachycephalic) is not borne out in the skeletal evidence from London (Figure 8). Though the database is minimal, this result is not surprising: most Normans were originally Vikings from Jutland and northernmost Germany. So far, DNA testing for the Early Saxon migration period has been unsuccessful, due largely to sampling problems. Researchers have however found morphological differences in skeletal material between cemeteries in different areas and even within individual cemeteries – for example in teeth, foot structure and stature.

Even with grave goods as cultural signifiers, it is often unclear who was who, as the native population adopted the same culture as the immigrants. Variations in dress and manner may represent social and political affiliations within the population's contemporary culture rather than past ethnic associations. In some cases the observed and measured differences in the skeleton may hold some significance quite unrelated to race, but dependent on diet, rank or family status. More work is needed in this area to test the feasibility of isolating 'ethnic' differences in skeletal material, though the melting pot probably saw much interbreeding as well as a mixing of cultures and ways of life.

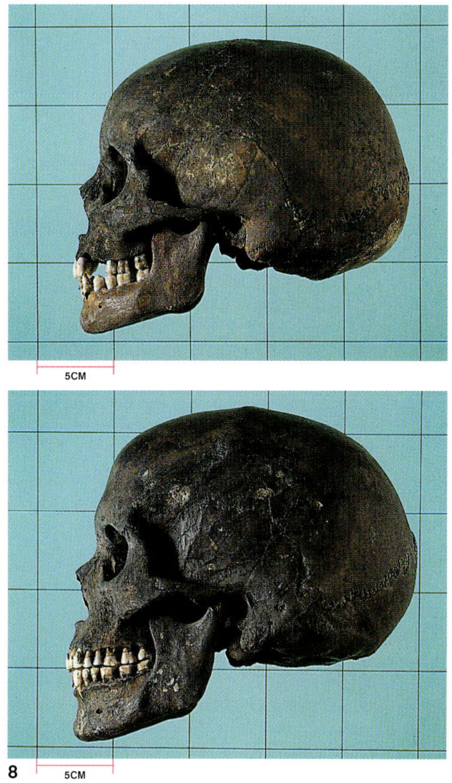

8

8 Little difference can be seen in the overall shape of these skulls. The top is a 13–16 year-old girl's skull of the late Saxon-Danish period. The lower skull is from a woman in her early twenties of the Norman period. The attributes of long-headedness (Dolichocephalic) and round-headedness (Brachycephalic), which in the 19th century were considered representative of Saxon or Norman origin, are found to a greater or lesser degree in all individuals and cannot be easily linked to specific groups.

PICTURING PEOPLE

PAST AND PRESENT PERCEPTIONS

What did the people of the Anglo-Saxon and Norman period look like? In general there is little visual or written material before the adoption of Christianity during the seventh century which brought with it literacy and the production of illustrated manuscripts. But these provide only a handful of contemporary images for the earlier centuries. In reconstructions of how people looked, their clothing, general manner and setting often reflects the society in which the image was produced more than the society it is trying to represent. Today, greater evidence is available which allows more accurate representations to be made. However, like those before us, we are limited by our own perceptions; the reconstructions we create may appear to future generations as subjective as our predecessors' attempts seem to us.

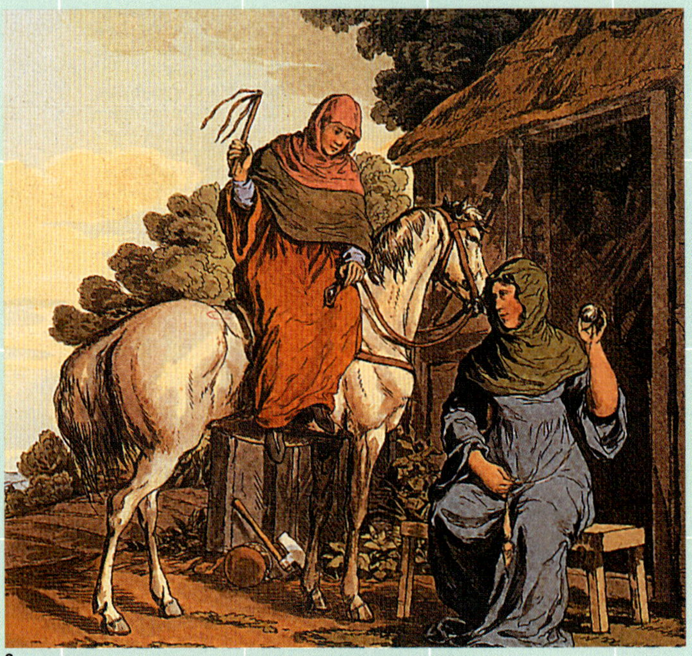

2

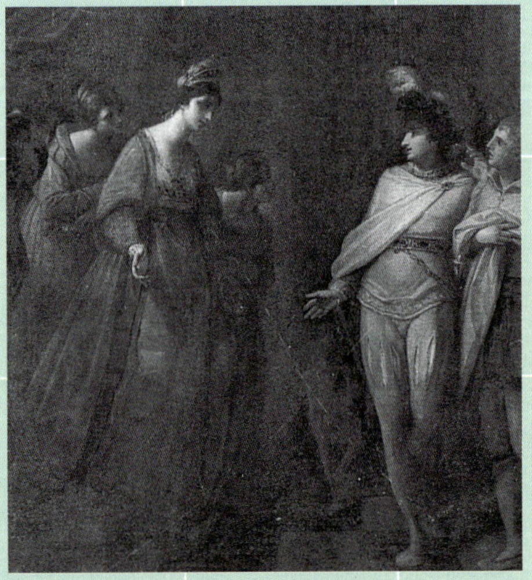

1

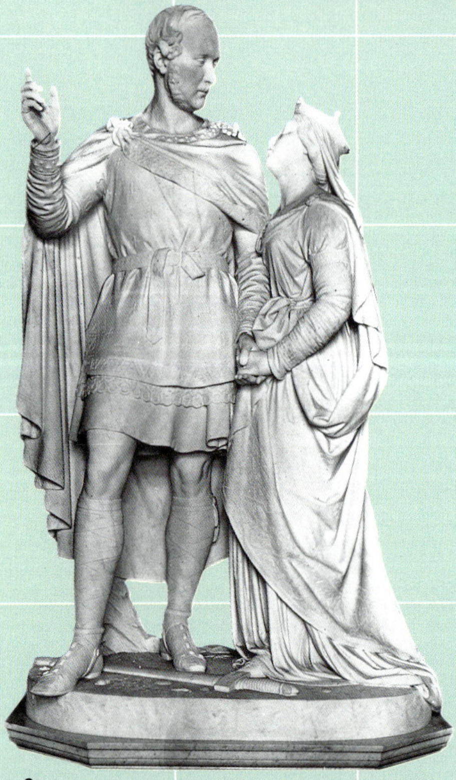

3

1 1770. *Elfrida, receiving King Edgar* (detail), by Angelica Kauffmann.

2 1814. *Anglo Saxon women of the VIII Century*, by Charles Hamilton-Smith whose aim was historical accuracy in both costume and set.

3 1868. Queen Victoria and Prince Albert posed as Anglo-Saxons for this statue sculpted by William Theed.

4 1628. Hengist and Horsa, the first Saxons to arrive in Britain, in an early portrayal by R. Verstegan.

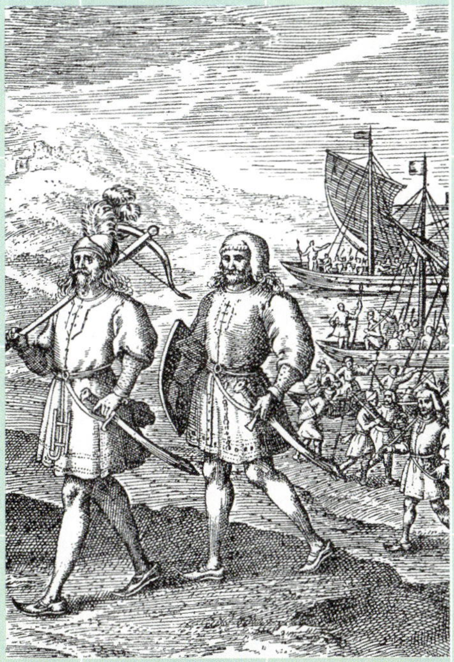

4

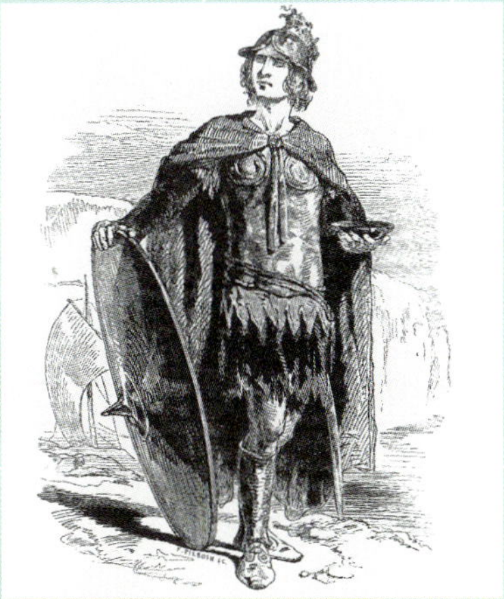

6

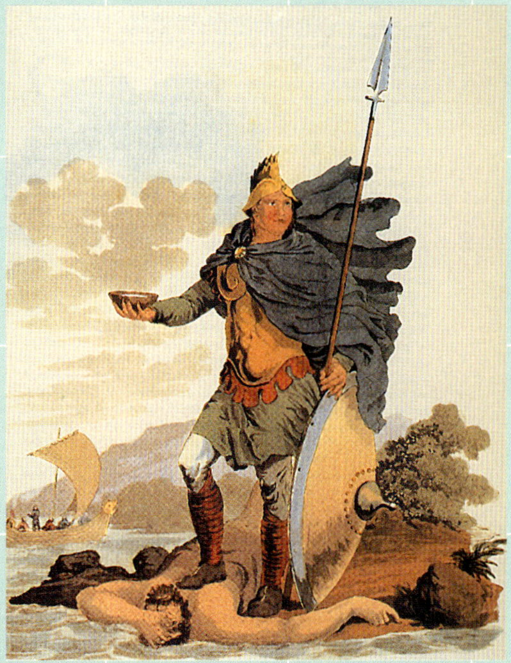

8

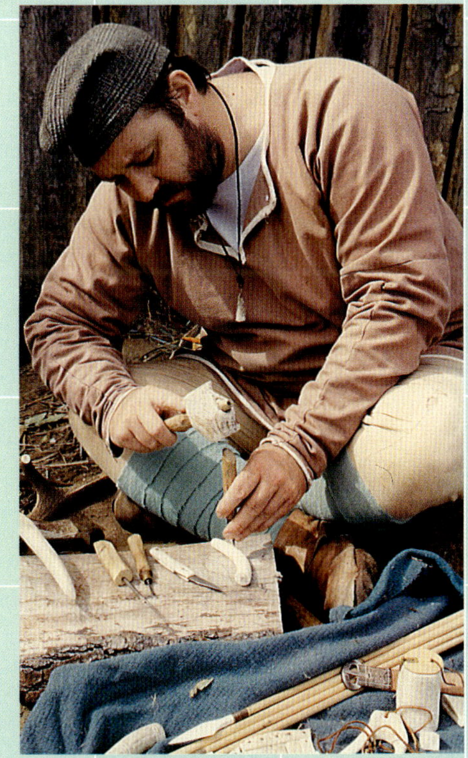

5

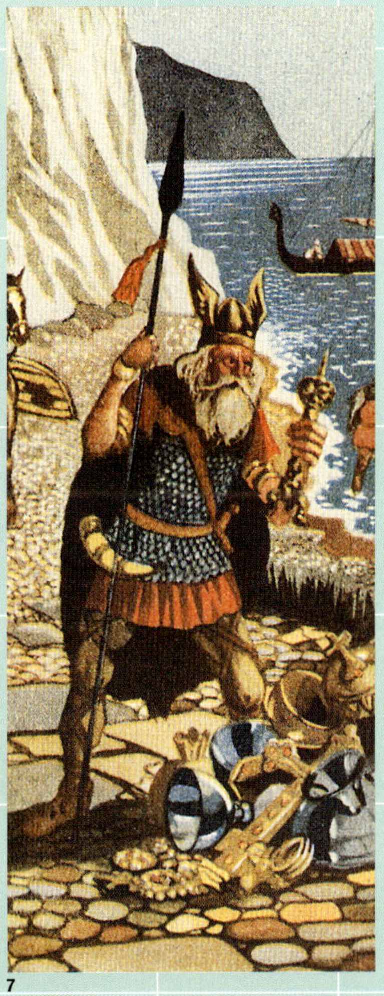

7

5 1987. Anglo-Saxon craft worker from West Stow Anglo-Saxon Village. At this reconstructed village in Suffolk people re-enact the life and activities of Anglo-Saxon times.

6 1849. An Anglo-Saxon Chieftain, from a publication entitled *The Anglo-Saxon*.

7 1953. Viking warrior raiding a Saxon village, by C.W. Bacon, from a popular children's book by R.J. Unstead.

8 1814. Costume of a Saxon Chief, by Charles Hamilton Smith.

MEDIEVAL BODIES

FAMINE AND PESTILENCE: THE CALAMITOUS FOURTEENTH CENTURY

by John Clark and Bill White

Medieval London was a magnet, drawing people to it not only from the Home Counties but also from the rest of England and beyond. By 1300 its population may have been approaching 100,000. It was by far the largest city in a largely rural England, and one of the largest in Europe. But for newcomers there were no streets paved with gold; many would have found only dire poverty. Food cost more in London than elsewhere. In 1338 a visitor found prices of essentials about 50 per cent higher in the city than in the country. Poverty was so widespread that in 1318 a wealthy citizen bequeathed money to give one penny to each of 2000 poor Londoners. Four years later 55 men, women and children were crushed to death in the crowds that gathered at the gate of Blackfriars, where alms were to be given out under the terms of the will of another pious Londoner. A number of the dead in the cemetery of St Nicholas Shambles, mentioned above, had a bone condition (cribra orbitalia) apparently brought on by chronic anaemia during childhood, perhaps from a diet lacking in iron. Of those whose age at death has been estimated, nearly 90 per cent had apparently died before they reached 45, and many had died in their teens and twenties. By contrast, where documentary evidence exists about the lives of wealthier people, a life-span of 50 years seems the medieval norm, with many living into their 60s or 70s.

1 A domestic tragedy: the skeleton of a young woman buried at St John's, Clerkenwell, contains the remains of her unborn child still within her pelvis. Although the birth process had begun, the labour was probably long and difficult, and mother and baby must have died of exhaustion.

By 1300 London was drawing on the agricultural produce of a large part of southern England and the midlands, up to 50 miles or more from the capital, in order to feed its population. London corn-dealers shipped grain to London by river from granaries in Henley-on-Thames in Oxfordshire and Faversham in Kent, and in years of shortage by sea from the East Anglian ports of Boston and King's Lynn. The City authorities controlled both prices and quality of basic foodstuffs. Each year samples of grain were purchased after the harvest at current market prices. Loaves were

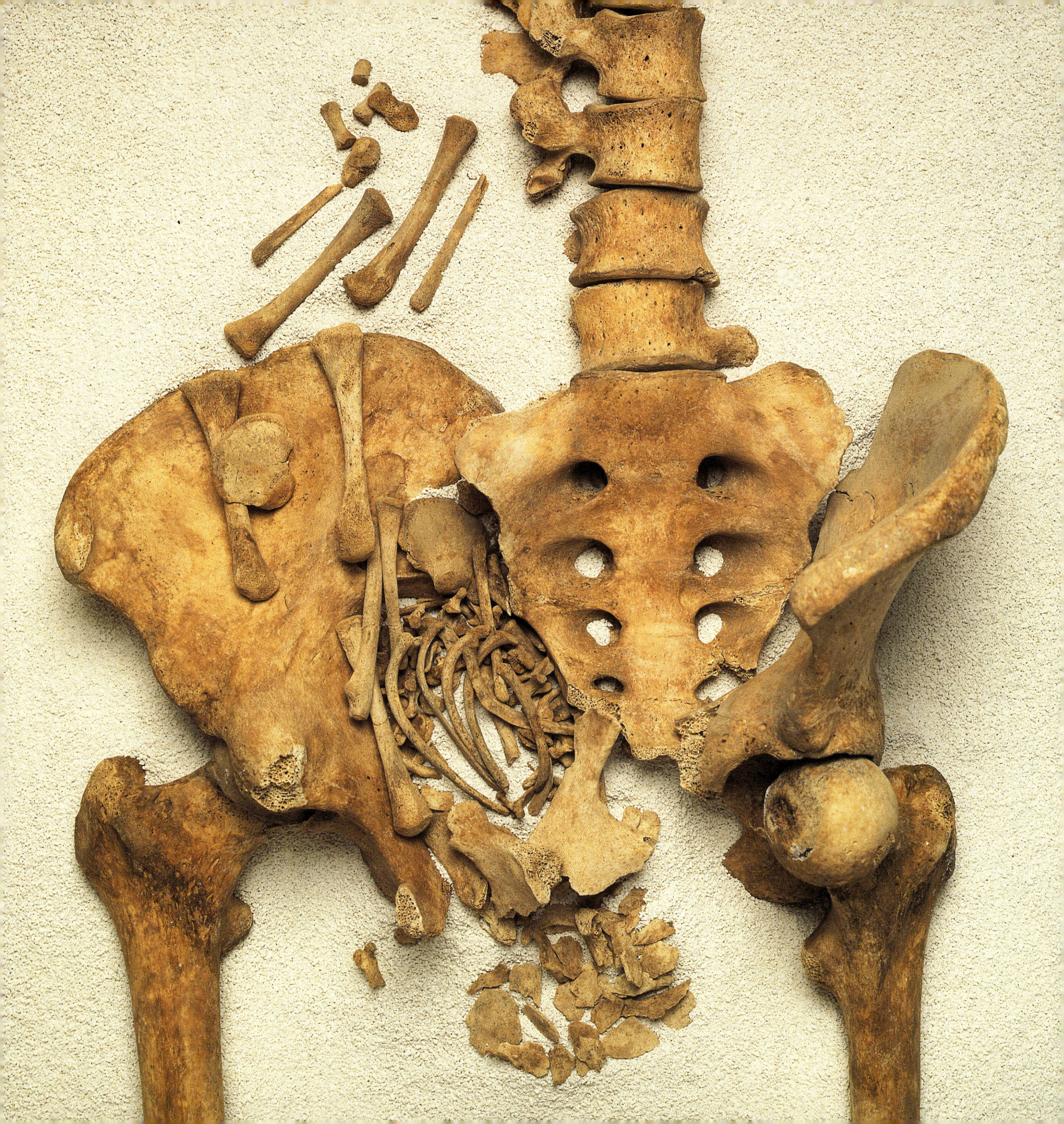

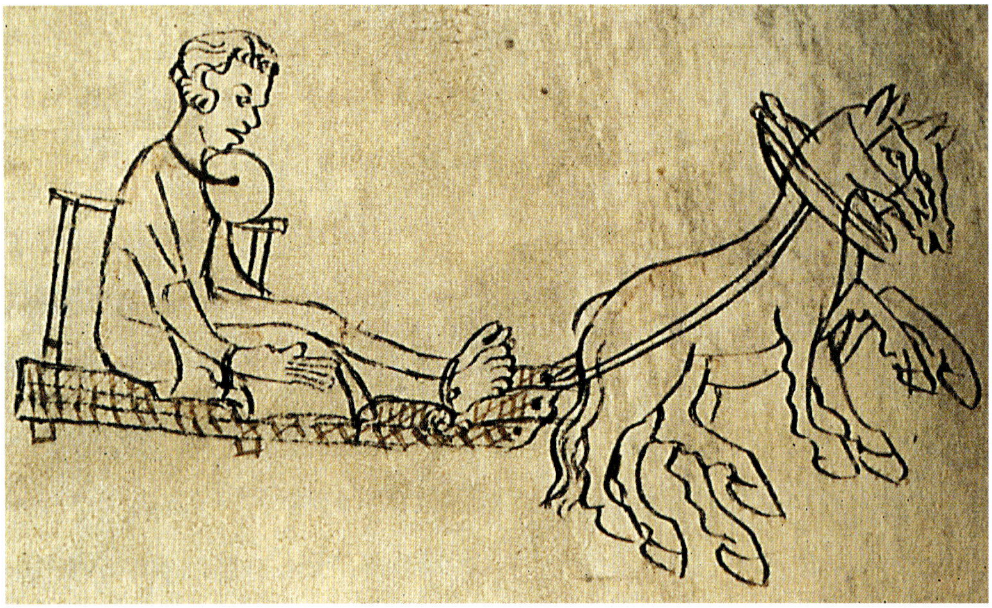

2

baked and a complicated calculation was applied to define the weight of a standard halfpenny loaf for the ensuing year (Figure 2).

Similarly, efforts were made to ensure the quality of drinking water. City regulations banned the digging of cesspits too close to wells, though seepages did occur. Thus, in 1422, a London baker was brought to court because he was baking bread with water from a 'horrible' well in his house 'to the great danger and nuisance of all who eat it'. As early as 1236 the City authorities had acquired rights to springs at Tyburn (close to today's Bond Street tube station) to supplement London's drinking water supply. Forty years later a pipeline was completed, running over two miles to feed a cistern in Cheapside 'so that rich and middling persons might have water to prepare their food and the poor for their drink'.

Yet all the City's attempts to ensure that people had access to clean water and cheap food could not protect them in times of poor harvest. In 1293–5 and again in 1308–9 grain prices rose alarmingly. And in 1315 disaster struck. A series of cold and wet seasons throughout northern Europe brought famine. In London grain prices – and with them bread prices – were suddenly double what they had been in even the worst of previous years. A London chronicler records starkly under the year 1316: 'This year was a great dearth of corn and other victuals, for a bushel of wheat was worth five shillings. And the poor people ate for hunger cats and horses and dogs.' There were rumours of cannibalism: 'And the poor people stole children and ate them.' In parts of England at least one in ten people starved to death or died from accompanying disease. No direct estimate of the effect on London is possible: the population may have risen at first as people from the countryside sought refuge from the famine. Yet overall there was a downturn in London's population. Long afterwards, survivors took to their graves the marks on their bones and teeth of the period of shortage and starvation they had lived through (see Figure 8).

2 **A London baker found guilty of selling underweight loaves is dragged through the streets on a hurdle, one of his loaves tied round his neck. An illustration from the City of London's *Assize of Bread*, containing regulations on the quality and weight of bread.**

IN SICKNESS AND IN HEALTH

The poor of medieval London had little access to medical aid when sick. 'Barber-surgeons' could treat wounds and broken limbs; midwives assisted in labour; home remedies and prayers for the intercession of saints were the only resource in time of illness. University-trained physicians, who treated illness as an imbalance of the 'humours', would usually be available only to the rich (Figure 3). Though London had several hospitals the modern words 'hospice' or 'asylum' might better reflect their functions: care rather than cure of the sick and dying, refuge for the needy, hospitality for poor travellers. Above all, hospitals were ecclesiastical establishments, staffed by clerics and providing for the spiritual needs of the inmates.

Among the earliest London hospitals were those, like St James (on the site of the later palace) and St Giles 'in the fields', built well away from the city to provide a refuge for sufferers from leprosy who were driven out of the towns and forced to beg along the roads. Though people suffering from a variety of skin diseases may have been wrongly identified as lepers, excavations in the cemeteries of medieval leper hospitals have revealed skeletons showing the telltale signs of the disease – distortion of the facial features, crippling erosion of the limbs – that made it so feared and abhorred throughout medieval Europe.

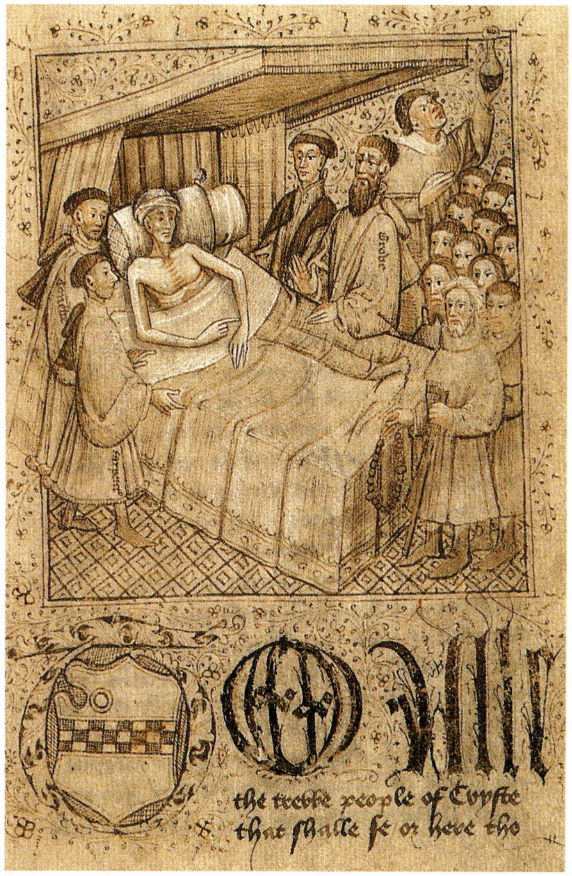
3

So far there have been no excavations on the sites of London's leper hospitals. However, between 1982 and 1991 archaeologists uncovered the remains of another early hospital outside the city gates: the 'new hospital' of St Mary Spital near Bishopsgate, founded in 1197 at the expense of prominent London citizen Walter Brunus (Brown) and his wife Roisia. It had 60, and later 90, beds, and in times of need several people were crammed in each bed. It became the largest hospital in medieval London, and one of the largest in England (Figure 4). It took in pilgrims and travellers, the poor and the sick. It also provided care for pregnant women – and for the child if the mother died. Infant burials and a stillbirth found in the hospital's graveyard may reflect this. Some of London's other hospitals made special provision for 'unmarried mothers'. At St Thomas's hospital in Southwark:

> that nobyl marchaunt, Rycharde Whytyngdon [Richard Whittington], made a newe chambyr with 8 beddys [beds] for yong wemen that hadde done a-mysse [amiss]... And he commaundyd that alle

3 **Richard Whittington, Mayor of London, on his deathbed in 1423. A physician stands at the back holding up a glass flask containing the patient's urine as an aid to diagnosis of his illness. From the *Ordinances* of the almshouse founded under the terms of Whittington's will.**

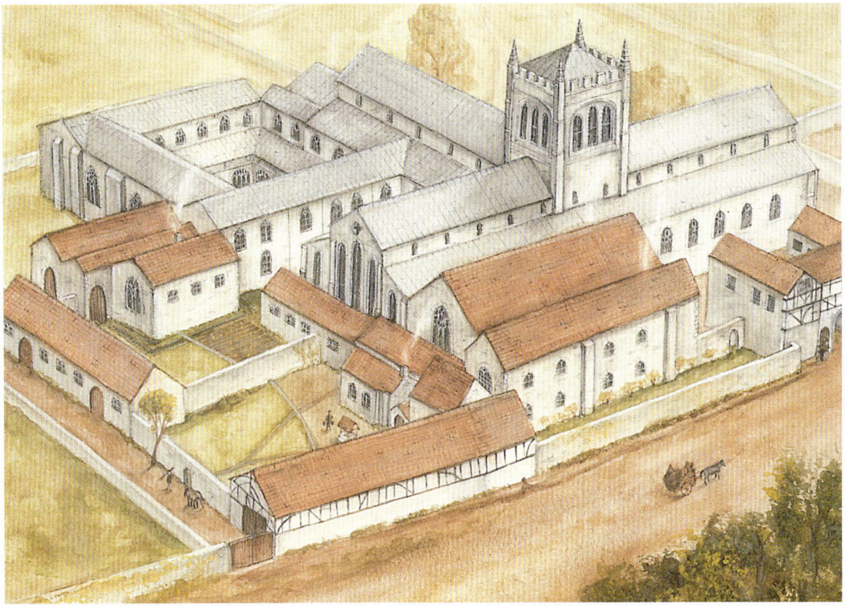
4

the thyngys that ben don in that chambyr shulde be kepte
secrete... for he wolde not shame no yonge women in
noo wyse, for hyt myght be cause of hyr lettyng of hyr
maryge [it might prevent her marriage].

At St Mary Spital archaeologists uncovered several distinct groups of burials. To the west of the thirteenth-century hospital building lay what was probably the main graveyard for hospital inmates at this time. Most were men; most had died under the age of 30. The condition of their bones shows that they had suffered from illness in childhood and were exposed to everyday knocks and stresses and probably to heavy manual labour from an early age. Some perhaps had been poor migrants seeking work in London.

By the fourteenth century hospital inmates appear to have had a higher life expectancy. Although hypoplasia of the dental enamel suggests that they had suffered severe disease or malnutrition in childhood they went on to lead long lives – and to suffer from other diseases, particularly tooth decay.

Burials in the hospital chapel, presumably those of the clergy and of wealthy patrons, reflect better health and nourishment. They had lived longer and their average height was 174cm (5ft 8in.), significantly greater than that for the men buried outside the church (169cm (5ft 6in.)). Good eating promoted height as well as girth! On the other hand, their teeth were generally in worse condition, presumably due to a diet rich in sugar. Three middle-aged men showed signs of a bone condition (diffuse idiopathic skeletal hyperostosis) that seems to come with a diet over-full of calories. Indeed, monks had a reputation for eating well. Geoffrey Chaucer's pen-portrait of a late fourteenth-century monk – of the same Augustinian order that ran St Mary Spital – must have been a familiar picture to his fellow Londoners:

His head was bald and shone like any glass,
And also his face, as if he had been anointed.
He was a lord, full fat and in good condition;

4 The hospital of St Mary Spital outside Bishopsgate, as it might have appeared at the end of the Middle Ages. Reconstruction painting by Kikar Singh.

His eyes were prominent and rolling in his head…

He was not pale like a tormented ghost.

A fat swan loved he best of any roast!

THE DANCE OF DEATH

Medieval doctors were helpless in the face of a horrifying and unfamiliar disease that burst upon Europe from the east in late 1347. Contemporary writers simply referred to the 'great pestilence' or the 'great death'. Today we call it the 'Black Death' and identify it as plague. Bubonic plague (named for the agonising and putrefying swellings or buboes that disfigure the victim's body), and the even more infectious pneumonic plague that can be spread by a sneeze, are both caused by a bacterium that normally infects rodents and their fleas. In Europe it seems to have been spread to humans by fleas usually found on black rats, which lived everywhere that humans did, and travelled with them on their ships. Without modern medical treatment 60 per cent of people infected with the bubonic form of plague are likely to die within ten days; pneumonic plague kills almost all its victims, and within two days.

Although medieval Europeans recognised that plague could be transmitted from person to person, some attributed its origin to a natural corruption of the air arising from putrefying corpses; to God's punishment for the sins of mankind; to the stars, in particular a catastrophic conjunction of three planets in the sign of Aquarius; or to deliberate action by 'foreign agents'. In Spain, Portuguese pilgrims were accused of poisoning wells, and in many parts of Europe Jews became the scapegoats.

Plague rapidly spread across Europe from the Mediterranean coast. In the summer of 1348 the first cases were reported in England. By one account it was a sick sailor on a ship from France, landing at Melcombe Regis in Dorset, who brought the disease to England. Certainly the infection seems to have spread outwards from the West Country. By March 1349 the plague was in full force in Surrey. But it had already reached London by other routes. Parliament, due to meet at Westminster in January 1349, was prorogued on the grounds that the plague had broken out in the area.

Estimates of the overall death toll vary widely: perhaps thirty to forty per cent of the population of England died within the year and a half that the plague raged, and it seems likely that the toll was higher in crowded towns than in the countryside. There is no reliable account of the immediate effects of the Black Death in London, yet some of its results are

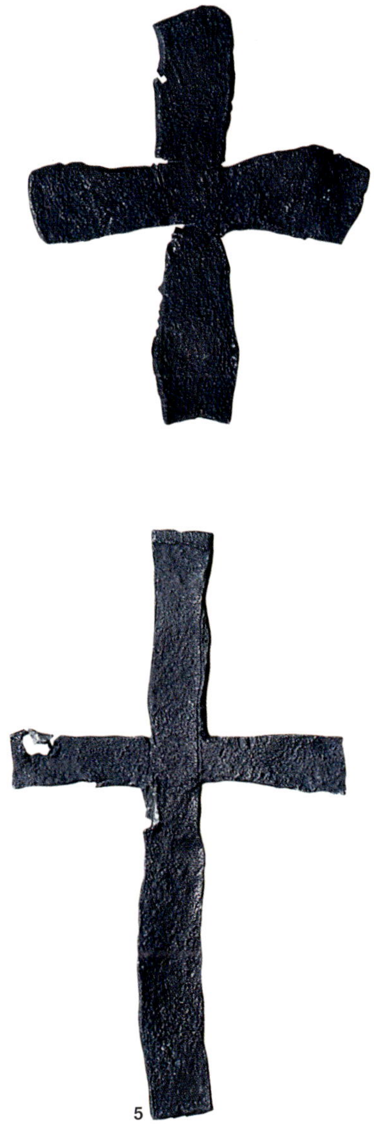

5

5 Two of the rough lead crosses found in a mass grave on the site of the medieval Grey Friars in 1905.

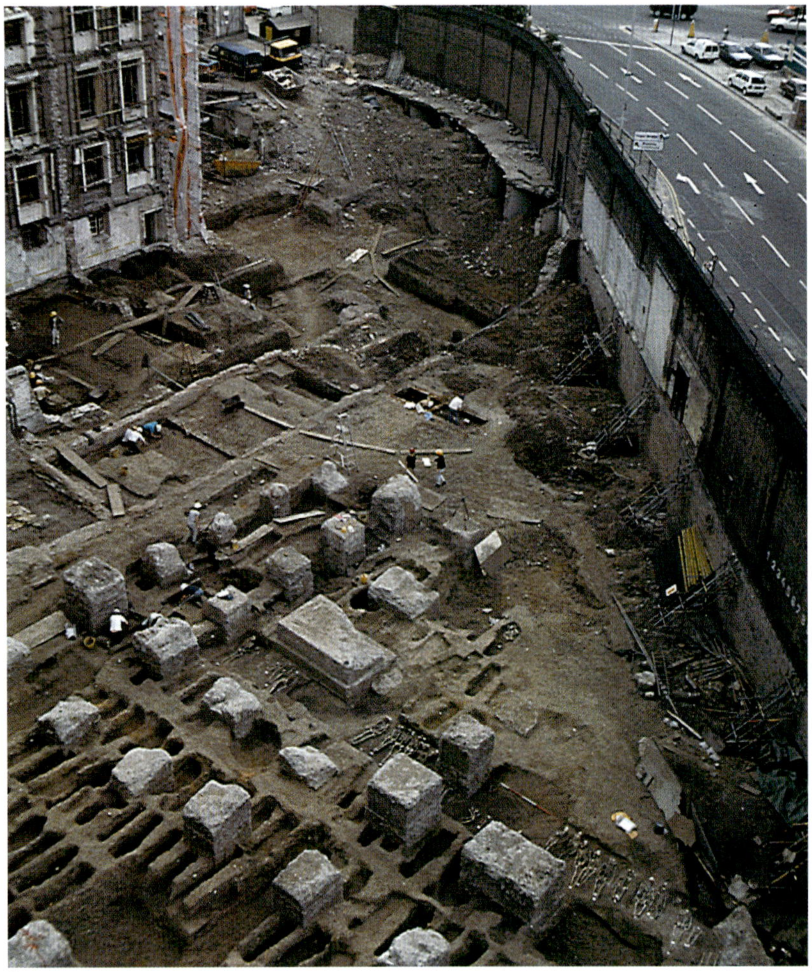

6

clear from contemporary records. At Westminster Abbey the Abbot died, together with 26 monks – fully half of the establishment. Among city businessmen, at least ten (and probably more) of London's 31 leading goldsmiths died of the plague.

Some medieval writers put the London death toll at over 50,000. A lower figure seems likely, but certainly the city's graveyards were soon full, and emergency measures were taken. In 1905 a mass grave was uncovered on the site of the priory of the Grey Friars north of St Paul's. It contained several hundred bodies, many of them accompanied by roughly made lead crosses (Figure 5). Further north, outside the city, Sir Walter Manny bought 13 acres of disused land near Smithfield to serve as a graveyard. Another was established at 'East Smithfield' near the Tower of London. Here excavations took place in 1986–8 on the site of what was later to be a Cistercian abbey and afterwards the Royal Mint, revealing the Black Death cemetery (Figure 6).

Although many burials had been placed in rows of individual graves, there was also a single pit containing the remains of eight adults and children, and three large trenches, one of them over 125 metres long (Figure 7). The bodies had been laid in these burial trenches up to five deep, but some were in coffins and all had been carefully placed. Clearly, in spite of the horrifying circumstances, the authorities were still controlling the proper disposal of the dead. One trench was dug well in advance and never fully used. Presumably the death toll had begun to fall.

Unlike the bodies from churchyards such as that of St Nicholas Shambles, the 600 excavated in East Smithfield did not represent 'natural' deaths over many years from a variety of causes, but the result of one catastrophe affecting a single generation of Londoners. Documentary sources suggest that the plague tended to kill especially the weak, the very young and the elderly, and that those in their twenties and thirties were

6 **The Black Death cemetery at East Smithfield under excavation.**

more likely to survive; study of the Black Death cemetery tends to bear this out. Overall, the dead of East Smithfield represent a cross-section of ordinary Londoners in the 1340s. They were rather shorter than the modern population, the average height of women being 158cm (5ft 2in.) and of men 167cm (5ft 6in.). Dental and nutritional diseases were rife, but degenerative diseases such as osteoarthritis were no more common than they are today. Limb fractures were very rare, indicating that living and working conditions were not harsh, and only one body showed marks of violence: a healed scalp wound resulting from a blow from an edged weapon.

The East Smithfield site is of international importance; it is so far the only fully analysed plague cemetery. Its skeletons may yet prove useful in modern medical research. A mutant gene (called CCR5-delta 32), which today offers some immunity to HIV infection, is thought to have its origins in the Black Death; research on the bones may serve to confirm this exciting hypothesis.

By late 1349 the worst of the epidemic was over. Yet the long-term effects were dramatic. London's population may have been reduced by half and there was another epidemic in 1361. This, 'the Children's Plague', seems to have affected particularly the young. If it was bubonic plague (which has been questioned) rather than some other infectious disease, it may have afflicted especially those too young to have experienced the first outbreak and to have developed some immunity – the children of those same young adults who had best survived the Black Death. Further outbreaks of plague were to follow, and it was not until after the final devastating Great Plague of 1665 and the Great Fire of the following year that London was to be free of danger.

London was able to recoup some of its losses of population. Immigration from the country and from smaller provincial towns continued as shortage of labour forced up wages. The population of London did not rise again for 150 years to the sort of level it had reached at the beginning of the fourteenth century. But with a smaller population the mass starvation of 1315–17 did not recur. There were bad harvests in 1437–40, but careful management of London's grain supply kept bread prices reasonable. Although the London chronicler records that 'the poor Commons were fain to make bread of barley or beans, peas and vetches etc', this time there were no reports of them eating cats, dogs and children. Medieval Londoners might never escape the conviction that sudden and gruesome death would strike at any time, but they had survived the worst that nature could inflict in what a modern American historian has called 'the calamitous fourteenth century'.

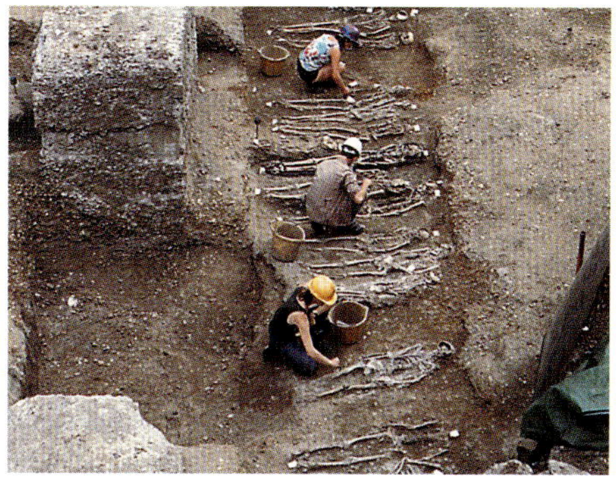

7

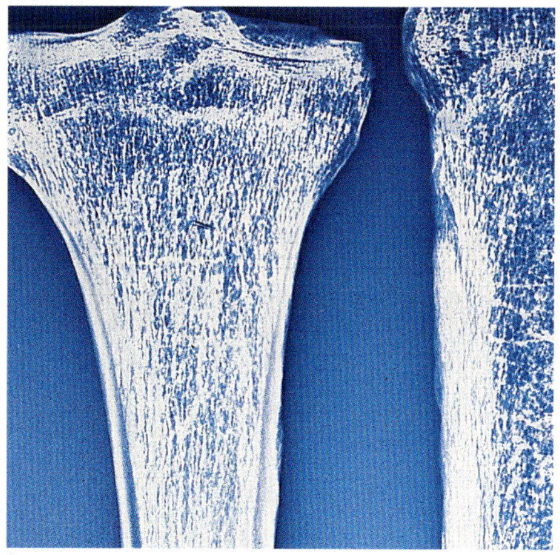

8

7 **Archaeologists excavating one of the mass burial trenches containing victims of the Black Death at East Smithfield.**

8 **A xeroradiograph of the leg bone of a middle-aged man who was buried in the Black Death cemetery at East Smithfield shows straight lines across the bone ('Harris lines'). These indicate that he had suffered interrupted growth as a child, probably during the famine of 1315–17.**

THE LITTLE PRINCESS

LADY ANNE MOWBRAY, DUCHESS OF YORK (1472–81)

In 1964 workers on a building site in Stepney broke into a vault in the area of the medieval nunnery of the order of St Clare, known as the Abbey of the Minoresses. In it lay a small lead coffin. An inscription showed that the coffin contained the body of Anne Mowbray, the young Duchess of York, who had died on 19 November 1481.

Anne Mowbray was born in 1472, the only child of John Mowbray, fourth Duke of Norfolk. On his death in 1476 she inherited great wealth and vast estates. In January 1478, when aged little more than five, she was married in great splendour to Richard Duke of York, the four-year-old younger son of King Edward IV, in St Stephen's Chapel, Westminster. Anne died at Greenwich when she was less than nine years old; Prince Richard, one of the two 'Princes in the Tower', disappeared during the reign of Richard III.

This rare opportunity to investigate the burial of a named person from the late Middle Ages was seized by Dr Francis Celoria (then of the London Museum), who assembled an interdisciplinary team of scientific experts to examine it in all its aspects.

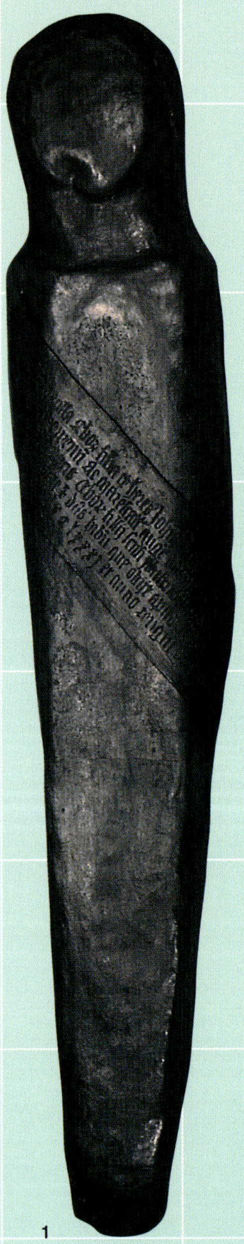

1

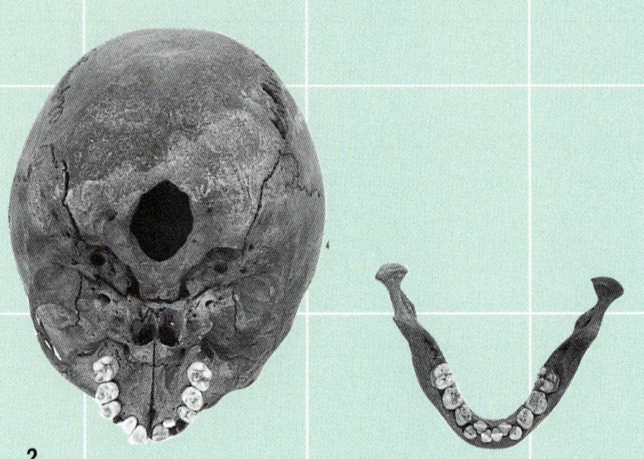

2

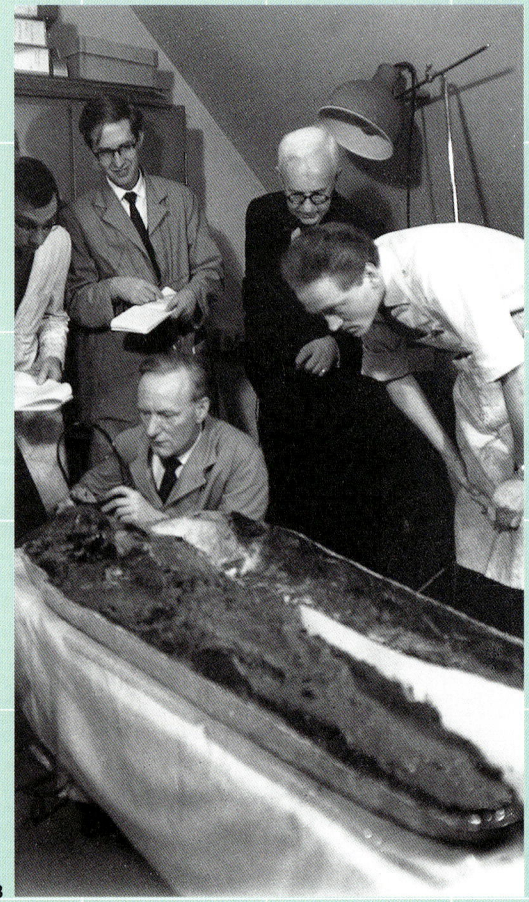

3

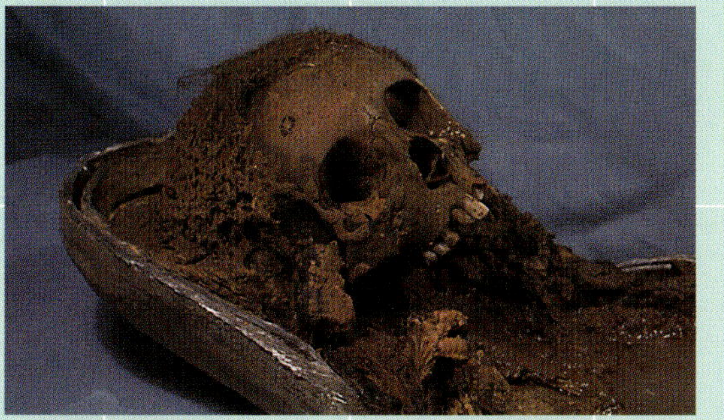

4

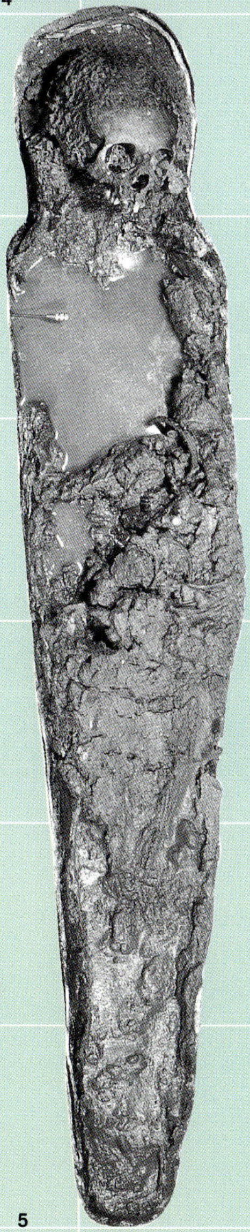

5

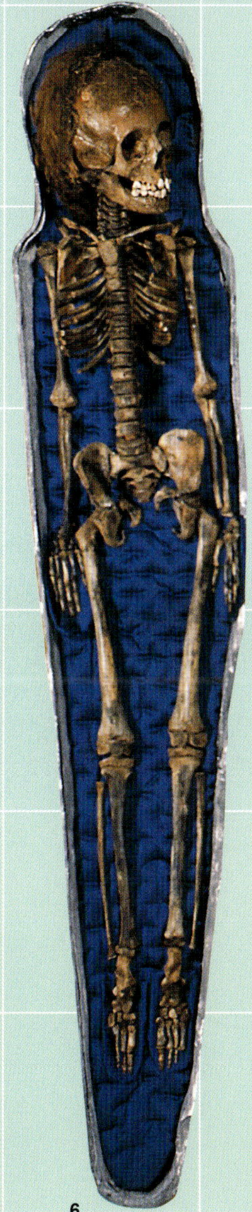

6

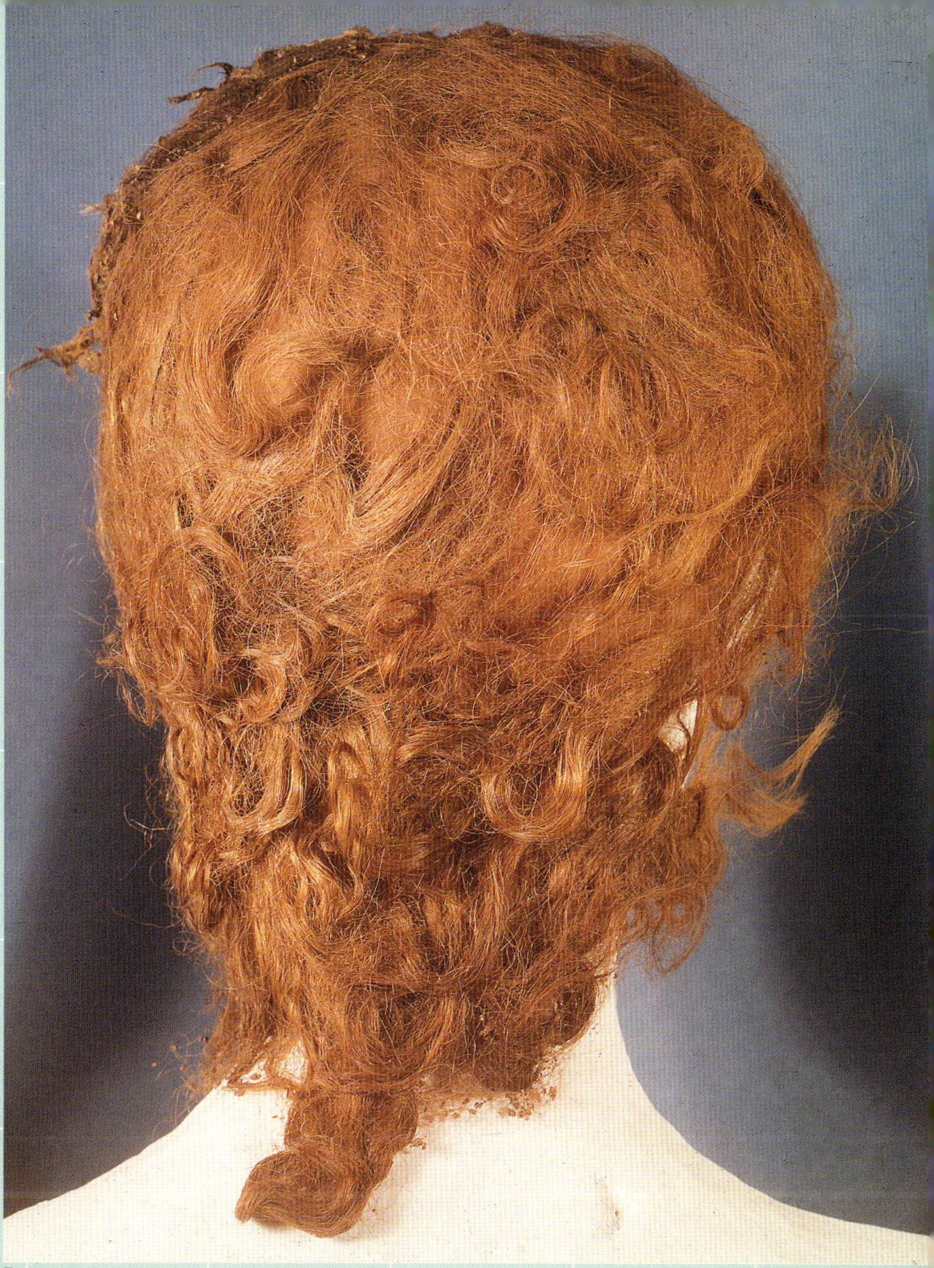

7

1 The coffin with its inscribed coffin plate.

2 The skull and lower jaw, showing the teeth.

3 Opening the coffin in the presence of the research team.

4 Anne's skull, in the coffin.

5 The coffin with top cut away showing the shrouded body within.

6 The body prepared for reburial. Anne was reburied in Westminster Abbey in May 1965.

7 Anne's hair – the colour is genuine, although the shade was probably originally darker.

A PORTRAIT GALLERY

OF MEDIEVAL LONDONERS

There are few illustrations of medieval London townsfolk. Images of royalty, nobility and the wealthy survive as tomb-monuments, but they are usually idealised likenesses rather than realistic portraits.

The face of the wooden effigy of King Edward III in Westminster Abbey is a rare example of medieval realism and may have been based on a death mask; the left side of his mouth is distorted, perhaps the result of the stroke from which he died.

Normally artists concentrated on details of costume or appearance that reflected the person's status, like Amy Lambard's fashionable narrow waist, tight sleeves and head dress stiffened with wire, Simon Eyre's scarlet fur-lined robe, and even the short forked beard sported by both John de Oteswich and Geoffrey Chaucer – a style worn also by King Richard II and very popular in the late fourteenth century.

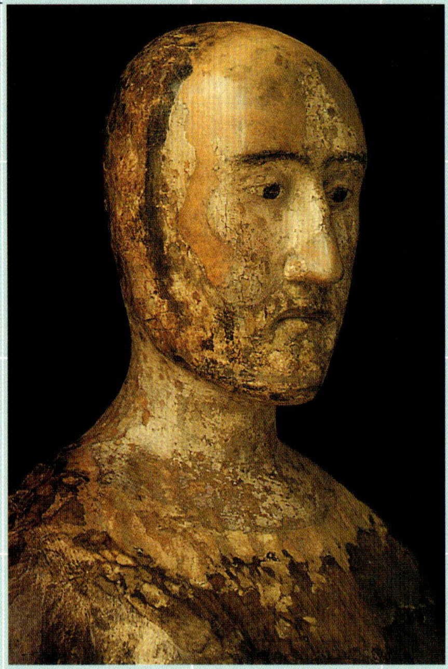

1

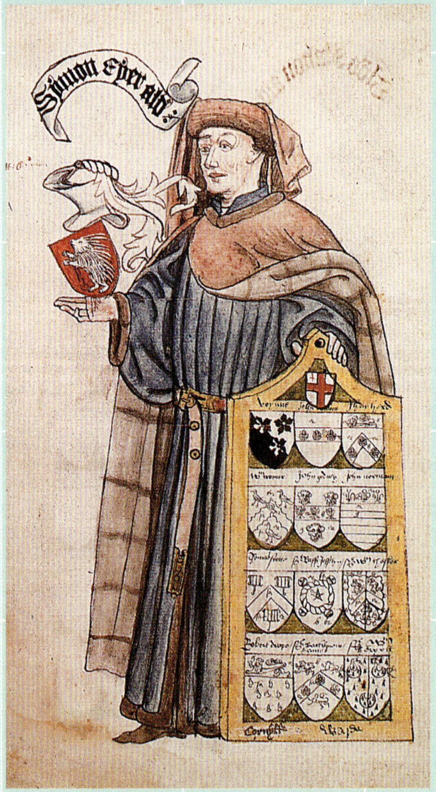

2

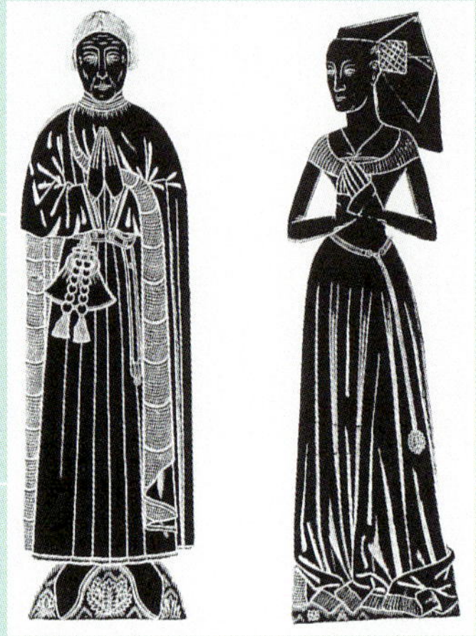

3

1 King Edward III (1312–77). This wooden effigy in Westminster Abbey was originally completed with a wig and a moustache and long beard of real hair, and dressed in royal robes. It was carried in the funeral procession and displayed during the lying-in-state at St Paul's Cathedral, and at Westminster Abbey where the King was buried.

2 Simon Eyre, Alderman of Cornhill Ward 1449–51.

3 John and Amy Lambard, 1487. John Lambard, mercer and alderman of London, was buried with his wife Amy under these fine funeral brasses in the parish church at Hinxworth, Hertfordshire, where he was born.

4 Eleanor de Bohun, Duchess of Gloucester (d1399). Funeral brass in Westminster Abbey.

5 John de Oteswich and his wife. Funeral monument in St Helen's church Bishopsgate, portraying a wealthy 14th–century London couple.

6 Geoffrey Chaucer, civil servant, customs official and court poet (*c.*1343–1400). This portrait appears in Thomas Hoccleve's *The Regement of Princes.*

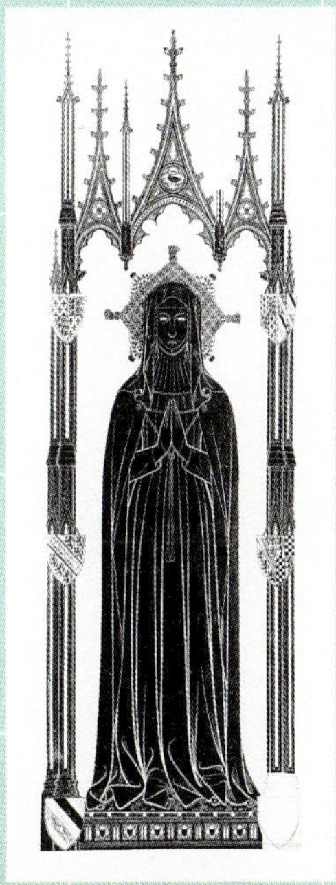
4

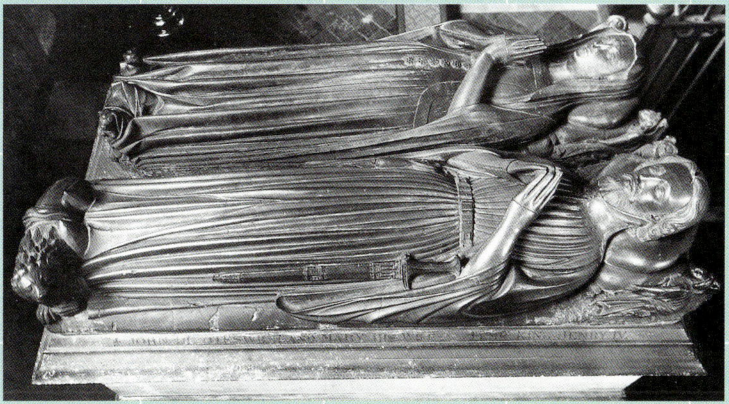
5

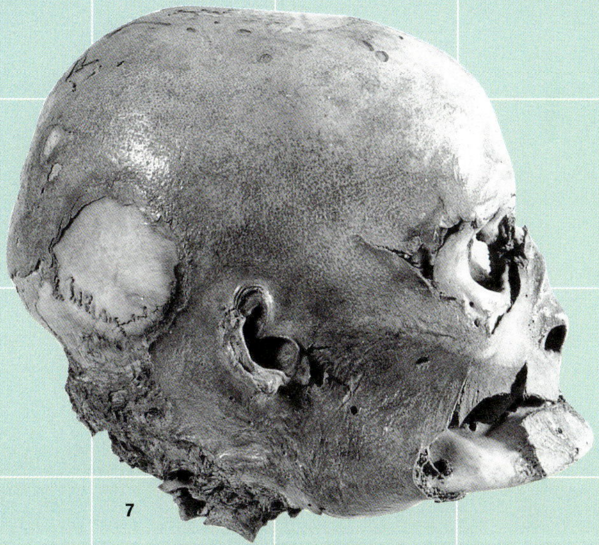
7

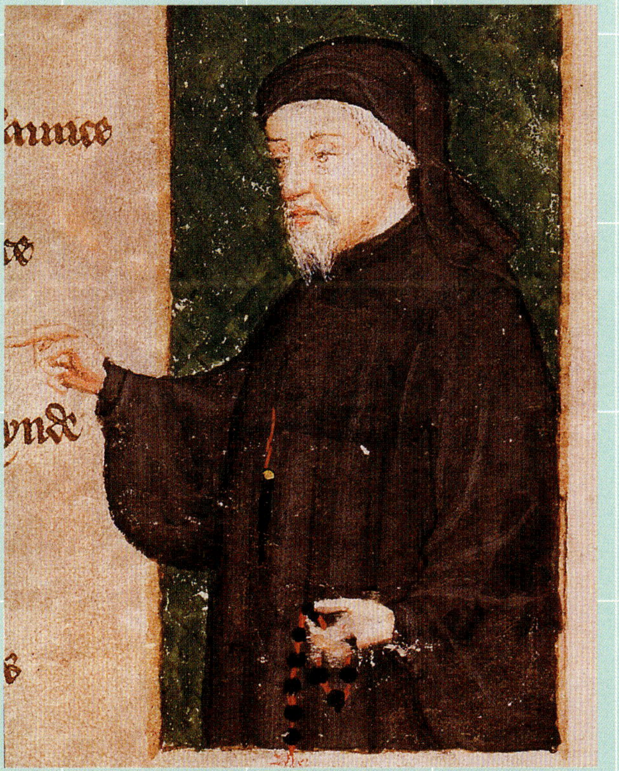
6

7 Simon of Sudbury, Archbishop of Canterbury (d1381). Sudbury was Chancellor to Richard II, and was generally blamed for the imposition in 1381 of the 'poll-tax' that sparked the rebellion known as the Peasants' Revolt. When the rebels reached London in June 1381 he took refuge in the Tower of London, but he was dragged out and beheaded on Tower Hill. The rebels paraded his head around the streets, then set it up above the gate on London Bridge. Eventually his head was returned to his home town, Sudbury in Suffolk, where it is preserved in the parish church of St Gregory.

TAILORED BODIES

MEDIEVAL AND TUDOR CLOTHING

by Kay Staniland

1 George, 5th Lord Seton (1531–85), portrayed by an unknown artist in 1558. His embroidered ensemble reflects both his wealth and his high status at the court of Mary, Queen of Scots. His hat of embroidered and spangled velvet is in sharp contrast to the excavated versions (see Figure 6). Note, too, the spangled plume.

For early Londoners clothing was simple in form and limited in quantity. A tunic at first constructed from a single length of cloth with a central hole for the head and seamed at the sides, with extra material eventually added for sleeves, was to evolve over a period of several hundred years into a more shapely and often very elegant garment. Capes and enveloping cloaks, combined with hoods and, less usually, hats, provided necessary protection from the elements. Short tunics were the most practical but in winter required leg coverings (hose); leather shoes and boots, and sometimes gloves, completed the ensemble. By the time the famous embroidery known as the Bayeux Tapestry was worked in the late eleventh century, longer tunics on men usually denoted high status. Women wore similarly cut ground-length tunics, usually with a veil-like covering on the head.

The underwear of both sexes was of linen and covered much of the body (sleeved shirt and breeches for men, sleeved, almost ground-length chemise for women). Thus clothing, a valuable possession in earlier times, was well protected from soiling from within; the underwear was easily washable, whereas the cleaning of upper garments, of wool or silk and often lined with furs, presented greater problems. The affluent simply bought new clothes and disposed of their unwanted garments as gifts; these were sometimes the prerequisite of retainers, whilst more elaborate and valuable garments might be presented to churches. The majority of the population is believed to have owned only a few garments.

Increasing wealth during the eleventh and twelfth centuries encouraged the expansion of trading links throughout Europe and, as a consequence, an increasing demand for luxury products. Clothing was one of the most expensive and cherished possessions of the medieval nobility and merchant classes, and was often used to demonstrate wealth and status. Excavated textiles from fourteenth-century London

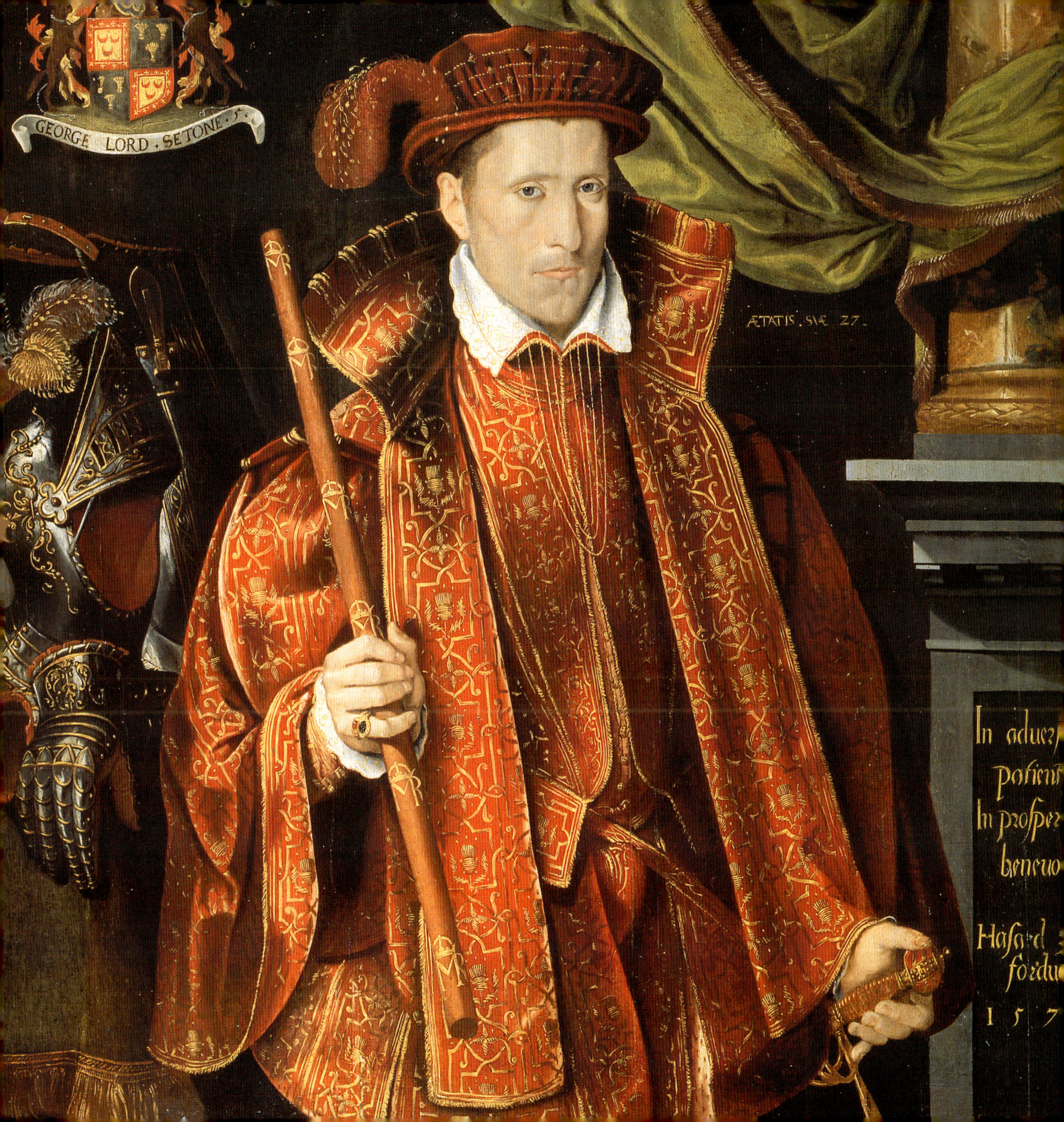
GEORGE LORD SETONE
ÆTATIS SVÆ 27

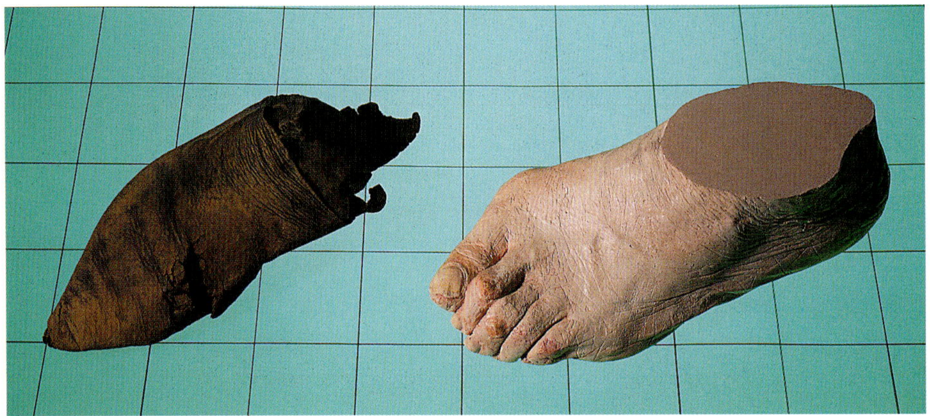
2a 5CM 2b

2 A leather shoe of the late 14th century (2a) excavated from the riverside at St Paul's. The large hole was caused by wear from a bunion (Hallux Valgus), swelling of the joint associated with displacement of the big toe (2b). This condition is worsened by narrow, pointed or badly fitting footwear; such pointed shoes were very fashionable at this time.

reveal the considerable range of clothes available and the high standard of stitching skills. They are too fragmentary to reveal much about the bodies of their owners but, like many later-surviving garments, seem generally to be on the small side – perhaps in part because clothing for slight figures has always been difficult to recycle.

In contrast, the assemblages of footwear from medieval London are large enough to provide useful statistical information about the size of feet at the time. The conclusions to be drawn so far indicate that medieval feet were not markedly different from modern ones, except that the largest may have been three to four sizes smaller. Wear marks and distortion evident in these shoes demonstrate the many ailments and deformities, from slight to major, which afflicted our predecessors: bunions, hammer toes, pigeon toes, arthritic toes, and abnormally arched feet and evidence of a shuffling gait have all left their mark on medieval boots and shoes (Figure 2). The changes wrought on the original work of the shoemaker by these medical conditions can be considerable and, perhaps more than all other artefacts, these shoes reveal the unchanging nature of the London body over many centuries.

By the fourteenth century changes in fashion became more recognisable and perhaps more frequent. Affluence had continued to spread throughout society, resulting in larger, more lavish wardrobes which brought in their wake sumptuary legislation, intended to control excess in dress as well as impose limitations on the clothing of each level of society. Tailors, experimenting with ways of fitting cloth smoothly to the body, were condemned for cutting up the precious hand-woven cloth in such a wasteful manner. It is possible to recognise for the first time an approach to dress, its transient novelties and changing form that we would now classify as 'fashion'.

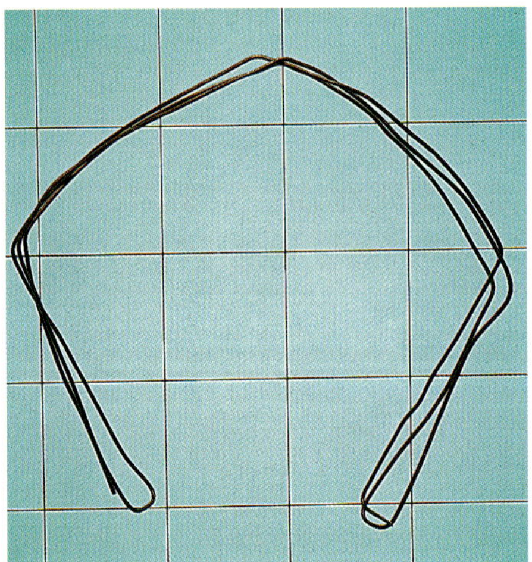
3 5CM

3 Wire stiffener for a 16th-century woman's head dress (see Figure 4), from an unknown London site.

For men this meant tightly fitted tunics, which quite quickly diminished in length as the century drew to a close, bringing their legs and leg-coverings to prominence for the first time. Padding 'improved' the shapeliness of these hip-hugging garments, which were fastened closely at the front with a multitude of fashionable buttons or with firm lacing. Women's dress contours were transformed in the same way, aided by the introduction of lacing in the eleventh or twelfth century; this device enabled torso-hugging garments to be slipped over the head without affecting the body underneath. As a counterpart to this new outline, especially the increasingly wide skirts, women's veils and headdresses became increasingly elaborate (Figure 4). This was to become a major feature in the fifteenth century and many examples can be seen in portraits and tomb effigies of the period.

Once the novelty of the short, tight doublet had run its course, men adopted loose-fitting short or long overgarments, often with long flowing sleeves; this helped to introduce a new, more masculine outline in the late fifteenth century. Tailors began to exploit their considerable armoury of cutting and shaping skills with the aid of padding, stiff interlinings, quantities of rich silks and velvets, gold braids and exotic furs. Like their female counterparts, men of fashion adopted larger hats to balance this new, larger-than-life image, and then abandoned them once this goal had been achieved.

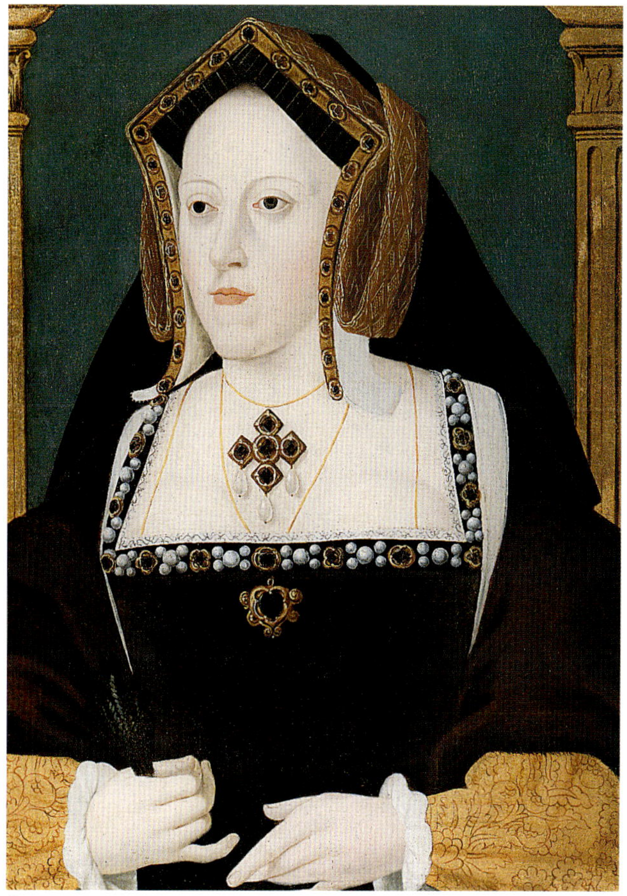

4

There are many more examples of complete or near-complete garments amongst the excavated textile finds from sixteenth-century London, but once more the sample is small and cannot be taken as an accurate guide to the body sizes of citizens or their offspring. Many of the items do seem to have been for those of a slighter build, but this may again be related to recycling problems; obesity is certainly not present in the sample. Significantly, these finds reveal the ways in which fashionable details still formed a part of the everyday dress of the merchants, craftsmen and their families who made up a significant part of Tudor London's population.

Contemporary portraits mostly record the appearance of the nobility, richly dressed in expensive, and often highly impractical, finery. By contrast, depictions of the less affluent are rare, but the excavated clothing is an important counterbalance to other sources of

4 Catherine of Aragon (1485–1536), first wife of Henry VIII, wearing one of the 'gable' head dresses typical of court wear in the 1530s and 1540s. These framed the face with rich fabrics and jewels, whilst the back of the head was concealed by a black bag-like structure. City merchants' wives imitated these court head dresses using plain cloth and fine linen.

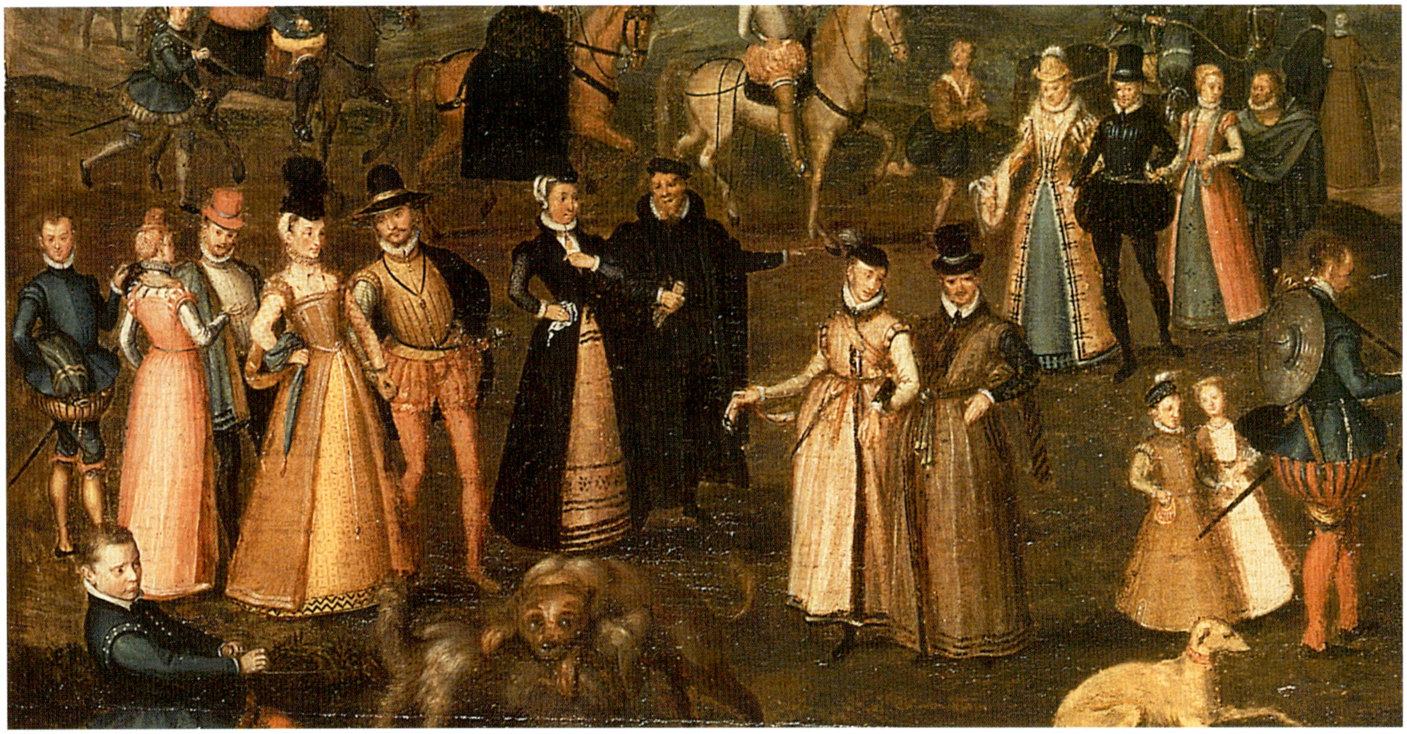

5

information and demonstrates the extensive use of wool, England's chief trading commodity (Figure 5). Practical and warm, it holds dye well, indicating that brightly coloured clothing was not denied to the lower classes. Similarly, trimmings of wool, silk or metal alloys replaced the expensive fashionable equivalents of the upper classes. Underwear was similar in style but made of cheaper and probably much less fine linen, which was worn plain rather than richly embroidered.

There are many knitted wool hats in these finds (Figure 6). They are of several distinct and, as Pieter Breugel illustrated in his paintings, possibly contemporary styles, though they may have been thrown away over a long period of time. Similar hats are to be seen in many Tudor portraits, including those of Henry VIII's courtiers painted by Hans Holbein. Often very stylish accessories imitating expensive versions in velvet or satin adorned with feathers and jewels, these were at the same time immensely practical and were the forerunners of the beret and the tam o'shanter. A succession of processes shrank and felted the knitting until it became waterproof; then the surface was brushed with teasels to draw up a fluffy nap (pile) which obscured the knitting. Surviving examples still have their ribbon trimming slotted through the knitting, whilst others have the slashed decoration

5 **Detail from *A Fete at Bermondsey*, *c.*1570 by Joris Hoefnagel. Women of noble birth wore simpler versions of fashionable dress: cloth and linen naturally predominated because they were practical. The affluent might have indulged in trimmings of velvet or satin and inexpensive furs.**

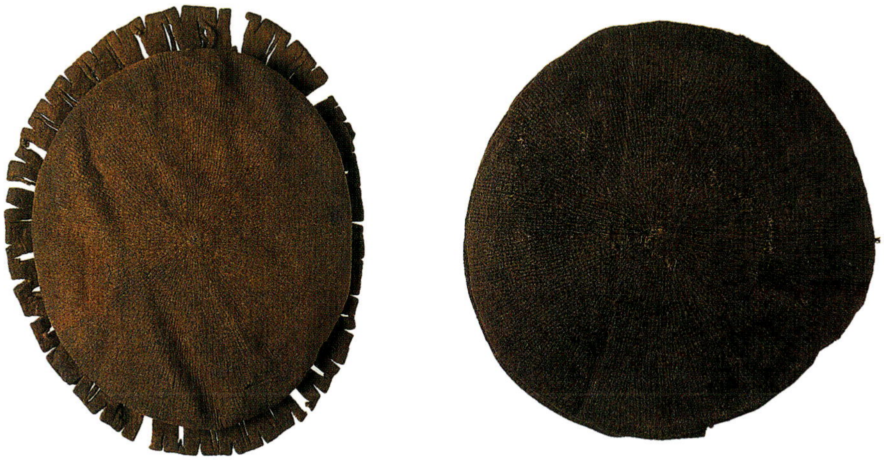

6

which is so typical of the period (Figure 6). Similar examples in cloth and felt have been excavated in London. One discarded cap fragment demonstrates how this heavily felted knitting could be recycled as an inner sole for a shoe.

Portraits show that both women and children also wore flat, brimmed hats – close-fitting silk bonnets, counterparts of the more numerous linen examples which represent the less formal dress of domestic or working life. Other examples of women's garments are few and mostly fragmentary. There was little that could not be cut up and recycled. Numerous metal hooks and perhaps eyelets have survived in archaeological contexts. These enabled bodices to be closely fitted to the female torso, but they were not fastened so tightly that they distorted the natural form of the body. Soon, however, during Elizabeth I's reign, bodices became long and stiff and not until the twentieth century were women to be free of such constriction – the one exception being a brief period during the early nineteenth century.

The origins of hand-knitting are obscure, but the technique seems to have appeared in western Europe in the early Middle Ages; it was possibly already used for caps in late fourteenth-century London. Up to the late seventeenth century all knitting was worked in the round, either on several needles or on a length of wire, and was shaped by decreasing or increasing stitches. The resulting network of threads was stretchy, expanding and contracting to fit closely to any part of the body. It was a revolutionary clothing development now very much taken for granted. For example, leg-coverings had for centuries been of bias-cut cloth which, even when cleverly cut from the finest cloth, failed to fit the leg neatly. The impact of new technology in knitting is striking, and soon men's

6 **Knitted woollen hats of the mid-16th century from unknown London sites. Such practical accessories were still trimmed with silk ribbons, and ornamental slashing was possible because the knitting had been so heavily felted and would not unravel. Although now various shades of brown, from the tannic acid in the soil, many of these hats were originally dyed in bright colours; for example, some appear a very reddish brown and were almost certainly dyed red with madder.**

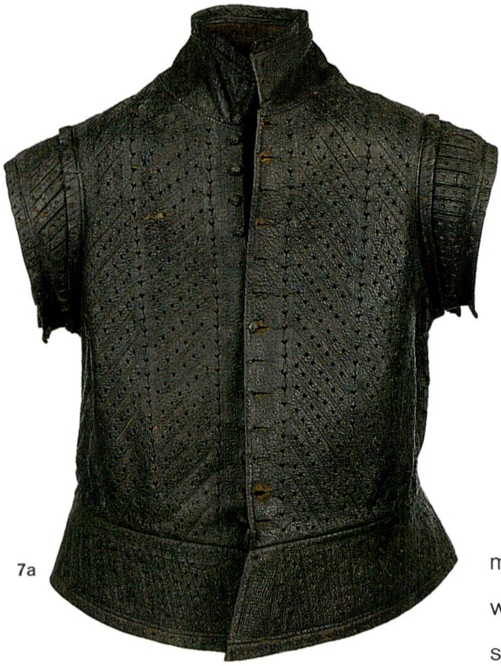

7a

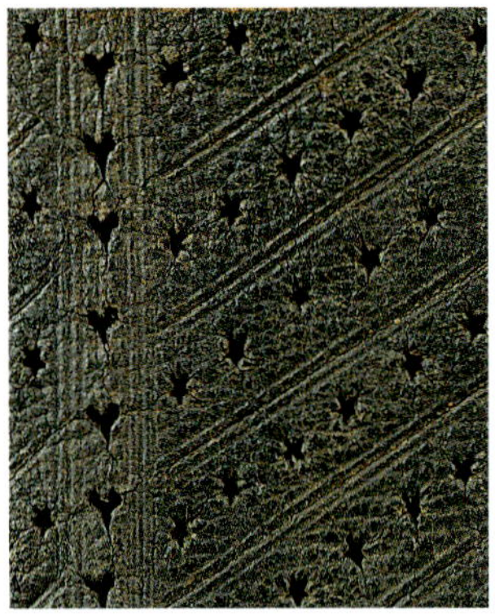

7b

legs became a focal point in fashionable dress. The early knitted stockings of London origin at first lacked the refined shaping seen in the expensive, finely knitted silk stockings imported from Italy and Spain. In contrast, however, these thick wool imitations already took into account the practical requirements of their less affluent owners: that most vulnerable point, the heel, was strongly reinforced by double-plied wool.

The combination of appearing fashionable while wearing practical clothes is also present in the decoratively slashed leather jerkins of the mid-sixteenth century which, to judge from the fragments excavated in London, were widely worn at all levels of society and by all age groups (Figure 7). Naturally the versions sported by the rich would have featured finer materials more skilfully ornamented and combined with expensive silks but yet again excavated finds underline Londoners' general eagerness for fashionable dress.

The most telling evidence of this impulse must be the numerous cod-pieces excavated in London in the 1920s (Figure 9). These may, in fact, merely represent the inner padding of rather more elegant examples, discarded when they became unfashionable in the later sixteenth century. The cod-piece seems to have developed from the simple triangular flap which covered the front opening of men's tights in fifteenth-century Europe. This became more conspicuous towards 1500, often bag-like and constructed of stiffer materials and ornamented with metallic laces. The large and heavily padded form of the cod-piece, made of the same material as the breeches, is particularly associated with Tudor dress between 1540 and 1560. A cunning repository for handkerchiefs and other small accessories, the cod-piece was a natural target for bawdy humour in Elizabethan and Stuart literature and it was sure to raise a laugh with the audiences of the Globe or Rose Theatres.

Perhaps the most poignant of the Tudor clothing finds are those associated with babies and children, rare in any period but almost unique in the field of sixteenth-century artefacts. Apart from a few tiny leather shoes of recognisably Tudor form, the surviving items of children's clothing are all of hand-knitted wool (Figure 8): what we would now call

7 A youth's brown leather jerkin of 1555–65 (7a). This was purchased in 1827 for use in a display at the Tower of London, but its earlier provenance is not known. It is ornamented with bands of scored lines containing punched heart or star motifs, and slashed diamonds on the neck sections. (7b): The moulded pewter buttons imitate the more expensive wooden versions which were ornamented with worked silk or gilt thread.

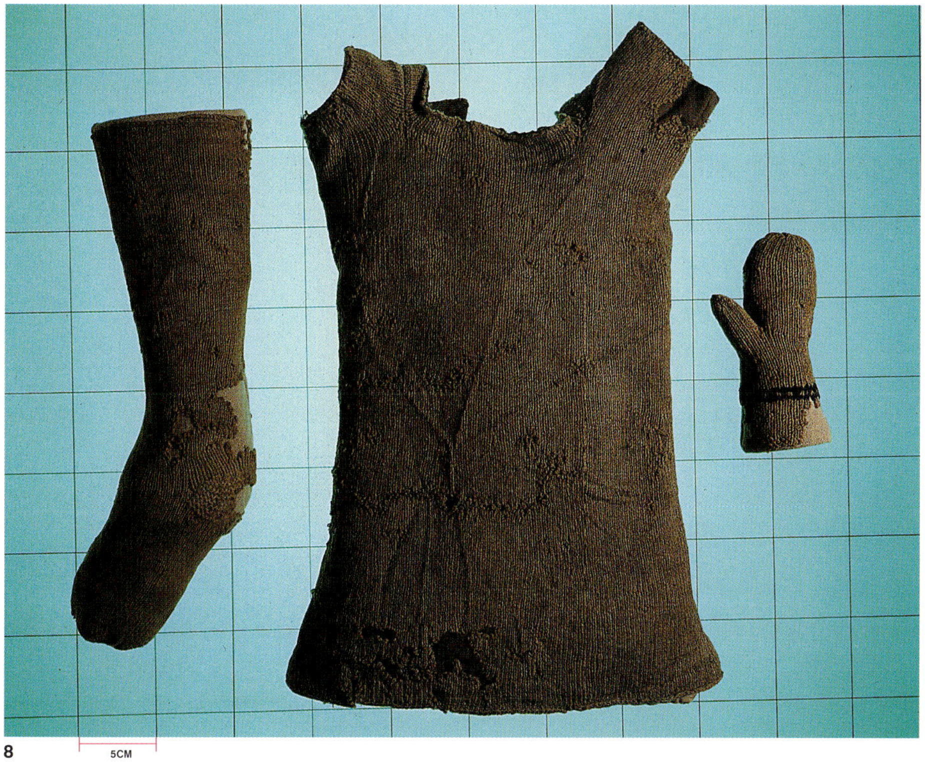

8

vests, but which were almost certainly termed 'waistcoats' at the time. Mittens and socks like the other knitted pieces, but miniature versions, were again constructed in the round on several needles; this suggests that the technique of knitting several shaped sections and sewing them together is a more recent development. Contemporary inventories reveal that these very practical items of clothing might be worn right across the social spectrum and were not expensive: perhaps this is why they show so few signs of being completely worn out when found several hundred years later.

Increasing quantities of historic clothing are preserved in museum collections and show the rise and fall of numerous short-lived fashions from the late sixteenth century to the present day. The story of such fashion changes, how they came about, how they built on the natural human frame, and in later periods even distorted it, is a fascinating and complex subject. The earlier stages, because they are more remote, are less fully understood, and London's excavated textile finds are therefore of outstanding importance. Not only do they provide invaluable technical information, but they may also demonstrate what Londoners wore and the way in which they strove to aggrandise their bodies with affordable imitations of sophisticated court fashions.

8 Infant's knitted sock,'vest', and mitten excavated in London, probably from the mid-16th century. These were knitted in a soft white wool and the mitten has a unique contrasting band, probably of naturally black sheep's wool. Several medieval paintings of the Virgin and Child show the Virgin knitting a similiar vest-like garment for her son, on three to five needles.

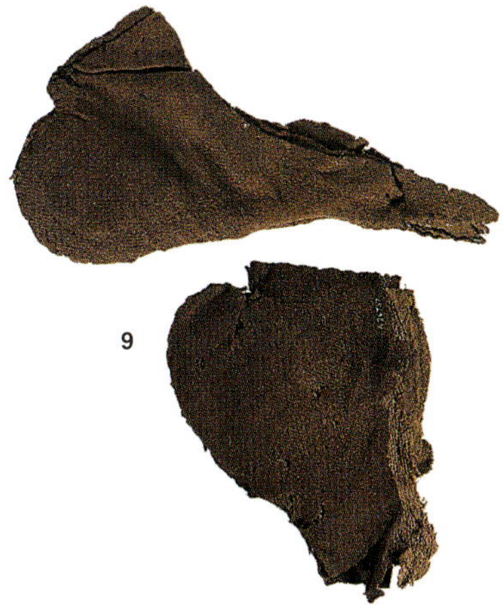

9

9 Cod-pieces formed of several layers of rough twilled cloth, excavated in Worship Street in the 1920s. These presumably date from the middle years of the 16th century. When first accessioned their purpose was not realised and they have for many years been classed as shoulder-wings from jerkins which, however, were not worn until later in the century and were of an entirely different shape.

TUDOR SEX APPEAL

MEN AND WOMEN AS SEX SYMBOLS

Wealthy Tudor Londoners showed off their bodies through elaborate and sensuous dress. Men and women wore alluring, seductive and brightly coloured materials. They disguised or flaunted their bodily shape by tailoring, corseting, padding and slashing of fabric. Often extravagant cod-pieces emphasised men's virility. Women wore elongated bodices cut low to reveal the bust. Stiff, structured underskirts or farthingales made their waists seem even smaller. This extreme fashion was uncomfortable but drew attention to female sexuality.

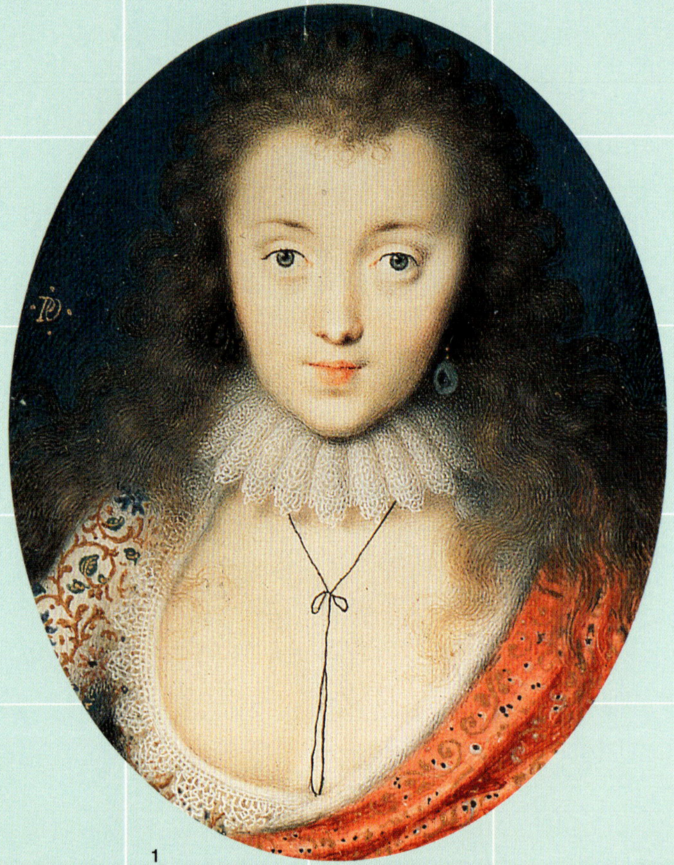

1

1 ***Venetia Stanley, Lady Digby***, **c.1615-17, by Peter Oliver. This miniature would no doubt have been an intimate keepsake. The lady's bodice is extremely low-cut and her cleavage emphasised by the black silk cord hanging between her breasts.**

2 ***Unknown woman***, **1569. Aged 21 years, this attractive young woman highlights the slimness of her waist by wearing a tight bodice and skirt which swells at the hips.**

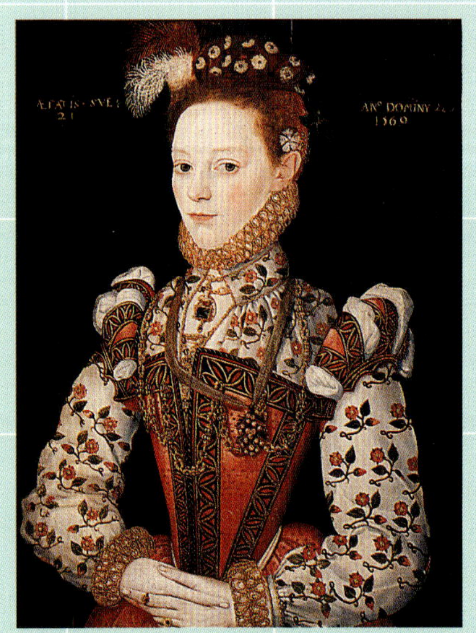

2

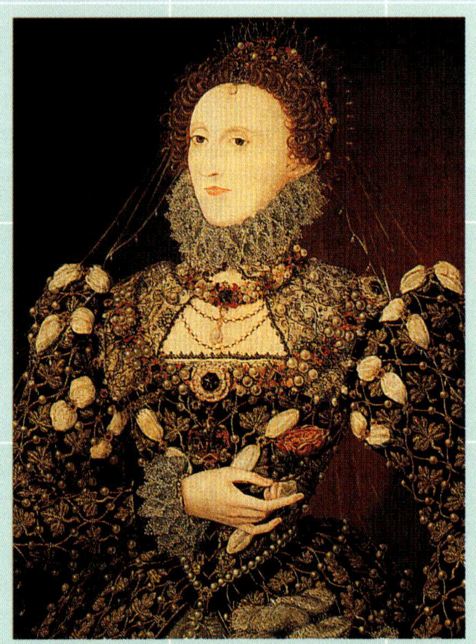

3

3 *Elizabeth I*, c.1575, attributed to Nicholas Hilliard. This portrait of Queen Elizabeth I is usually referred to as the 'Phoenix portrait' because of the pendant jewel worn on her breast.

4 *Henry VIII*, c.1537, after Hans Holbein the younger. The king's stance, broad shoulders and large cod-piece show off his strength and masculinity.

5 *Dancing scene*, c.1600. In 1562, Alessandro Magno, an Italian visitor to London, noted how: '... in dances, men hold women in their arms and hug them very tightly, and for each dance they kiss them in a very lustful way'. Once believed to represent Elizabeth I and the Earl of Leicester, this painting is now thought to show a French dancing scene.

6 *Henry Howard, Earl of Surrey*, c.1546, by an unknown artist. Luxuriously dressed in the Italian fashion, Surrey wears a cod-piece made of the same material as his trunkhose.

7 *Young man among Roses*, c.1588 by Nicholas Hilliard. The man wears a doublet with a shaped padded front known as a peascod belly and short trunkhose revealing very slender long legs.

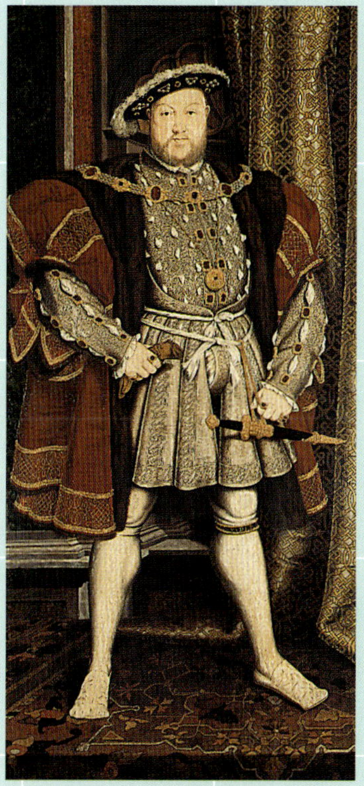

4

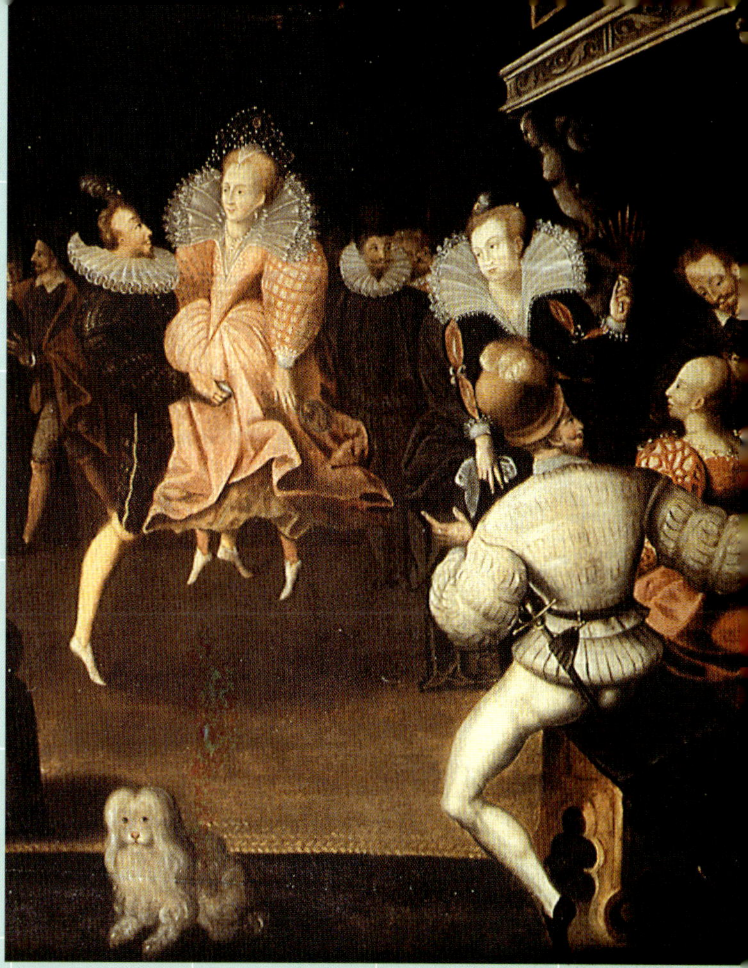

5

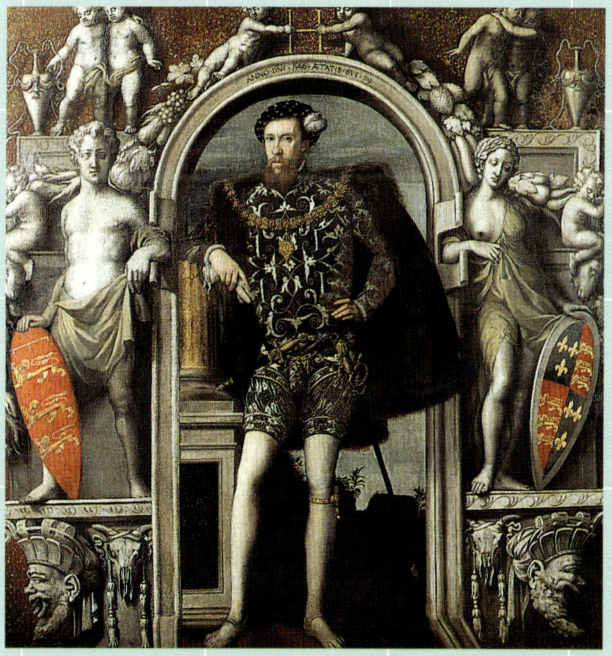

6

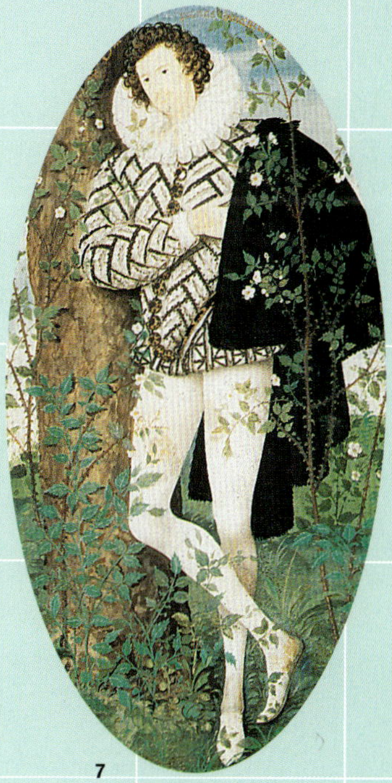

7

GEORGIAN AND VICTORIAN BODIES

A LONDON LOOK?

by Alex Werner, Janice Conheeney and Karen Fielder

What did Londoners look like in the eighteenth and nineteenth centuries? The paintings, watercolours and prints of London life by artists such as Hogarth, Rowlandson and Frith reveal the varied appearance of the London populace. But what were the distinctive characteristics of Londoners compared with those who lived in the country or on the Continent? Such questions were often answered more directly by foreign commentators than by local writers. Visitors to London were able to spot particular everyday traits and mannerisms of posture, appearance and dress, although there were subtle characteristics which distinguished one level of London society from another that went unnoticed by foreigners. Often their writings were selective, concentrating only on the main London attractions or meeting places such as Vauxhall Gardens, the Royal Exchange or Covent Garden. Here, however, they encountered a broad spectrum of inhabitants on the streets and noted their salient features. There are many general descriptons of Londoners to be found in the art and literature of the period, but like most of the essays in this book, the analysis of human skeletons is employed to gain further insight into the lives and afflictions of eighteenth- and nineteenth-century Londoners.

Justification for the excavation of burials from the recent past has been a matter of some controversy. Strict laws govern the disturbance of cemeteries and permission to excavate is granted only in very special cases, usually when a site is being redeveloped. There are a number of reasons why it is important to study post-medieval skeletons, not least because evidence such as alteration in the average build and appearance of people, or changes in disease pattern, would be lost. Significantly for future research, the accuracy of osteological techniques can be tested by comparing the resulting data with contemporary documentary sources. Overall, the skeletal record is important in relation to the other sources of the period

1 An election-day crowd in Covent Garden (detail from *Westminster Election of 1788* by Robert Dighton).

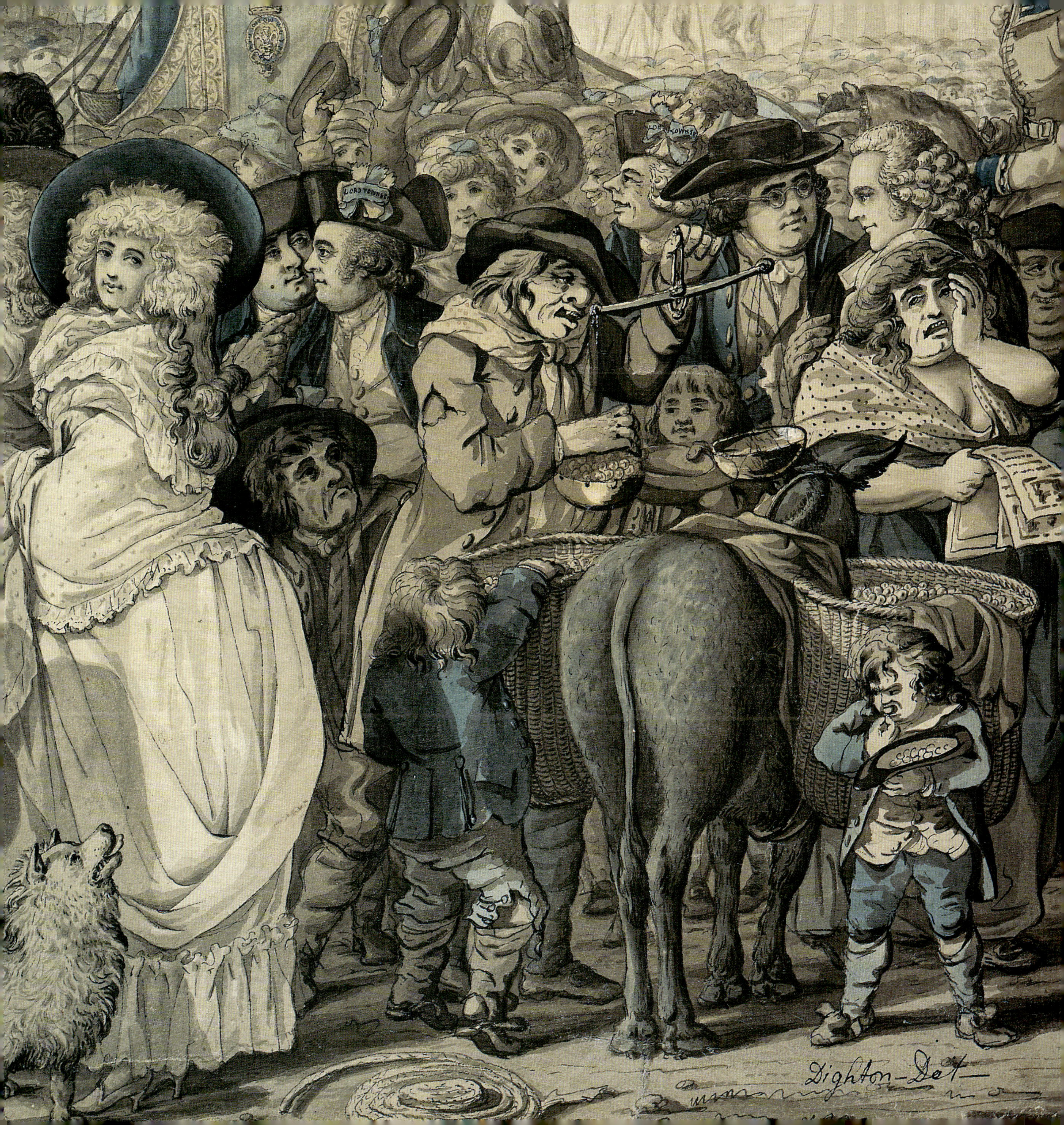
Dighton Del

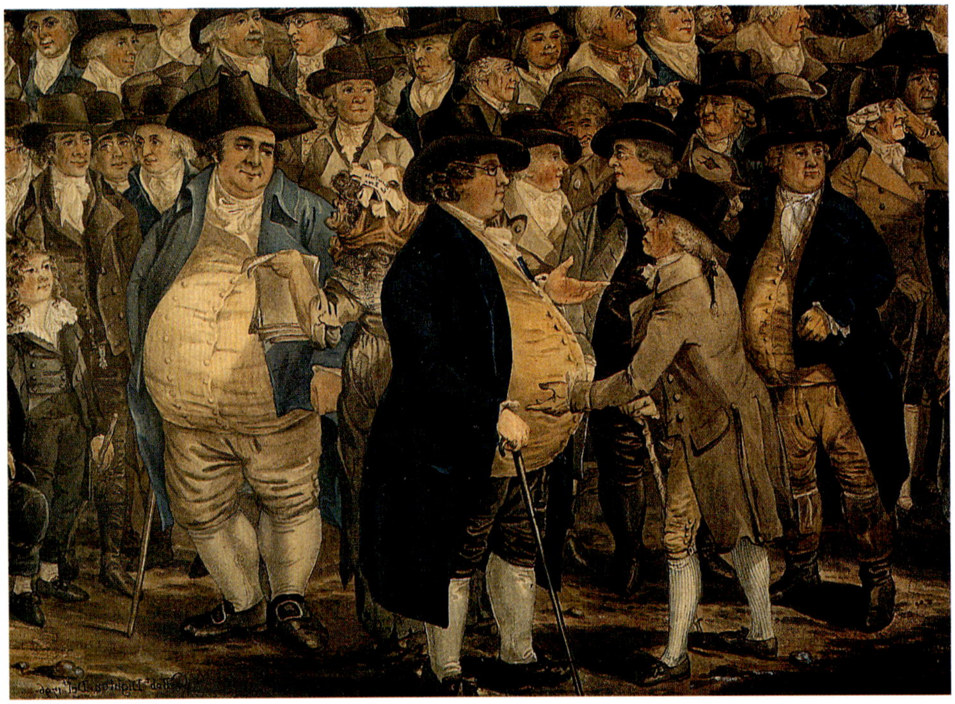

2

for understanding how people lived, worked and died in London.

There was (and still is) a frenetic pace to London life. For some writers and visitors, this was a noteworthy feature affecting how Londoners looked. Henry Mayhew remarked on the 'living stream' of people who passed him by in the streets, stating that 'their very pace and destination are different; there is a walk and business determination distinctly London'. The narrator of Edgar Allan Poe's short story *The Man of the Crowd*, seated in the bow window of a London coffee house at dusk, focused on 'the continuous tides of population' passing in the street and became interested in 'the innumerable varieties of figure, dress, air, gait, visage, and expression of countenance'. Washington Irving also felt that this driving force gave Londoners 'a look of hurry and abstraction.' One of the most apposite descriptions was made in 1837 by John Hogg in his study of London people:

> The appearance of the people in the streets of London is one of the first things that attracts the notice of strangers. The native inhabitants, or those who have been born in the metropolis, and whose forefathers have resided in it for two or three generations, are somewhat under middle size, but their limbs and features are generally well formed. They are of spare habit, but rather muscular; they are characterised by firmness of carriage, and an erect, independent air; they move with a steady, measured step, and generally a very brisk pace. The features are generally very strongly marked, and pointed; the eye in particular presents an openness and fullness that is remarkable. The tout-ensemble of the countenance bears an air of keenness, animation, and intelligence, that distinguish the Londoner from his country neighbour.

2 **Corpulent gentlemen, 1796 (detail from a Robert Dighton watercolour).**

The reference to short stature is confirmed by the measurement of the human skeletons. The average height of a group of skeletons recently excavated at St Bride's Lower

Churchyard, Farringdon Street, was 171cm (5ft 7 1/4in.) for men, and 157cm (5ft 1 3/4in.) for women and at Christ Church, Spitalfields was 168cm (5ft 6in.) and 155cm (5 ft 1in.) respectively. For the latter sample, measurement of the forearm bone was taken into account in the calculation. The forearm was short relative to the length of the leg bone and it is believed that this might be a characteristic peculiar to the Huguenot immigrants. The estimates of the St Bride's sample were all calculated from the length of the femur. Clearly, Londoners of this period were shorter than their modern day counterparts (175cm or 5ft 9in. and 162cm or 5ft 5 3/4in. for males and females respectively) and this deficit in height was more apparent in the female. Perhaps women's growth was more compromised by adverse conditions during their developmental years, and thus they failed to achieve their maximum growth potential.

By examining the skeletal record with regard to overall body shape, it can be shown that males were generally larger than females as would be expected in any population. However, in terms of the actual sexing characteristics the difference was not as pronounced as in samples from the Roman and Medieval periods; males and females were closer in natural body shape than those of an earlier date. This would imply that, generally, neither sex had particularly marked muscle development which perhaps contradicts the general descriptions made by John Hogg.

Hogg's observation of people's alertness, which suggested a healthy state, was also countered by Matt Bramble in Tobias Smollett's *Humphry Clinker* (1771) when he spoke of the 'languid, sallow looks' that marked out 'the inhabitants of London.' According to him, the pressure and stress on the body, the polluted air, adulterated food and the generally unhealthy nature of City life was revealed, above all, in the pale complexions of Londoners. Bramble found it difficult to explain the attractions of city life. Country people were drawn to London by the prospect of domestic work:

> They desert their dirt and drudgery, and swarm up to London, in hopes of getting into service, where they can live luxuriously and wear fine clothes, without being obliged to work; for idleness is natural to man.

Unfortunately, London was a 'centre of infection' and was noisy. Henry Mayhew spoke of city people being 'bombarded with sound' like living 'in a mill,' until the sound became 'the normal state' for them. Space was at a premium and they found themselves, as Bramble noted:

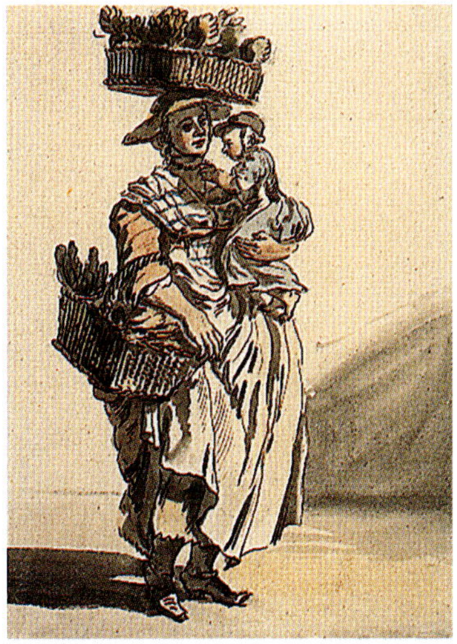

3

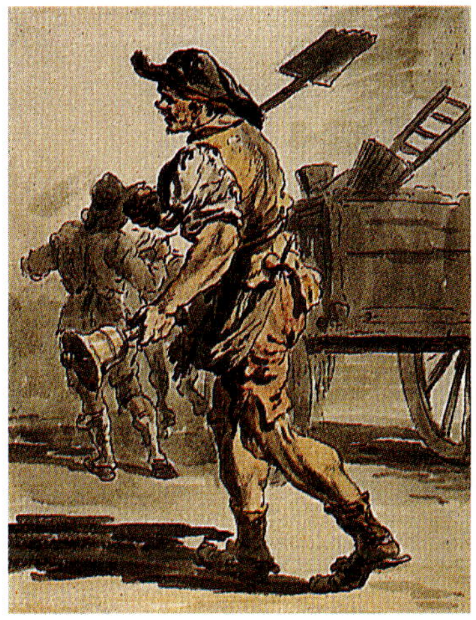

4

3 **A London green-vegetable seller carrying a child, 1759, by Paul Sandby.**

4 **A London coalman, 1759, by Paul Sandby.**

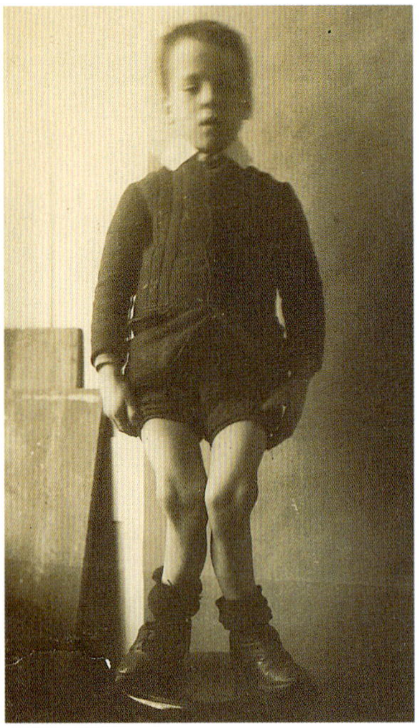

5

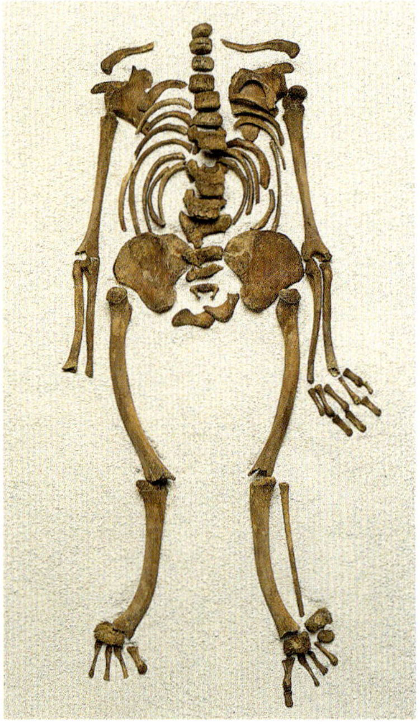

6

> pent up in frowzy lodgings, where there is not enough room to sling a cat . . . breathe the steams of endless putrefaction . . . gross acid of sea-coal . . . a pernicious nuisance to lungs of any delicacy of texture.

Smoke and pollution cannot have helped those suffering from bronchitis and asthma. In the mornings, it was remarked that the cities of London and Westminster and the borough of Southwark were 'cover'd by a Cloud of Smoak, most People being employed in lighting Fires'. The use of coal fires for heating and for industrial processes made smogs and fogs prevalent. Rainwater was reported sometimes to be 'black' in colour. The streets were also 'unpleasantly full either of dust or mud', the result of houses being demolished and the enormous numbers of coaches and carts rolling in the streets night and day. This made walking along the streets hazardous in wet weather although the pavement or 'elevated footpath' (this was a special feature noted by visitors) helped to lessen the risk of being splashed with dirt. In summertime, carts carrying water barrels pierced with holes watered the streets to keep the dust clouds to a minimum.

One very apparent visual effect of the frequent smogs would have been the badly bowed limbs of some of the inhabitants, symptomatic of childhood rickets (Figures 5 and 6). Rickets results from a lack of vitamin D derived either from the diet or, more significantly, from sunlight. The condition appears to have been unselective in the class of child it afflicted: cases were recorded at Christ Church, at Marylebone cemetery, a high-status burial site in west London, and at St Bride's Lower Churchyard where over 15 per cent of children suffered from the condition. The effects of the disease would have been cyclical, children recovering during spring and summer and relapsing in winter.

5 **Boy aged 11 showing deformity of the legs due to rickets, c.1891.**

6 **Skeleton of a child suffering from rickets, with typical bowing of the long bones, from Broadgate.**

KEEPING CLEAN

Cleanliness was a feature of upper-class Londoners. The well-to-do picked and cleaned their teeth and washed their hands, arms, faces, necks and throats (and possibly their private parts, though this is not specified) most days in cold water. The dental heath of those individuals buried at Christ Church and at St Bride's Lower Churchyard was poor with a high rate of tooth loss and caries being prevalent in the remaining teeth. This would suggest that there was lack of oral hygiene made worse by a diet that caused tooth decay and required little chewing. Illustrations of the London populace show large numbers of both young and old with a sunken-mouthed appearance (Figures 1,12,16). This is reflected in the skeletal evidence, showing that a substantial proportion of the St Bride's sample was toothless by middle age. Some had the benefit of cosmetic help, especially at Spitalfields where dentures or bridges were still in place in nine people, and two had gold fillings. Dental appliances may have been more common than this and been removed at death. Only one person had a gold filling at St Bride's Lower Churchyard, and no dental appliances were discovered. At Marylebone cemetery, like Spitalfields, a relatively wealthy burial ground, a woman had an incisor from another person wired into a gap in her front teeth (Figure 7), a form of 'Waterloo teeth' (this term refers to the practise of extracting teeth from those killed in battle). This may indicate the ability to afford restorative work of this kind, and therefore imply a difference in the appearance of the two groups of people in life. Even those who had retained their teeth would have had noticeable decay and in some cases, no doubt, severe halitosis. A not uncommon feature of the St Bride's sample was a hole apparent between the canines and first premolars when the top and bottom teeth are clenched: a characteristic usually attributed to smokers who habitually gripped clay pipes between the teeth.

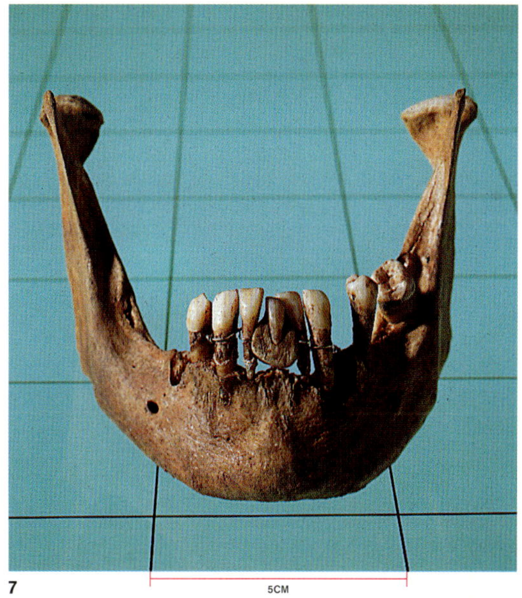

7

The wealthy had their bed-linen and undergarments changed on a regular basis. They employed nurses to take care of their infants and children. The daily routine included washing them 'all over with a sponge and warm water'. Great attention was given to making children 'hardy' by gradually subjecting them to less warm water until they liked 'to be washed with cold'. Washerwomen were employed, often working in the very early hours of the morning, to wash all the household linen in tubs in the wash-houses and backyards. Houses were kept clean by servants washing down the stairs, kitchen and entrance steps every day. It was far more difficult for working people to clean their living quarters or to stay clean themselves. Reference was made to the wives of journeymen-mechanics washing their husbands' shirts so that they might appear 'like Christians' though they lived 'like Brutes'. Water was made available only a few times a week at public stand-pipes. Poor people congregated with their pails in courts and alleys queuing up to

7 A false tooth in a woman's lower jaw, recovered from Marylebone cemetery. The false tooth is human and wires make use of the woman's surviving teeth as anchors to hold it in place.

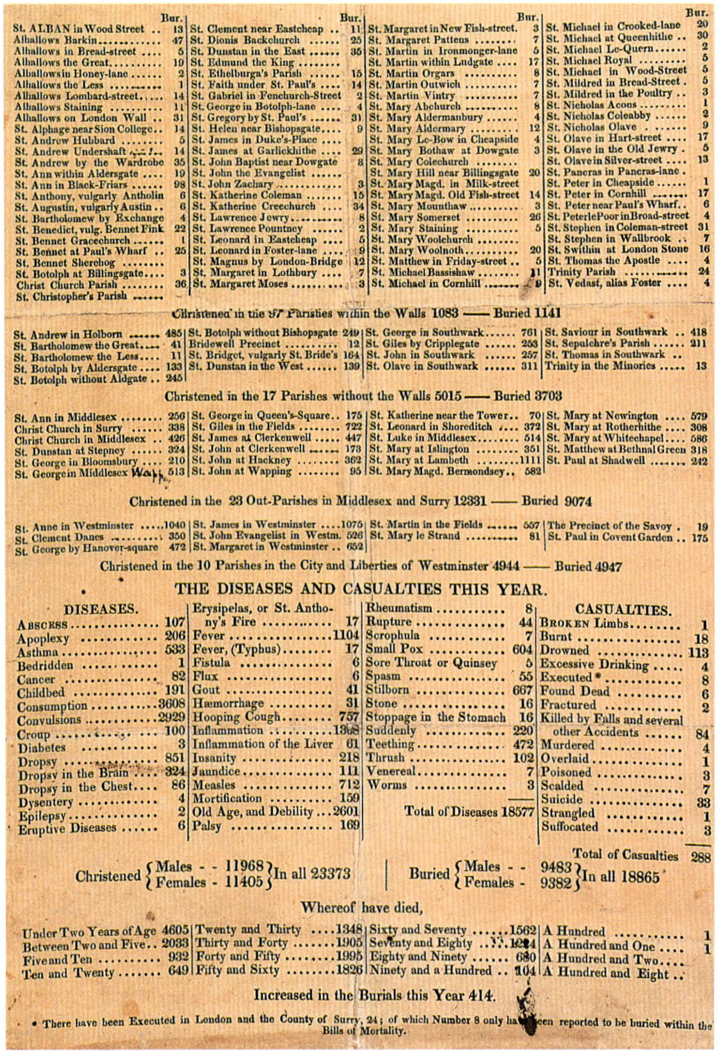

	Bur.		Bur.		Bur.		Bur.
St. ALBAN in Wood Street ..	13	St. Clement near Eastcheap ..	11	St. Margaret in New Fish-street.	3	St. Michael in Crooked-lane	20
Alhallows Barkin	47	St. Dionis Backchurch	25	St. Margaret Pattens	7	St. Michael at Queenhithe ..	30
Alhallows in Bread-street	5	St. Dunstan in the East	35	St. Martin in Ironmonger-lane	5	St. Michael Le-Quern	2
Alhallows the Great	19	St. Edmund the King		St. Martin within Ludgate	17	St. Michael Royal	5
Alhallows in Honey-lane	2	St. Ethelburga's Parish	15	St. Martin Orgars	8	St. Michael in Wood-Street	5
Alhallows the Less	1	St. Faith under St. Paul's	14	St. Martin Outwich	7	St. Mildred in Bread-Street	5
Alhallows Lombard-street	14	St. Gabriel in Fenchurch-Street	2	St. Martin Vintry	7	St. Mildred in the Poultry ..	3
Alhallows Staining	11	St. George in Botolph-lane	4	St. Mary Abchurch	8	St. Nicholas Acons	1
Alhallows on London Wall ..	31	St. Gregory by St. Paul's	31	St. Mary Aldermanbury	4	St. Nicholas Coleabby	2
St. Alphage near Sion College ..	14	St. Helen near Bishopsgate	9	St. Mary Aldermary	12	St. Nicholas Olave	9
St. Andrew Hubbard	5	St. James in Duke's-Place		St. Mary Le-Bow in Cheapside	4	St. Olave in Hart-street	17
St. Andrew Undershaft	14	St. James at Garlickhithe	29	St. Mary Bothaw at Dowgate	3	St. Olave in the Old Jewry	5
St. Andrew by the Wardrobe	35	St. John Baptist near Dowgate	8	St. Mary Colechurch		St. Olave in Silver-street	13
St. Ann within Aldersgate	19	St. John the Evangelist		St. Mary Hill near Billingsgate	20	St. Pancras in Pancras-lane	
St. Ann in Black-Friars	98	St. John Zachary	3	St. Mary Magd. in Milk-street		St. Peter in Cheapside	1
St. Anthony, vulgarly Antholin	6	St. Katherine Coleman	15	St. Mary Magd. Old Fish-street	14	St. Peter in Cornhill	17
St. Augustin, vulgarly Austin ..	6	St. Katherine Creechurch	34	St. Mary Mounthaw	3	St. Peter near Paul's Wharf ..	6
St. Bartholomew by Exchange	4	St. Lawrence Jewry	8	St. Mary Somerset	26	St. Peter le Poor in Broad-street	4
St. Benedict, vulg. Bennet Fink	22	St. Lawrence Pountney	2	St. Mary Staining	5	St. Stephen in Coleman-street	31
St. Bennet Gracechurch	1	St. Leonard in Eastcheap	5	St. Mary Woolchurch		St. Stephen in Wallbrook ..	7
St. Bennet at Paul's Wharf ..	25	St. Leonard in Foster-lane	9	St. Mary Woolnoth	20	St. Swithin at London Stone	16
St. Bennet Sherehog		St. Magnus by London-Bridge	12	St. Matthew in Friday-street ..	5	St. Thomas the Apostle	4
St. Botolph at Billingsgate	3	St. Margaret in Lothbury	7	St. Michael Bassishaw	11	Trinity Parish	24
Christ Church Parish	36	St. Margaret Moses	3	St. Michael in Cornhill	9	St. Vedast, alias Foster	4
St. Christopher's Parish							

Christened in the 97 Parishes within the Walls 1083 —— Buried 1141

St. Andrew in Holborn	485	St. Botolph without Bishopsgate	249	St. George in Southwark	761	St. Saviour in Southwark ..	418
St. Bartholomew the Great	41	Bridewell Precinct	12	St. Giles by Cripplegate	253	St. Sepulchre's Parish	211
St. Bartholomew the Less	11	St. Bridget, vulgarly St. Bride's	164	St. John in Southwark	257	St. Thomas in Southwark ..	
St. Botolph by Aldersgate	133	St. Dunstan in the West	139	St. Olave in Southwark	311	Trinity in the Minories	13
St. Botolph without Aldgate ..	245						

Christened in the 17 Parishes without the Walls 5015 —— Buried 3703

St. Ann in Middlesex	256	St. George in Queen's-Square ..	175	St. Katherine near the Tower ..	70	St. Mary at Newington	579
Christ Church in Surry	338	St. Giles in the Fields	722	St. Leonard in Shoreditch	372	St. Mary at Rotherhithe	308
Christ Church in Middlesex ..	426	St. James at Clerkenwell	447	St. Luke in Middlesex	514	St. Mary at Whitechapel	586
St. Dunstan at Stepney	324	St. John at Clerkenwell	173	St. Mary at Islington	351	St. Matthew at Bethnal Green	318
St. George in Bloomsbury	210	St. John at Hackney	362	St. Mary at Lambeth	1111	St. Paul at Shadwell	242
St. George in Middlesex Wapp.	513	St. John at Wapping	95	St. Mary Magd. Bermondsey ..	582		

Christened in the 23 Out-Parishes in Middlesex and Surry 12331 —— Buried 9074

St. Anne in Westminster	1040	St. James in Westminster	1075	St. Martin in the Fields	557	The Precinct of the Savoy	19
St. Clement Danes	350	St. John Evangelist in Westm.	526	St. Mary le Strand	81	St. Paul in Covent Garden ..	175
St. George by Hanover-square	472	St. Margaret in Westminster ..	652				

Christened in the 10 Parishes in the City and Liberties of Westminster 4944 —— Buried 4947

THE DISEASES AND CASUALTIES THIS YEAR.

DISEASES.						CASUALTIES.	
Abscess	107	Erysipelas, or St. Anthony's Fire	17	Rheumatism	8	Broken Limbs	1
Apoplexy	206	Fever	1104	Rupture	44	Burnt	18
Asthma	533	Fever, (Typhus)	17	Scrophula	7	Drowned	113
Bedridden	1	Fistula	6	Small Pox	604	Excessive Drinking	4
Cancer	82	Flux	6	Sore Throat or Quinsey	5	Executed *	8
Childbed	191	Gout	41	Spasm	55	Found Dead	6
Consumption	3608	Hæmorrhage	31	Stilborn	667	Fractured	2
Convulsions	2929	Hooping Cough	757	Stone	16	Killed by Falls and several other Accidents	84
Croup	100	Inflammation	1368	Stoppage in the Stomach	16	Murdered	4
Diabetes	3	Inflammation of the Liver	61	Suddenly	220	Overlaid	1
Dropsy	851	Insanity	218	Teething	472	Poisoned	3
Dropsy in the Brain	324	Jaundice	111	Thrush	102	Scalded	7
Dropsy in the Chest	86	Measles	712	Venereal	7	Suicide	33
Dysentery	4	Mortification	159	Worms	3	Strangled	1
Epilepsy	2	Old Age, and Debility	2601	Total of Diseases	18577	Suffocated	3
Eruptive Diseases	6	Palsy	169			Total of Casualties	288

Christened { Males - - 11968 / Females - 11405 } In all 23373 | Buried { Males - - 9483 / Females - 9382 } In all 18865

Whereof have died,

Under Two Years of Age	4605	Twenty and Thirty	1348	Sixty and Seventy	1562	A Hundred	1
Between Two and Five ..	2033	Thirty and Forty	1905	Seventy and Eighty	1224	A Hundred and One	1
Five and Ten	932	Forty and Fifty	1995	Eighty and Ninety	680	A Hundred and Two	
Ten and Twenty	649	Fifty and Sixty	1826	Ninety and a Hundred ..	104	A Hundred and Eight ..	

Increased in the Burials this Year 414.

* There have been Executed in London and the County of Surry, 24; of which Number 8 only ha[ve b]een reported to be buried within the Bills of Mortality.

8

collect sufficient water. At river stairs, coal-heavers, porters and Thames-side industrial workers such as glassworkers were to be seen 'washing their Dirty Carcasses'.

WATER, DIET AND DISEASE

It is difficult to judge how pure the water supplied by private water companies was at this period, and whether there was a risk to health. The quality deteriorated once water closets began to be installed in the early nineteenth century. This resulted in a greater discharge of effluent into the Thames and unfortunately many of the water companies drew their water from this same source. Unboiled water tended not to be drunk. Matt Bramble referred to human excrement as being the least offensive content of 'Thames water'; rather it was 'the drugs, minerals, and poisons, used in mechanics and manufacture, enriched with the putrefying carcasses of beasts and men; and mixed with the scourings of all the wash-tubs, kennels, and common sewers, within the bills of mortality' that made it so dangerous and unpleasant.

Some water-borne diseases such as cholera do not cause any skeletal change. However, the effects of a polluted water supply may be a contributing factor in the presence of cribra orbitalia (a condition of the eye-sockets). This condition possibly reflects an iron deficiency, which may in turn be the result of chronic diarrhoea. It can be present in any age group, but tends to be more frequently found in children. At Christ Church just over a third of those whose skull survived suffered from cribra orbitalia, compared with about one in six in a seventeenth-century group of London skulls recovered from Moorfields early in this century. One possible explanation for this high rate is the increased exposure to infection as the urban environment deteriorated. In the sample from St Bride's Lower Churchyard, 14 cases were detected, a much lower rate than at Christ Church. It has been suggested that the wealthier classes took to cooking in brass– and tin–lined copper pots, and so no longer took up iron from their cooking utensils, or perhaps some were hand-feeding their infants,

8 Bills of Mortality for 1821–2 listing the causes of death. Note the high child mortality and the longevity of some Londoners.

which may have been hygienically or nutritionally prejudicial to health. In either case, a proportion of pale, sickly looking children would have been apparent in the population.

Another disease, which in its more advanced stages could have affected the appearance of a person, and which has an environmental component, is tuberculosis. This disease thrives in conditions of overcrowding, squalor and poverty. Four cases were reported at St Bride's Lower Churchyard, three of them affecting the spine. It has been claimed that brucellosis was more common in the seventeenth century and tuberculosis in the eighteenth and nineteenth centuries, though we know that untreated cow's milk, a principal source of brucellosis, was drunk in the eighteenth century.

Beer or 'small beer' was the standard everyday drink – it was even given to children: 'beer, nothing but beer, is drunk'. It was claimed that more grain was consumed in England for making beer than for making bread. Londoners were great drinkers of non-alcoholic beverages also, chocolate, tea and coffee being very popular. Despite this, drunkenness was common and intoxicated men and women were often to be seen stumbling along the street (see Figure 9). The presence of drunk people on the streets may be borne out by the pattern of fractures suffered by the people in the St Bride's Lower Churchyard, of whom just under 10 per cent had at least one fracture. Almost half of these were rib fractures, commonly caused by stumbling or brawling. There were many drinking clubs which met once if not twice a week. Clergymen drank and smoked in public places, and a foreign visitor described them as 'stout and ruddy', their general appearance suggesting that they led 'a pleasant and not fatiguing life'. Liquors were viewed as 'a sort of poison', and César de Saussure, a Swiss visitor to London, noted that they were believed to be a necessary evil because of the 'thickness and dampness of the atmosphere'. Gin-drinking was considered to be one of the main causes of theft and robbery in London. Henry Fielding complained that when the 'wretches' were brought to trial, they had to be confined until they became sober. He wrote of 'the dreadful effects' of those 'who swallow pints of this poison' and his misfortune in having 'to see, and to smell' them every day.

Londoners consumed large quantities of meat, especially beef and mutton. It would, however, be incorrect to say that all citizens over-indulged in food and drink. The poor would not have been able to afford meat on a regular basis, though gin and beer were relatively cheap. Many of the painted and engraved portraits of prosperous Londoners show them to have been corpulent if not overweight (see Figure 2).

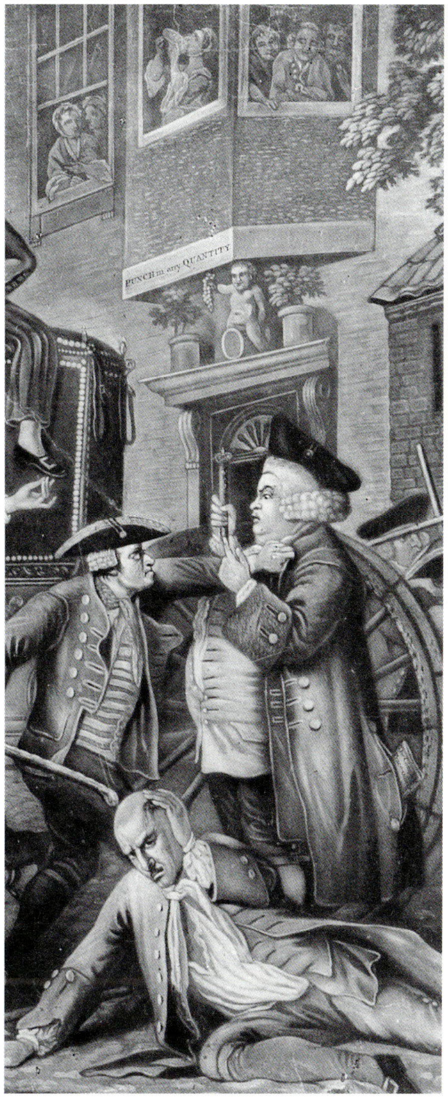

9

9 **A sailor is attacking a constable, and another constable has been knocked down with a blow to the head, 1768. (Detail from *A Rescue* or the *Tars Triumphant*, a print after the painting by John Collett).**

MALE AND FEMALE, YOUNG AND OLD

There were differences in the composition of the population as derived from the St Bride's Lower Churchyard and Christ Church Spitalfields samples. In the latter, the analysis suggested that there were almost equal numbers of men and women in the population. In the former, it was found that there was a greater proportion of adult men at a ratio of 1.6 males to every female. This may have been a local phenomenon; a reflection of the contribution of the Fleet Prison and the nearby workhouse to the population of the St Bride's Lower Churchyard. Such burials were not identified explicitly in the parish records, but a number of poor burials paid for by the parish were recorded.

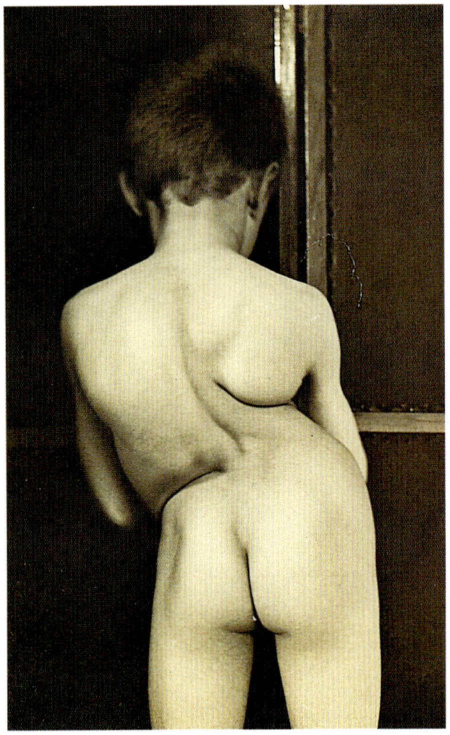

10

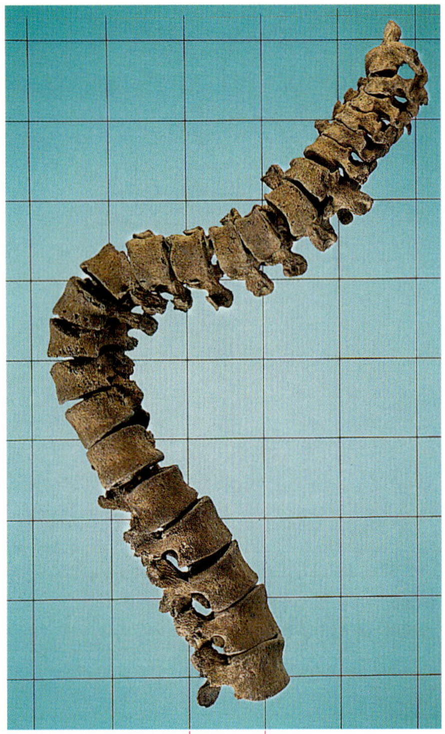

11

5CM

Of the juveniles present in the St Bride's Lower Churchyard sample, nearly three-quarters were less than five years of age, and half were less than one year old. Predicted age structures based on normal populations suggest that a greater proportion of the juvenile deaths should have been in the less-than-one-year group. This apparent deficit may be the result of the smallest infant burials being often packed at the top of stacks of coffins in the Churchyard, almost as though they were being used to fill up spaces. These may have been the first to be damaged in the intervening period between burial and excavation. The discrepancy could also imply that the stresses placed on children's health continued even after the crucial first year. Despite the high infant mortality in the St Bride's sample, one in five reached maturity. Perhaps this supports the theory that if a person survived childhood then they had a good chance of living a long life (see Figure 8).

10 Young man suffering from curvature of the spine, c.1893.

11 Spinal column showing the curvature of the spine resulting from collapse of the vertebral body due to weakening by osteoporosis.

Ten cases of diffuse idiopathic skeletal hyperostosis (DISH) were recorded in the St Bride's sample. The skeletal changes resulting from the condition (principally fusion of the spine) would usually not be apparent in life. A possible causal factor is obesity, which, if confirmed, would suggest that even among this relatively poor community there were some overweight individuals. The condition is also age-related, in that it tends to affect older men, further evidence for the contention that the elderly formed a significant proportion of the population. Other conditions present at St Bride's Lower Churchyard which are indicative of a sizeable older age group include Paget's Disease and osteoporosis. Paget's Disease commonly affects those over 50 years of age, and men more than women. Only a few cases would present any symptoms, usually pain, though it may induce bowing of the legs and an increased susceptibility to fractures. Eleven people were affected. Eight people suffered from osteoporosis, seven of them women. Osteoporosis involves a loss of bone substance with increasing age, and is most common in post-menopausal women. The bone condition itself would not be visible, but some of effects certainly would: here six of the seven women had a noticeable curvature of the spine owing to the collapse or fracture of weakened vertebrae. Over 50 per cent of adults in the St Bride's Lower Churchyard sample were affected by osteoarthritis, and the pattern was similar at Spitalfields. Men and women were almost equally affected, and though, in most cases, the presence of the condition would not have been evident, in a few cases pain, degeneration and possible lack of mobility may have made the sufferer move somewhat stiffly and awkwardly.

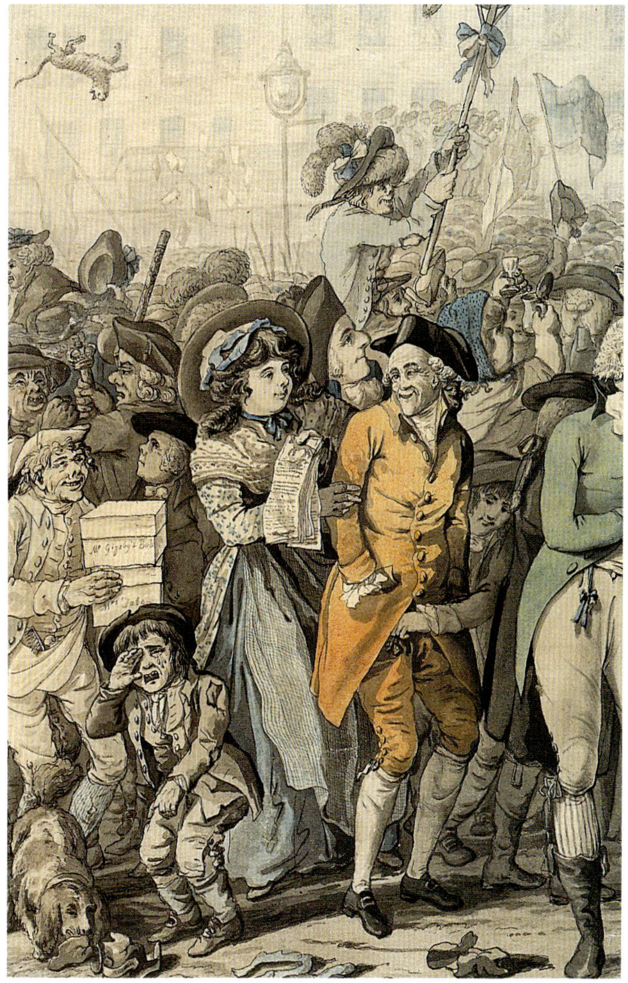

12

APPEARANCE

In the eighteenth century it was noted that most men were not too concerned about their clothes, except that they should be clean and made of good quality cloth and linen. A visitor, Carl Philip Moritz, walking from Charing Cross to the Royal Exchange, observed how 'persons from the highest to the lowest ranks' were 'almost all well-looking people, and cleanly and neatly dressed'. Dress was quite plain and this style extended to all classes of society with the exception of the very wealthy. Another foreign visitor observed in 1722 that 'the dress of the English is like the French but not so gaudy; they generally go plain but in the best cloths and stuffs and wear the best linen of any Nation in the World'. The search for practical, comfortable clothes resulted in gentlemen adopting the types of

12 **The London populace at its most boisterous, with a dead cat being thrown in the air (detail from *Westminster Election of 1788* by Robert Dighton).**

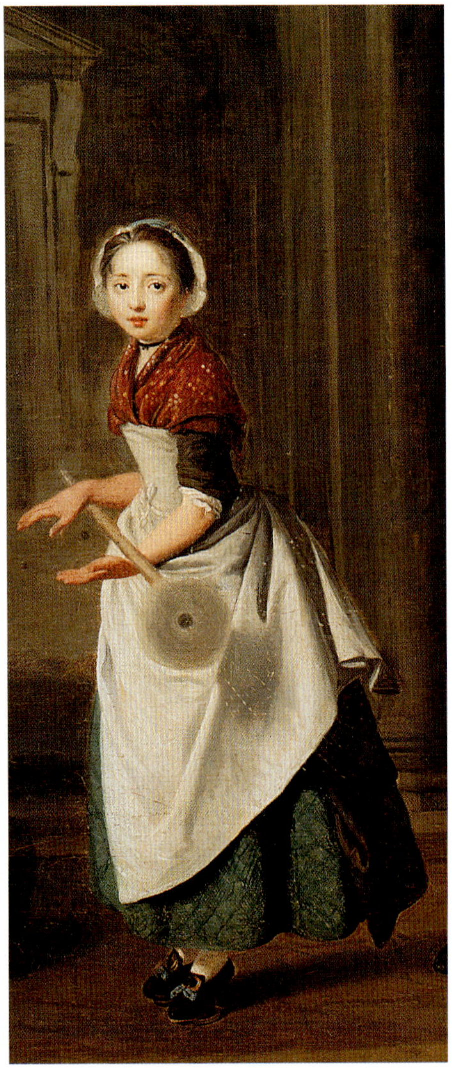

13

clothes worn by working men such as the frock (coat). This made it difficult to identify a person's status or profession, for according to Mayhew there was 'little to distinguish him from the crowd of well-dressed and well-mannered persons'.

Any form of extra decoration, such as gold or silver lace on a coat or a hat with a plume, was considered ostentatious and derisory. Individuals wearing such costume, usually described as 'French', were sometimes abused verbally in the street and ran the risk of having mud thrown at them. They were wise to travel by coach or sedan chair if they wished to avoid such hazards. Londoners in a crowd were felt to be loud, crude and unruly, often portraying signs of drunkenness and debauchery (see Figure 12).

Women were generally more flamboyant in their dress than men but still less showy than their continental counterparts. Fashions of dress changed regularly during the eighteenth and nineteenth centuries. Oliver Goldsmith produced an amusing set of letters purportedly written by a Chinese philosopher residing in London to his friend in the East. He observed with puzzlement the changing fashion styles:

> Today they are lifted upon stilts, tomorrow they lower their heels and raise their heads; their cloaths at one time are bloated out with whalebone; at present they have laid their hoops aside and are become as slim as mermaids.

César de Saussure noted the pride and care that women took in their 'slim, pretty figures,' and how in the morning they put on 'a sort of bodice' which encircled 'their waist tightly'. In the streets and parks they walked at a brisk pace 'more in order to show their clothes than for the pleasure of exercise.' Englishwomen were noted for their good figures. This was often attributed to their enjoyment of exercise such as riding and walking. Oliver Goldsmith's Chinese sage also expressed surprise at the attention he received from the opposite sex in the streets, no doubt prostitutes, meeting with 'more invitations . . . in one night' than 'at Pekin in twelve revolutions of the moon'. Many commentators described the well-dressed servant girls who wore silks on Sundays and were often mistaken for their mistresses (Figure 13). By the nineteenth century, formal and standardised uniforms were introduced for female servants. Employers sometimes stipulated the wearing of simple clothes when attending church on a Sunday, and even 'hood-shaped bonnets.' Towards the end of the century, with the decline of servants entering domestic service, they found it even more difficult to impose dress codes.

13 **A well-dressed servant girl spins her mop, c.1764. (Detail from *A City Shower* by Edward Penny)**

CORSETS AND CRINOLINES

The years between 1840 and 1900 saw the most dramatic changes in the fashionable female form. Tiny corseted waists and dome-shaped skirts worn over growing numbers of heavily starched and stiffened petticoats characterised the 1840s and 1850s. The introduction of the lightweight steel-cage crinoline in 1856 came as a welcome relief from the insufferable weight of the petticoats. Not only did it allow greater mobility and free movement of the legs, it also enabled skirt widths to increase to ever more monstrous dimensions, reaching their maximum in the early 1860s. However, kneeling, bending and sitting whilst wearing these garments was problematic, as was passing through doorways and boarding omnibuses. More embarrassingly, the buoyant crinolines were liable to lift in a strong gust of wind, or even turn inside out, revealing an immodest glimpse of the drawers worn beneath. The fashion permeated to the working classes, where domestic servants in crinolines collided with furniture, ornaments and fire grates as they went about their chores.

The width of the skirts to some extent offset the need for a tiny waist, but after 1863 the crinoline subsided, and the skirt drapery shifted to the back of the dress where it was supported by an arrangement of half hoops and later by a bustle, a false bottom consisting of horsehair pads. Some manufacturers turned their attention to producing healthy garments. One of the best known of these was Madame Roxy Caplin of Berners Street. Caplin prided herself on garments designed on the basis of a scientific examination of the body and its geometrical measurement, and her hygienic corset was awarded a medal at the Great Exhibition of 1851. Arguments raged for and against the corset, and whilst Caplin argued that corsets were 'beneficial to the weak, delicate and imperfect', and 'absolutely indispensable when properly constructed', others described the wearing of stays as 'the greatest folly of civilised life'. Even the medical profession could not agree on the harmful effect of the tightly laced corset. Some blamed all manner of diseases and disfigurements on them, while others argued that if ladies were to cease wearing corsets they would not only lose a vital means of bodily support but be guilty of utterly immoral behaviour. The wearers themselves seemed resigned to their discomfort, as

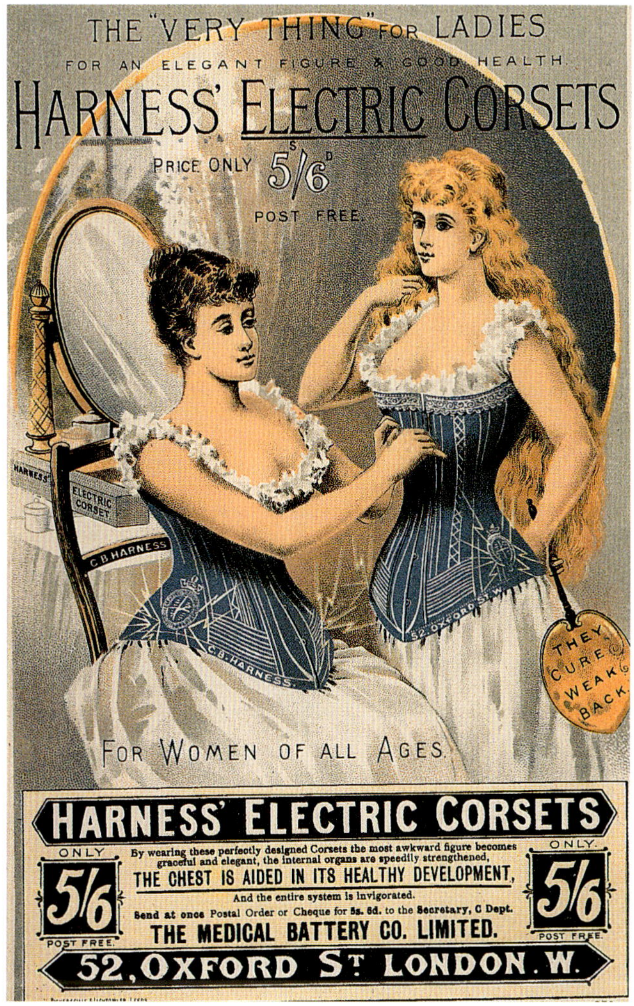

14

14 Corset advertisement, 1891. Patented in 1891, the battery-driven electric corset claimed not only to produce an elegant figure, but also to 'exercise a most beneficial influence upon respiratory and other organs', and to remedy debilities such as rheumatism, neuralgia and indigestion.

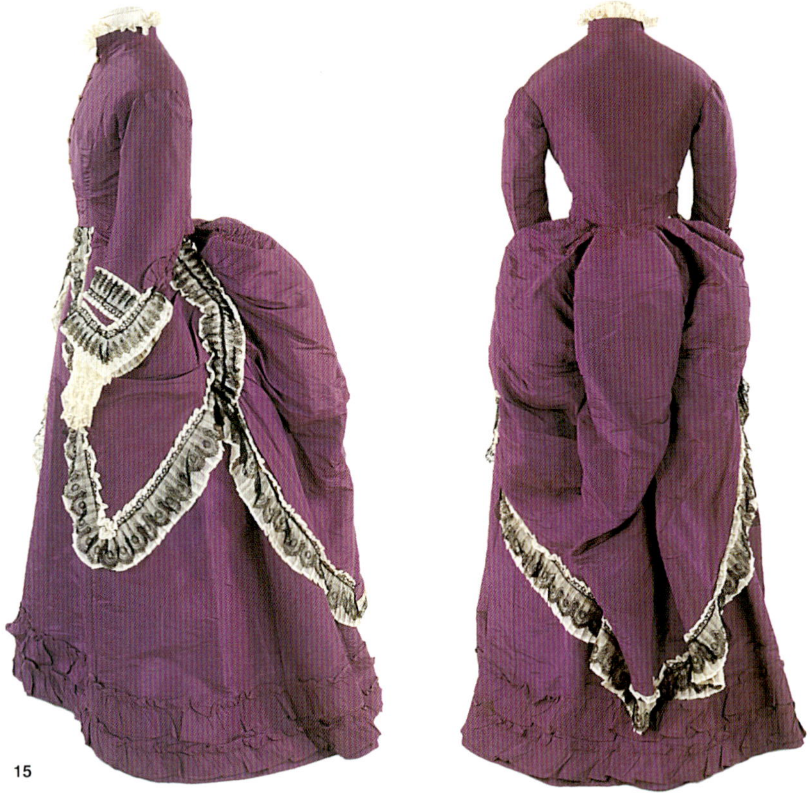

15

in the following account in *The Englishwoman's Domestic Magazine* in May 1867:

> I was placed at the age of fifteen at a fashionable school in London, and there it was the custom for the waists of the pupils to be reduced one inch per month until they were what the lady principal considered small enough. When I left school at seventeen, my waist measured only thirteen inches, it having been formerly twenty-three inches in circumference.

The writer apparently suffered no pain after the first few minutes when she was laced into her corset by a maid, and the only ill effects which she ascribes to the garment were occasional headaches and a loss of appetite. A fellow pupil, a well-built girl, left school with a fourteen-inch waist, and despite the need for two strong maids to lace her in, and her fainting twice on one occasion while they struggled to make the stays meet, suffered not one day of ill health.

Tightly laced ladies were prone to faint at the slightest provocation owing to the effects of the 'waist screw'. In one such incident, described in *The Habits of Good Society* (1859), a physician was called away from a family meal to attend a young lady who had fainted during a dinner party and whose companions were unable to revive her. When the physician arrived, he drew out his penknife, and exclaimed, 'Ha, this is tight lacing!' adding, 'no time to be lost'. 'He cut open the boddice of the dress; it opened, and, with a gush, gave the poor young lady breath; the heart had been compressed by tight lacing, and had nearly ceased to act.'

The account continued its denigration of tight lacing: 'the liver, lungs, the powers of the stomach, have been brought into a diseased state by this most pernicious habit. Loss of bloom, fixed redness in the nose, eruptions on the skin, are among its sad effects.' The author claimed that 'seven women in ten were crooked', and 'whole families leaned on one side or the other'. To date, no example from the skeletal record has been discovered

15 **Fashionable day dress, c.1875. This gown was produced under the name of Madame Elise, dressmaker, of Regent Street who came to public notice in 1863 when one of her seamstresses died as a direct result of dire working conditions.**

where the actual rib cage of an individual has been deformed by corsetry. It is possible that cases may have been overlooked because, as a rule, the rib cage is not reconstructed and measured for inclusions in the indices which are commonly used to describe body shape.

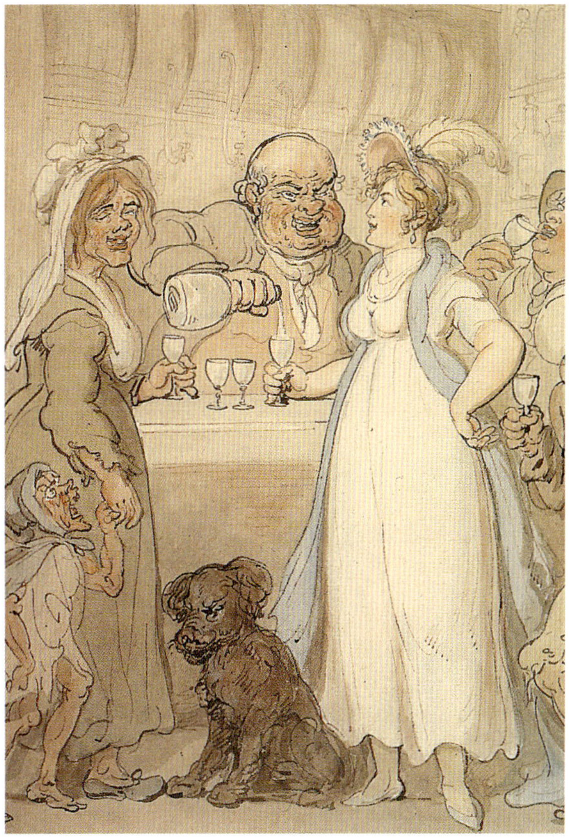

16

FACIAL COMPLEXION

Most women were noted to have 'white complexions', though whether because of keeping out of the sun, applying make-up or because of diet and lifestyle is unclear. Country girls clearly differed from their London counterparts with their complexions being likened to 'lilies and roses'. Cosmetics made use of by London women included: 'rouge' or red paint to add colour to an impaired complexion, white lead paint to make the skin paler, especially in the neck area, pomatum for the dressing of hair, and pastes for the hands. Perfumes were used liberally and included 'hungary water,' 'jessamy' and the perfumed powder 'pulvil'. And this was not just confined to women. Men made use of similar scents to sweeten their clothes and disguise their body odour.

Women powdered and curled their hair, plucked their eyebrows and even applied lengths of mouse-skin:

> . . . her eyebrows from a mouse's hide,
> Stuck on with art on either side . . .
> (Jonathan Swift, 'The Lady's Dressing Room', 1730).

They applied patches made of silk to their faces, often to cover up the ravages of smallpox. Smallpox was one of the main killer-diseases in the eighteenth century but does not show up in the skeletal record. It has been estimated that it accounted for ten per cent of all deaths in London at that period. Many of those who survived the disease were left pockmarked for life. This visible facial scarring was so common in towns and cities that it was rarely remarked upon. In Cleland's *Memoirs of a Woman of Pleasure* the heroine loses both her parents to the disease, as well as succumbing to it herself 'in a village near Liverpool'. Luckily, she had only a mild attack and recovered 'entirely unmark'd'. Later in the book, the face of one of her clients in London was 'mark'd with the small-pox, but no

16 **A young attractive woman is introduced to the 'pleasures' of gin drinking, c.1810 by Thomas Rowlandson.**

more that what added a grace of more manliness to features rather turned to softness and delicacy'.

HAIR AND WIGS

Simple headdresses were made of cambric or lace. Fashion styles changed frequently, particularly in relation to hair. In the 1770s, hair decoration became very elaborate and was extended to a great height. Satirical prints focus on the impracticality of these structures, described in *The Gentlemen's Magazine* as 'Babel-towers of hair as high as if they meant to reach the sky'. George Stevens remarked that 'wigs, as well as books, are furniture for the head & both wigs & books are sometimes equally voluminous' (Figure 17).

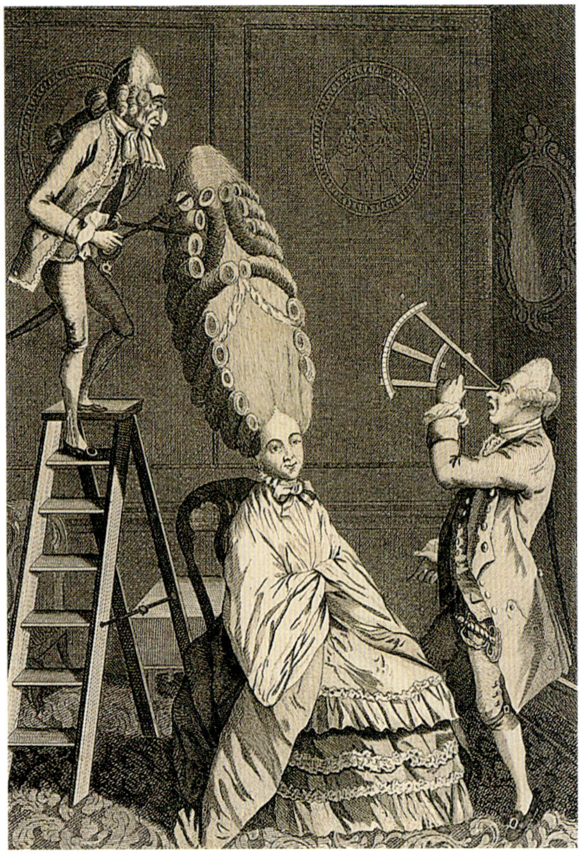

17

In eighteenth-century London most men had their heads shaved and wore wigs. This fashion was supposed to have originated in France in the 1630s when Louis XIII went prematurely bald. However, there were good hygienic reasons as well; lice could be kept under control more easily and wigs could be cleaned. In prints of the period men's bald pates seem unnatural, and putting on a wig in the morning and taking it off at night would have been as natural as brushing the hair today. There were many names for the different types of wigs which came in all shapes and sizes. Hogarth's print *The Five Orders of Perriwigs* illustrates those worn at the coronation of George III. Wigs were made of human or animal hair, sometimes of mohair and silk, of feathers, and even sometimes of iron or copper wire. They were often supplemented by pigtails or 'queues', ribbons and bows. They could be 'full-bottomed', which were the most elaborate and costly, their appearance being of 'a mass of curls', as described by the Cunningtons, 'framing the face, then falling around and below the shoulders', rising 'high above the forehead, generally in two horns, one on each side of a centre parting'. Artisans and tradesmen wore simpler forms of wigs such as the 'cut wig' or the 'bob wig'. A glance at the style and quality of a wig could reveal much about the social status of the owner, but by the 1790s wigs were going out of fashion, and hair had begun to be worn naturally. Faces were on the whole clean-shaven; in paintings and engravings of the period it is very rare to find a bearded figure. In the course of the nineteenth century the focus shifted to the length of the whiskers and beards, the curls of the moustaches and the position of the hair-parting.

17 A seated lady has her hair curled and dressed to a towering height, c.1770.

LIFTING THE CURTAIN: THE NINETEENTH CENTURY

The squalid and unhealthy living conditions of the London poor are better documented in the nineteenth century than in the eighteenth. Dorothy George, in her seminal work, *London Life in the Eighteenth Century*, notes Francis Place's comments of 1824 on the considerable improvement in the physical condition of poor children: 'there are no such groups of half-starved miserable, scald-headed children with rickety limbs and bandy legs as there were in the days of my youth' (the term 'scald-headed' suggesting congenital syphilis (Figure 19)). Doctors of the period witnessed a similar improvement due to the 'greater cleanliness and less crowded state of the inhabitants'. But, as George noted, 'everything is relative'. London life continued to be hazardous to health, especially to the young and the old. Severe poverty and overcrowding were to be found in many parts of the metropolis throughout the nineteenth century. Such a visible disease as rickets, particularly associated with the industrial revolution and urban life, was to remain prevalent in London well into the twentieth century.

The cholera outbreaks of 1832, 1849 and 1866 in the metropolis drew attention to London's slums. The writings of Dr John Simon in the 1850s 'lift the curtain' on the appalling living conditions:

> . . . such unclean confusion of bodies and bodily functions, such mutual exposure of animal and sexual nakedness, as is rather bestial than human. . . . To children who are born under its curse it must often be a very baptism into infamy.

It was felt that people became hardened to disease despite their terrible surroundings and unbearable lifestyle. He witnessed how 'birth and death went side by side; where the mother in travail, or the child with small-pox, or the corpse waiting internment has no separation from the rest'. In 1849, on a visit to Jacob's Island in Bermondsey, Mayhew described the air as 'stagnant and putrid', and the inhabitants as having 'blanched cheeks . . . white as vegetables grown in the dark'. They drank from a stream into which ran the sewage from their houses. Something of the unfolding tragedy is revealed in the story told of a man that they met who had caught scarlet fever and recovered only to be struck down with typhus. Miraculously, he recovered but was again laid low by the disease. His child had died from cholera and his wife was in the workhouse suffering from the same condition. Many healthy and industrious families were reduced to a state of such abject poverty through illness.

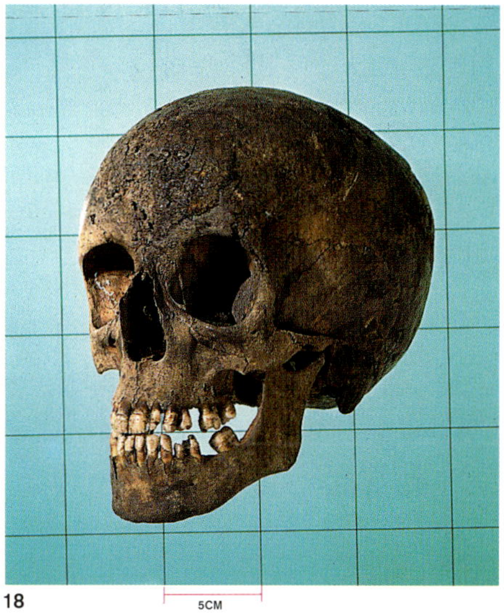

18

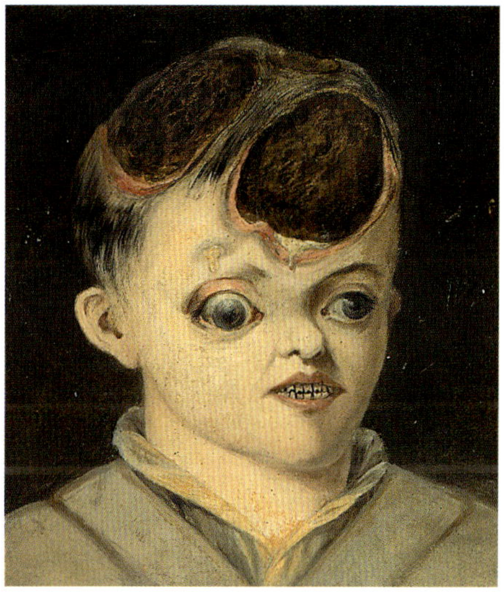

19

18 Female syphilitic skull with multiple erosive lesions (from Red Cross Way, Southwark).

19 An undergrown girl, aged 16 years, showing effects of congenital syphilis, c.1885.

FASHION VICTIMS

CORSETS AND CRINOLINES

In the eighteenth and nineteenth centuries, a variety of body-forming devices were employed to achieve the desired shape, including buoyant crinolines, rear-enhancing bustles and wasp-waist corsets. At times the tyranny of fashion reached such extremes that the outward appearance produced by the artificial boning, frames and pads bore no relation to the flesh and bones of the natural body enclosed within.

Men and women endured pain, discomfort and inconvenience to maintain an up-to-date body shape. Even George IV regularly pulled his portly figure into shape with a body-belt or corset. A surviving pattern of one made for him in 1824 survives in the Museum of London's collection, revealing a 50-inch waist. Sometimes, the corset was used in conjunction with other items to create the latest body outline such as 'the Grecian Bend', a popular style of the 1870s. The combined effect of high-heeled shoes or boots, a tiny waist and rear protrusion of bunched-up fabric, was to tilt the upper part of the body forward in a hen-like posture, which caught the attention of the medical profession.

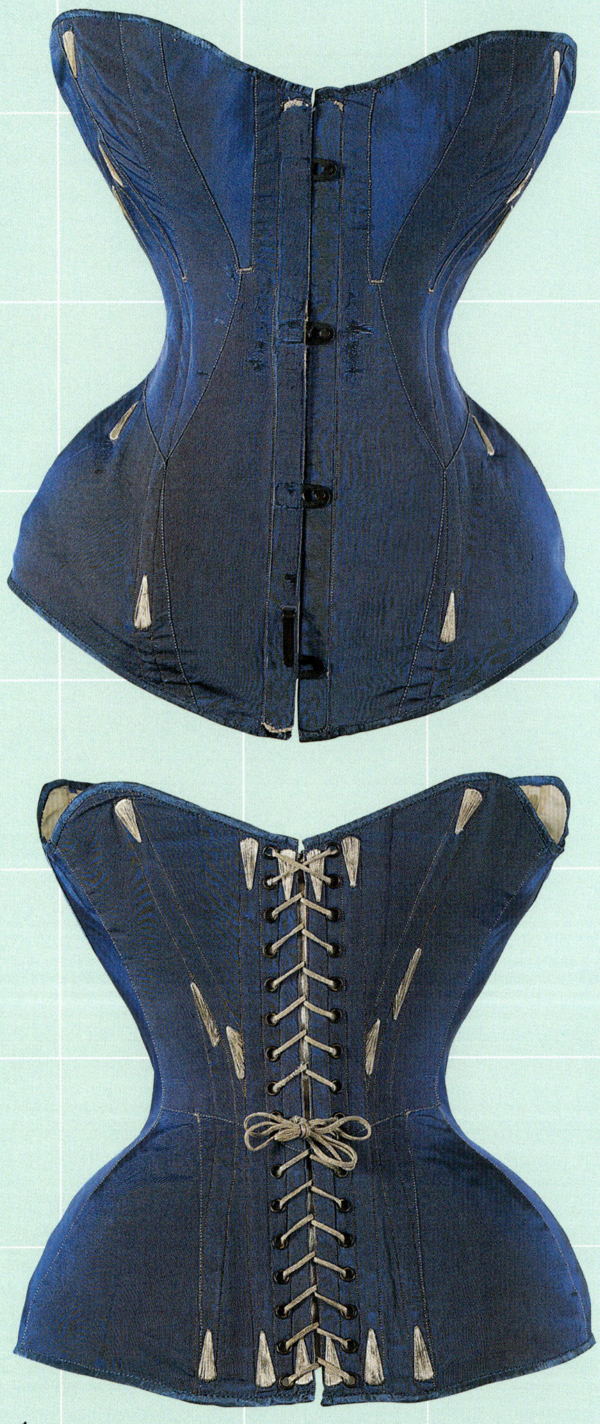

1

1 **Corset, *c.*1851.** This corset was sympathetically designed by Madame Roxy Caplin with minimal, flexible boning to achieve fashionable curves without 'confining the female figure in a cruelly narrow prison of whalebone and steel'. However, it could still produce a waist circumference of 19 inches.

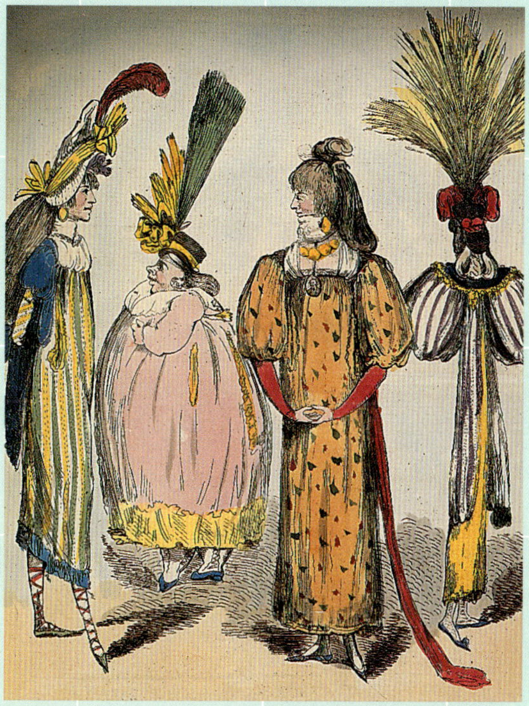

2 Gauzy, formless gowns became popular in the late 18th century, so that the natural curves of the body were almost lost among swathes of diaphanous fabrics.

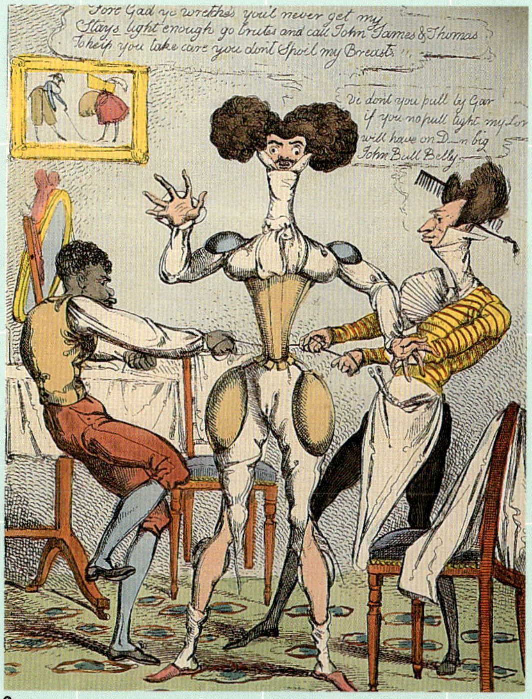

3 ***Lacing a Dandy*, 1819.** Men were not immune to the lure of fashion, and fashion-conscious dandies squeezed themselves into corsets in order to maintain a modishly trim figure.

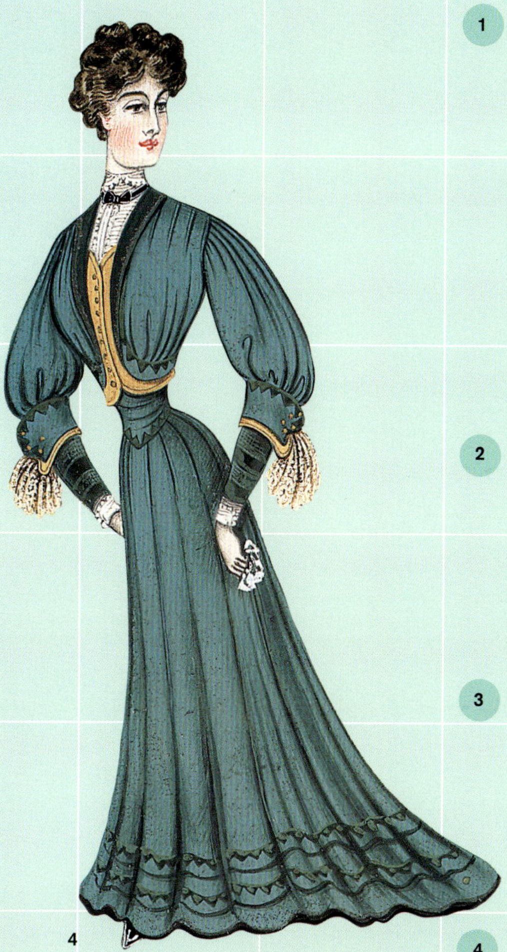

4 **Lewis and Allenby fashion design, *c.*1900.** The tiny waist and swan-like curves were achieved by the wearing of a long-line, flat fronted corset which threw the bust forward and forced the hips backwards.

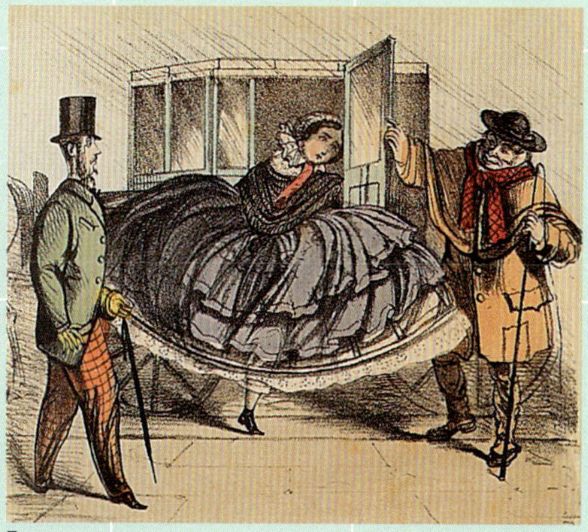

5 ***Crinoline - its difficulties and dangers*, *c.*1860.** Crinolines reached such monstrous dimensions in the early 1860s that normal progress through doorways and into cabs and omnibuses was seriously impeded.

EUGENICS

READING THE FACE AND BODY

By the late nineteenth century there was widespread concern about the social and physical degeneration of the British people, and reports on London's poor by social commentators such as Henry Mayhew and Charles Booth fuelled these fears. It was widely believed that both mental and physical characteristics were inherited between generations. Francis Galton, cousin of Charles Darwin, was fascinated by the idea that, as in phrenology, mental qualities could be 'read off' the body. He pioneered the science of eugenics, believing that a physical study of the population would reveal its mental condition.

Galton believed that the quality of the nation's population could be improved by reducing the 'undesirables' whilst allowing those of high 'civic worth' to multiply. Galton divided the population into classes according to their value to society and compared these with figures produced by Charles Booth in his study of the population of London in the 1880s and 1890s. Booth's lowest classes, consisting of 'criminals, loafers and casual earners', corresponded to Galton's lowest classes of 'undesirables', whose procreation was to be discouraged.

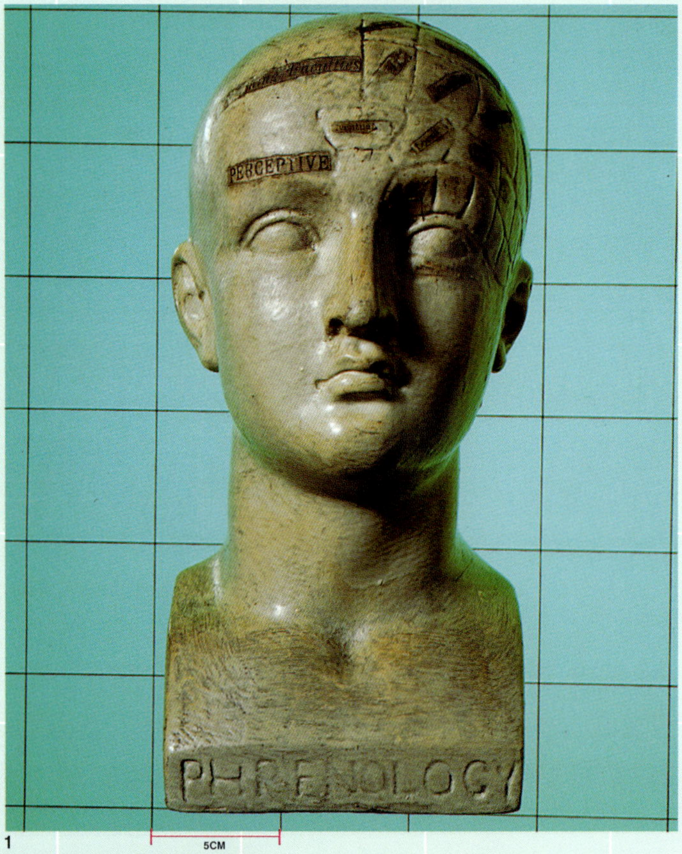

1

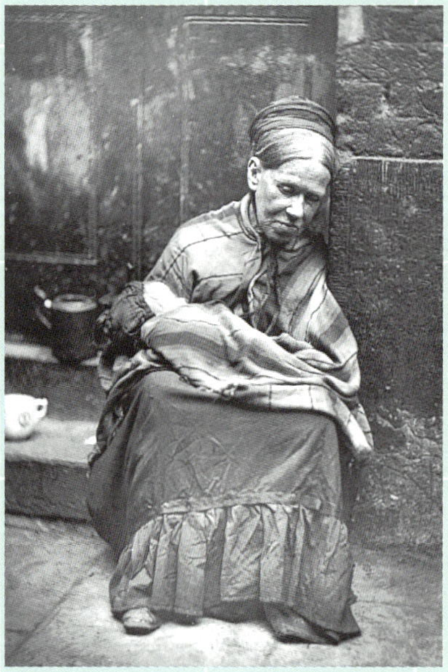

2

1 Phrenological head, 19th century.

2 *The "crawlers"*, photograph by John Thomson, 1877. In 1903 Jack London noted the 'ghettoising' of the London poor in the East End: 'a short and stunted people is created, . . . a pavement folk . . . lacking stamina and strength . . . [the] women and children are pale and anaemic, with eyes ringed darkly, who stoop and slouch, and are nearly twisted out of all shapeliness and beauty'.

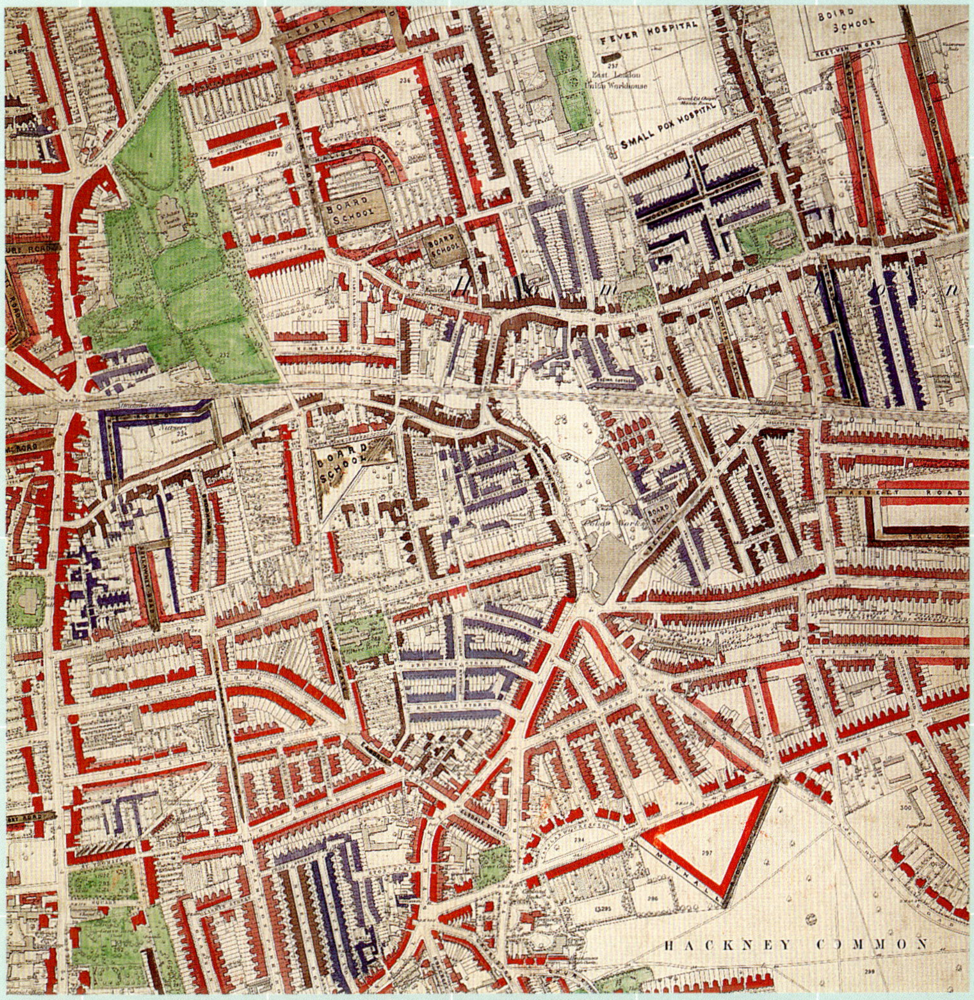

3

3 Charles Booth's ***Map of Poverty***, Hackney area, 1889. Charles Booth produced a map of the London poor, on which he located social types by colour coding the streets. The very poor and 'semi-criminal' class are indicated in dark blue and black respectively.

4 Francis Galton's photographs of criminals from the Millbank Penitentiary, 1877. Galton believed that criminal mentality revealed itself in the faces of criminals (4a). He developed the technique of composite photography (4b) to eliminate individual peculiarities to produce an 'average' face.

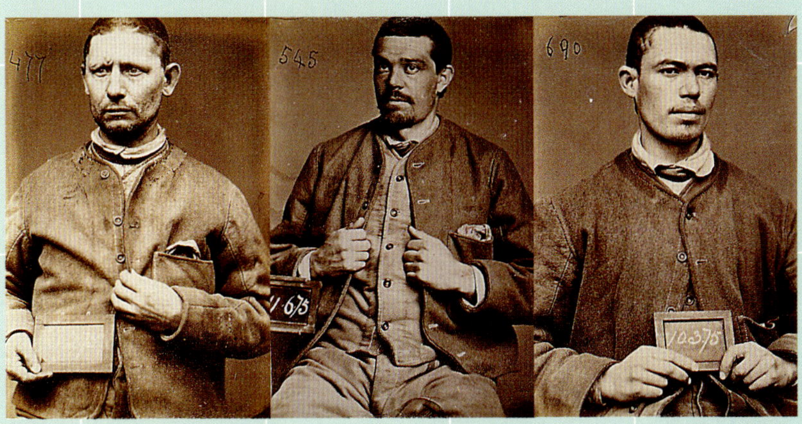

4a

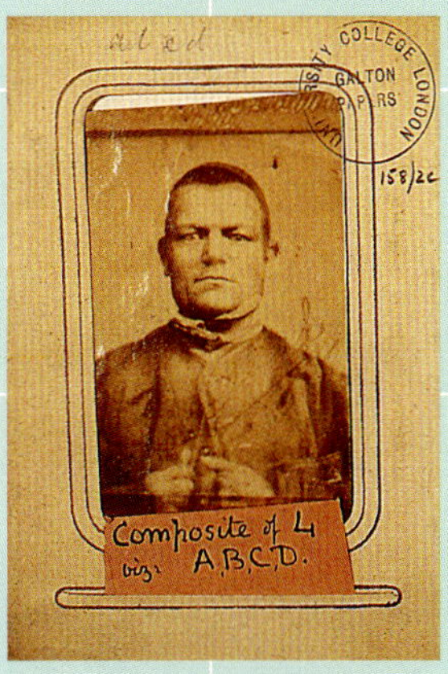

4b

LONDONERS NOW

by Torla Evans, John Chase and Richard Stroud

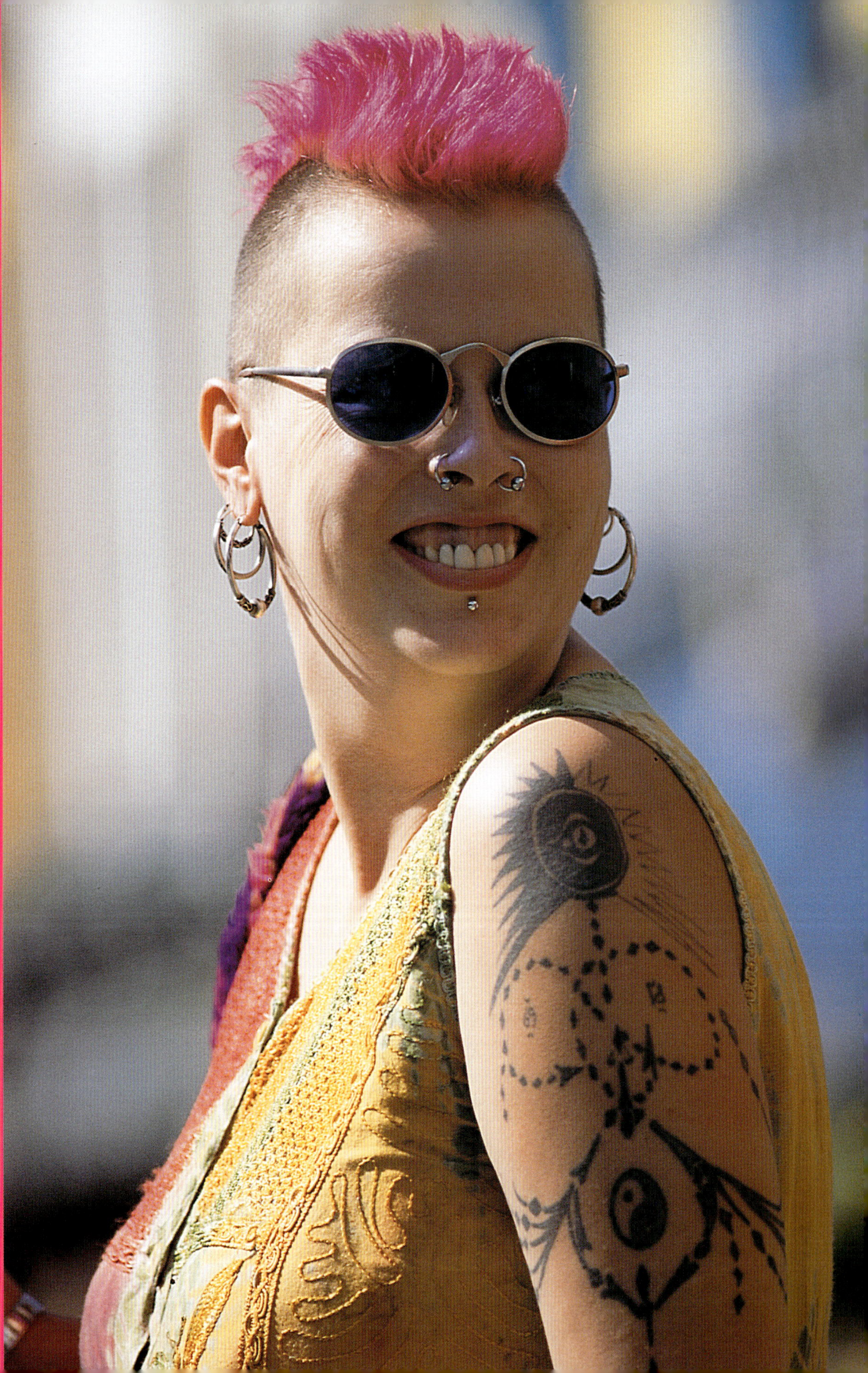

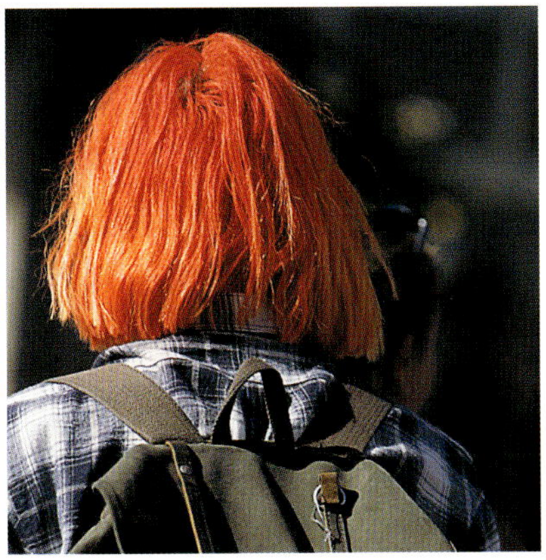
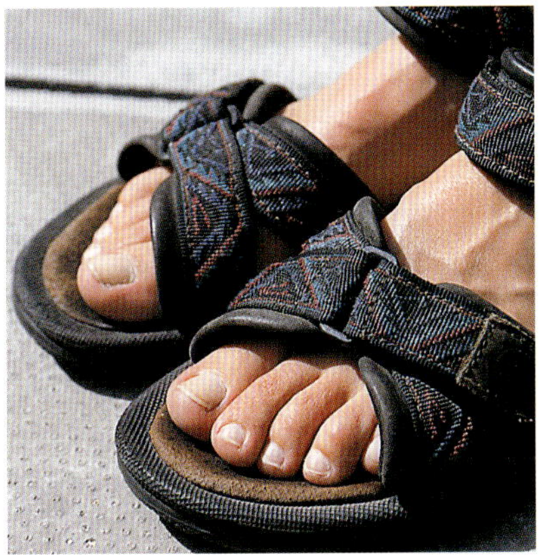
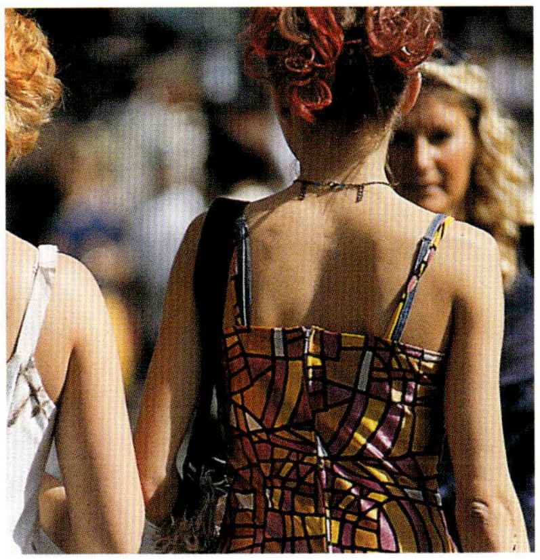
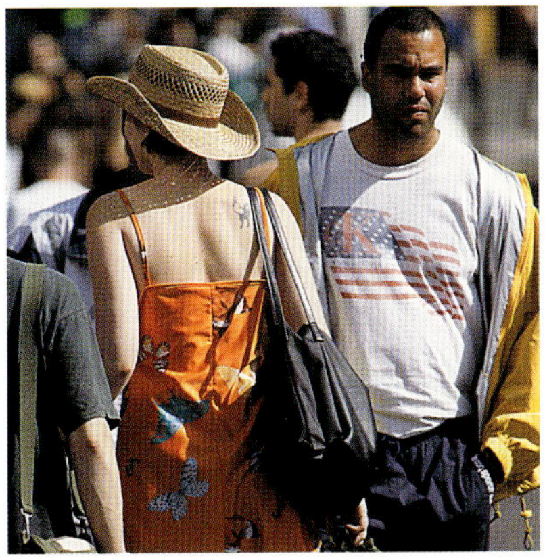
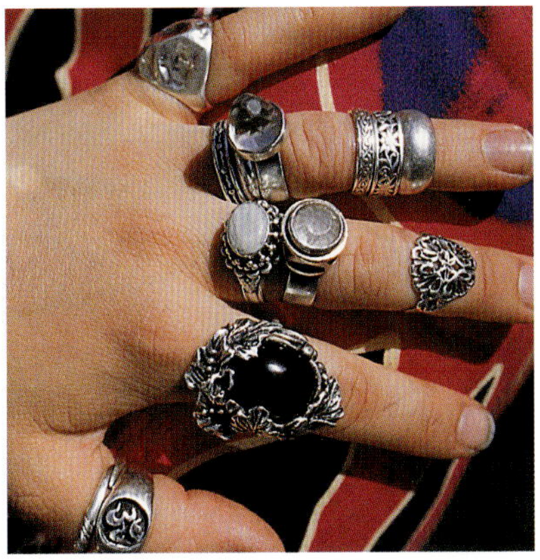
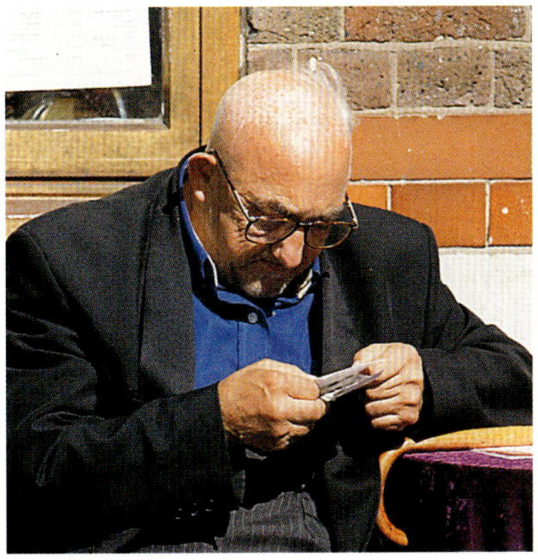
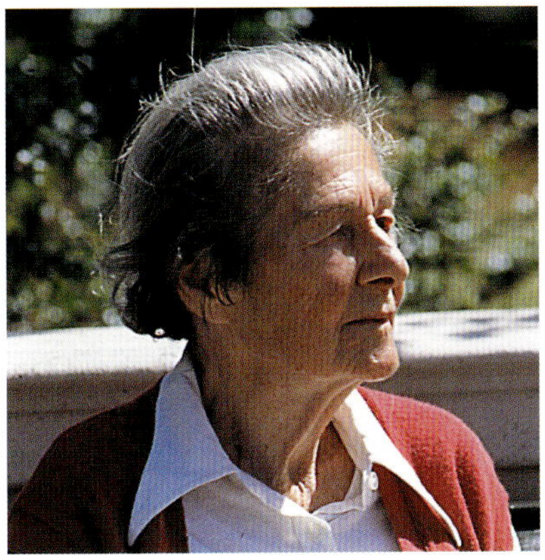
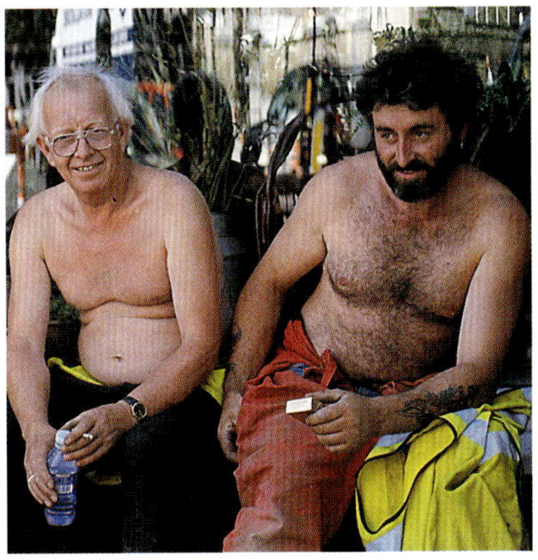
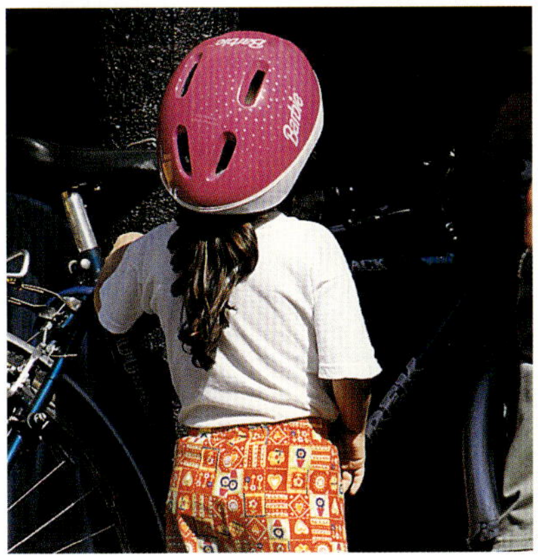
Barbie

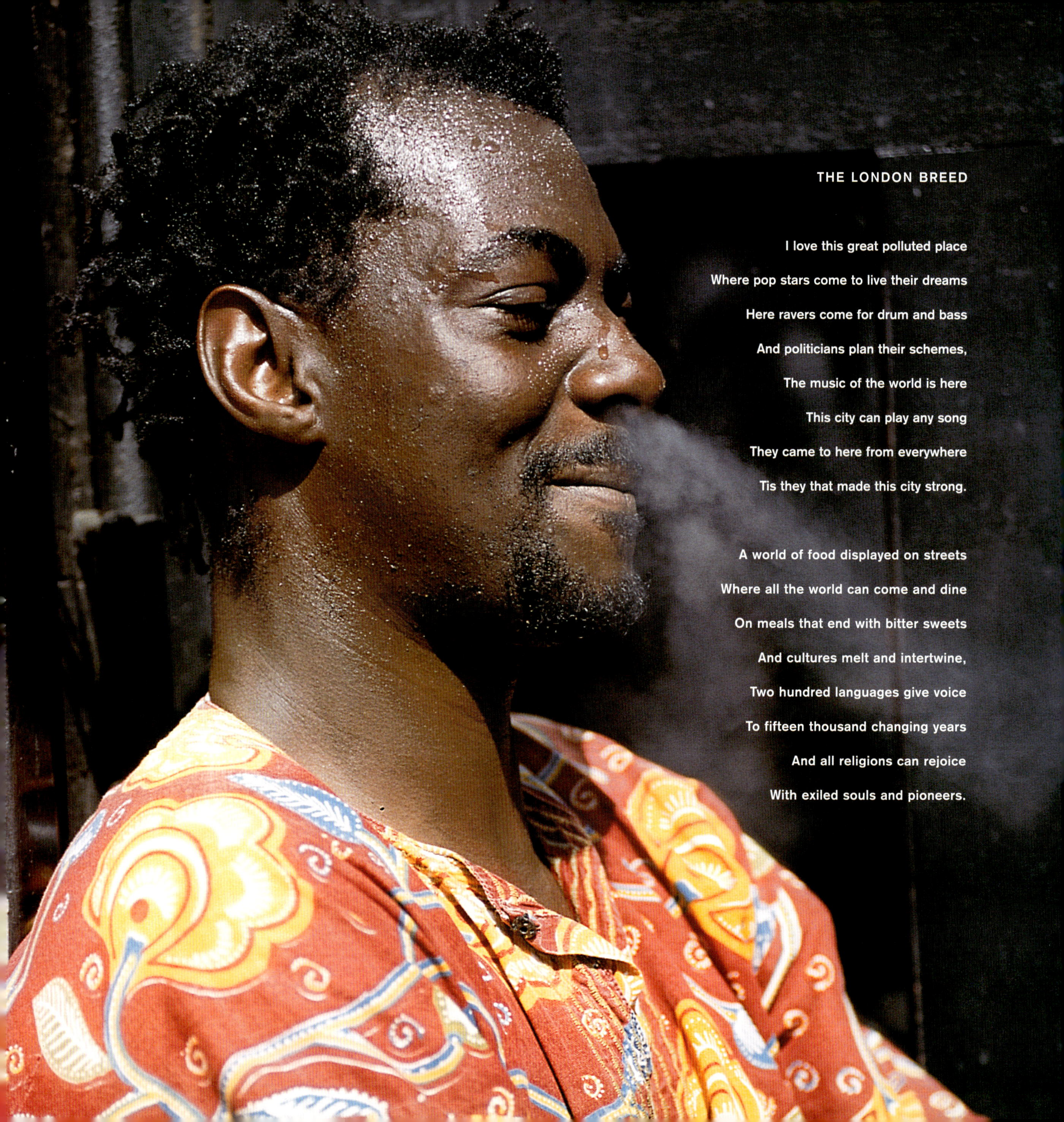

THE LONDON BREED

I love this great polluted place
Where pop stars come to live their dreams
Here ravers come for drum and bass
And politicians plan their schemes,
The music of the world is here
This city can play any song
They came to here from everywhere
Tis they that made this city strong.

A world of food displayed on streets
Where all the world can come and dine
On meals that end with bitter sweets
And cultures melt and intertwine,
Two hundred languages give voice
To fifteen thousand changing years
And all religions can rejoice
With exiled souls and pioneers.

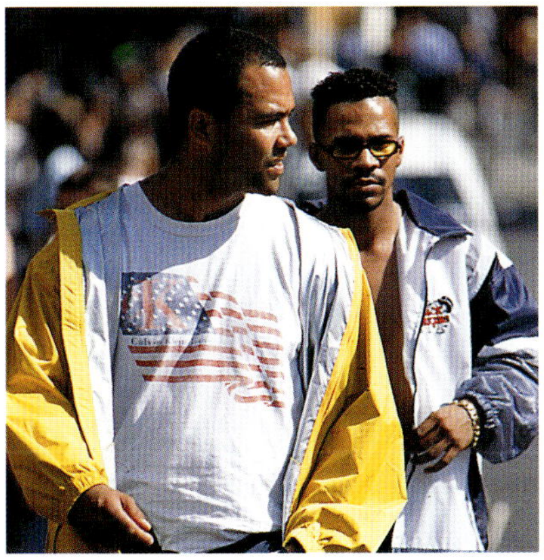

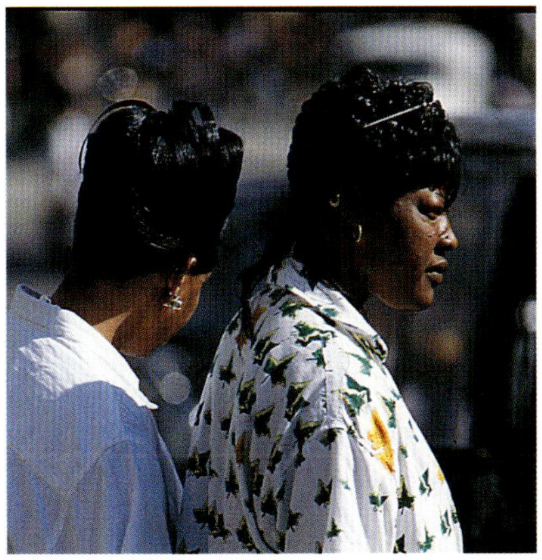

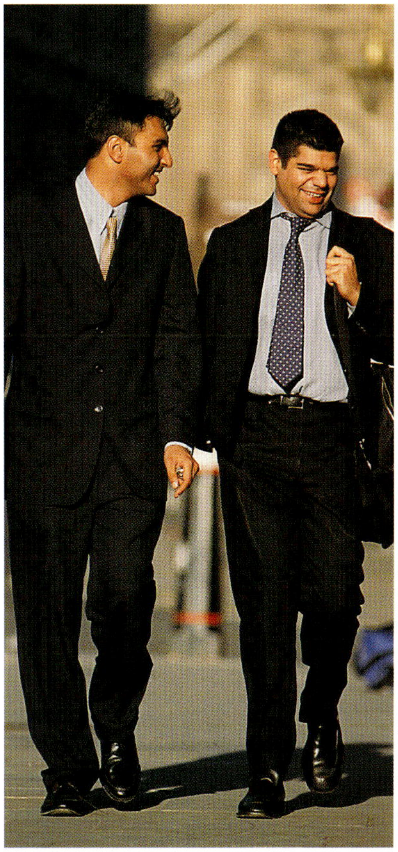

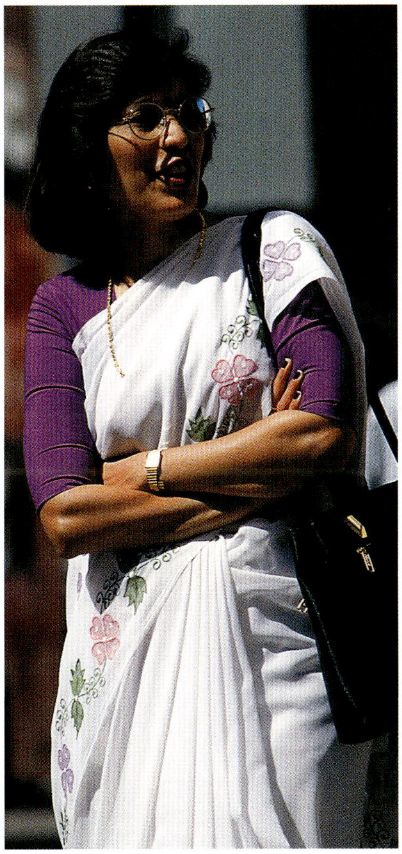

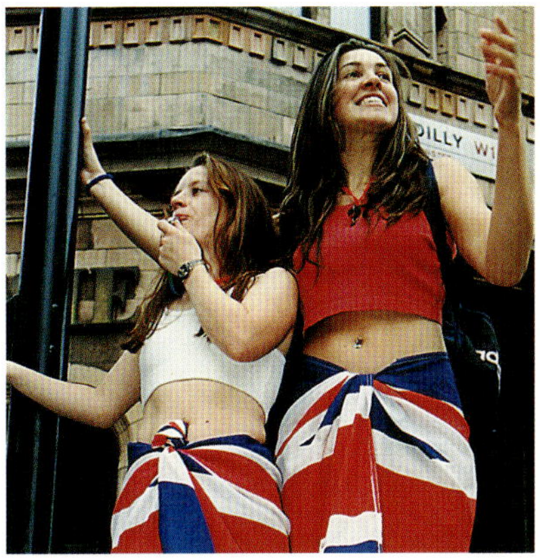

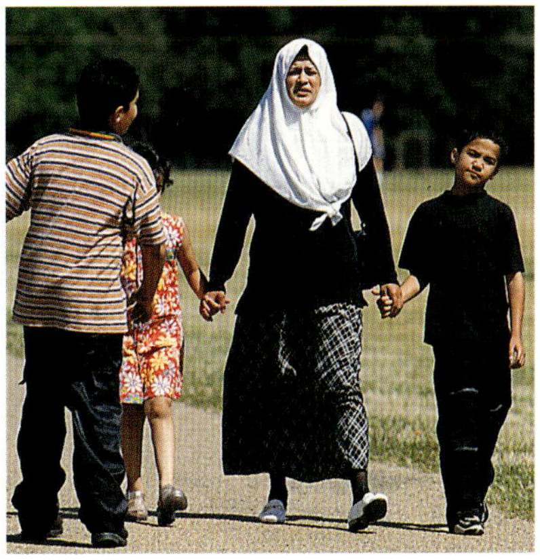

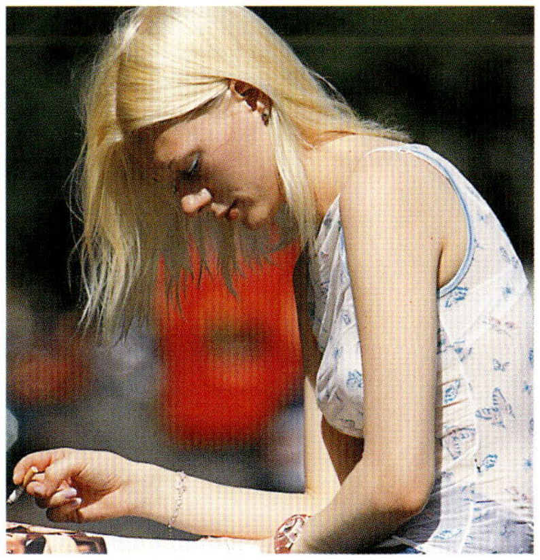

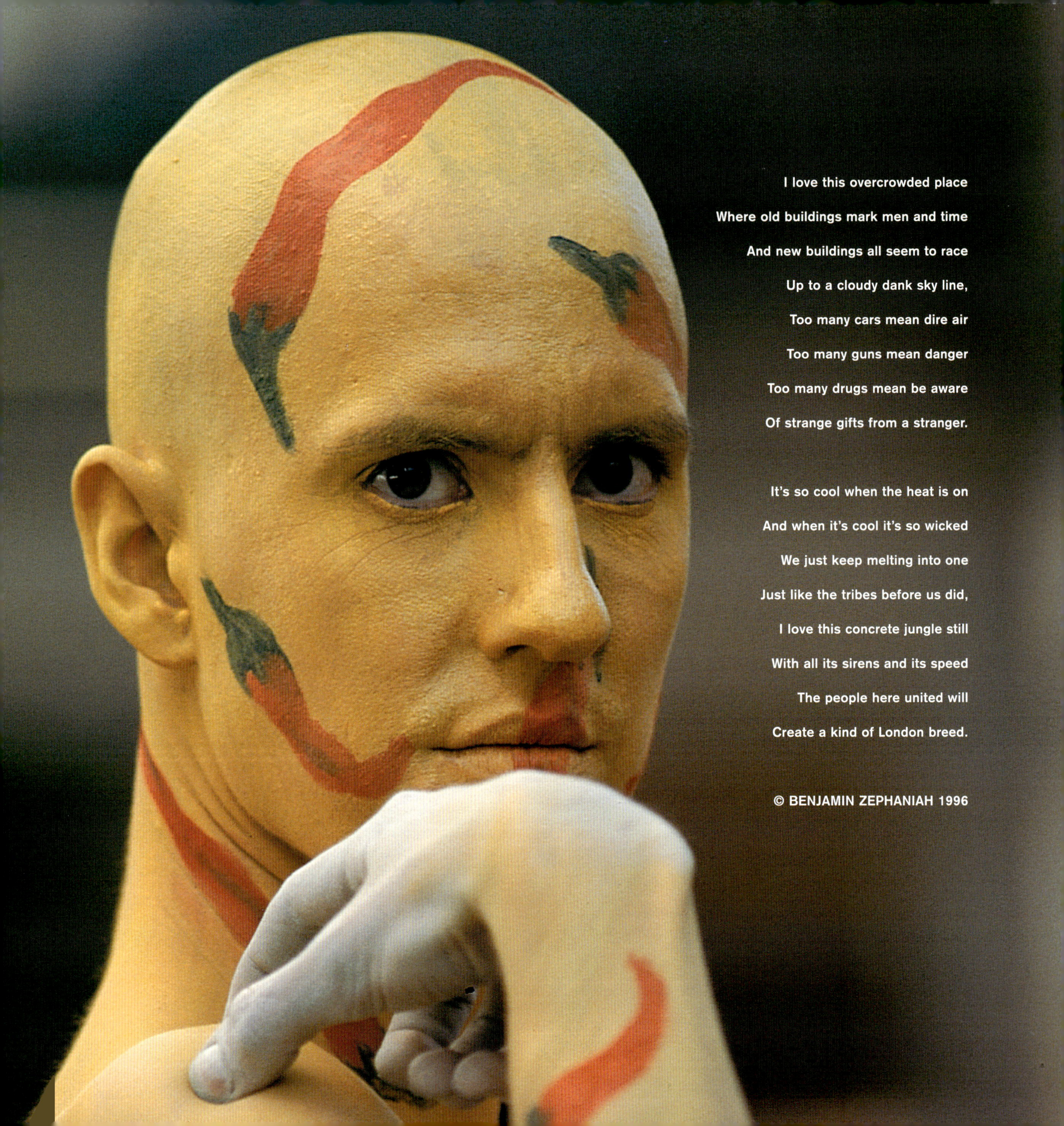

I love this overcrowded place
Where old buildings mark men and time
And new buildings all seem to race
Up to a cloudy dank sky line,
Too many cars mean dire air
Too many guns mean danger
Too many drugs mean be aware
Of strange gifts from a stranger.

It's so cool when the heat is on
And when it's cool it's so wicked
We just keep melting into one
Just like the tribes before us did,
I love this concrete jungle still
With all its sirens and its speed
The people here united will
Create a kind of London breed.

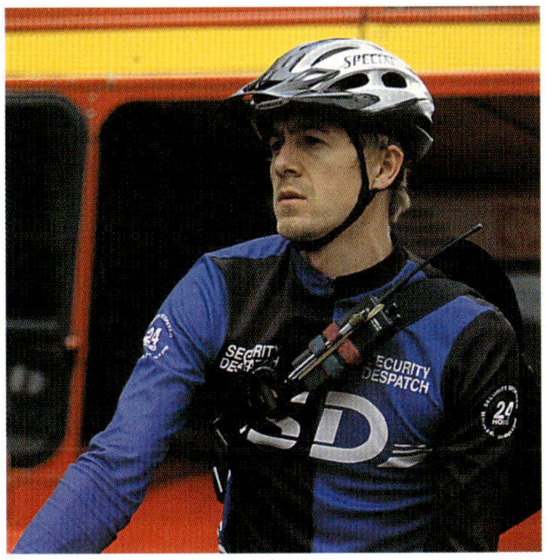
SECURITY DESPATCH

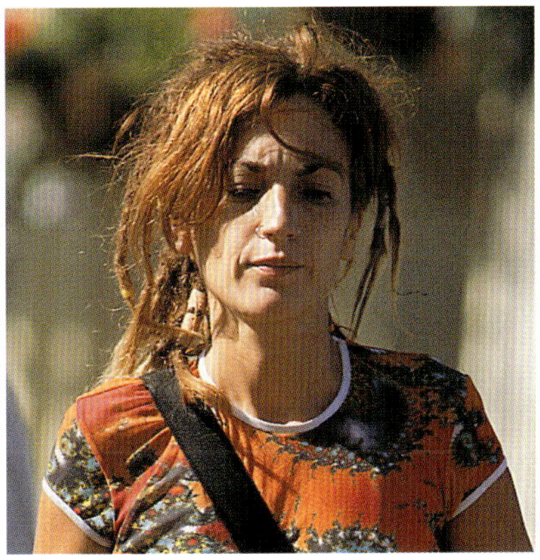

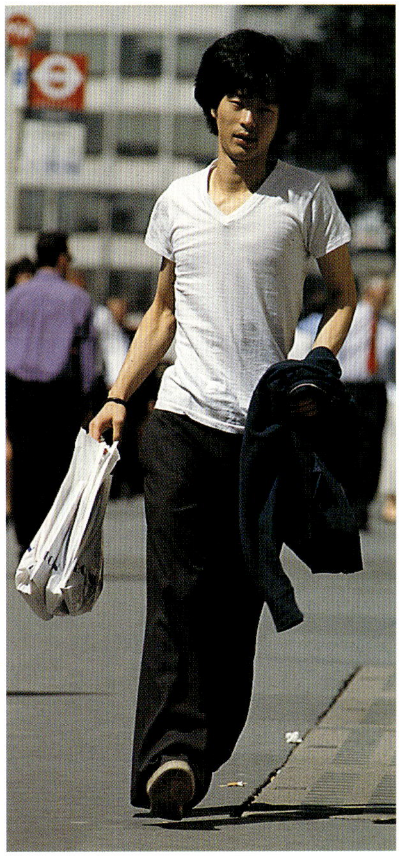

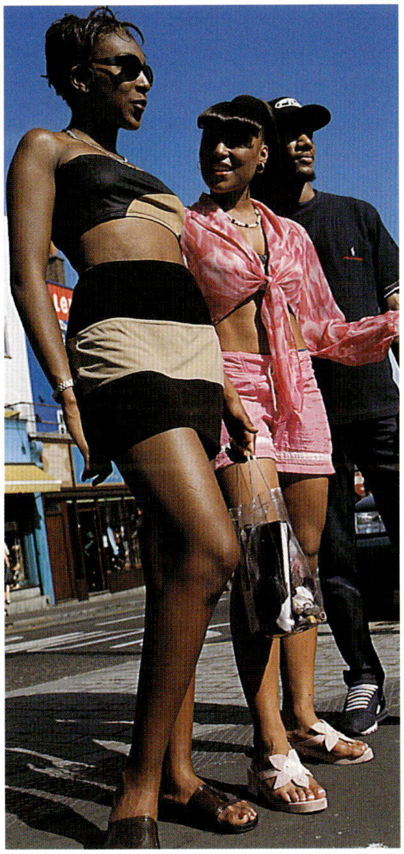

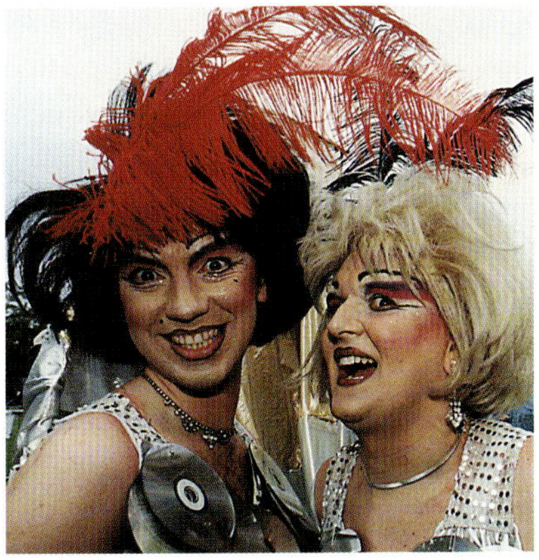

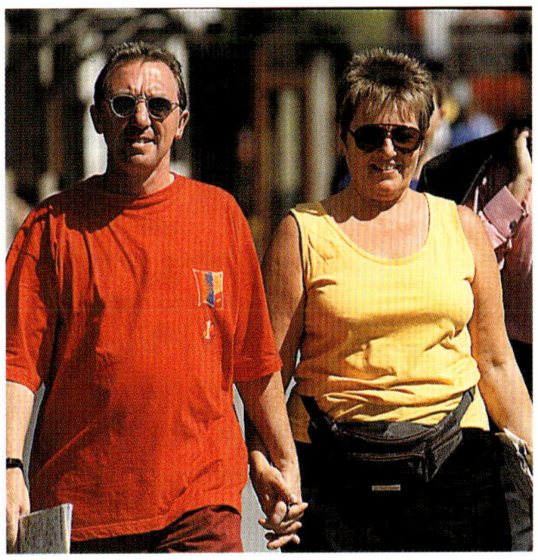

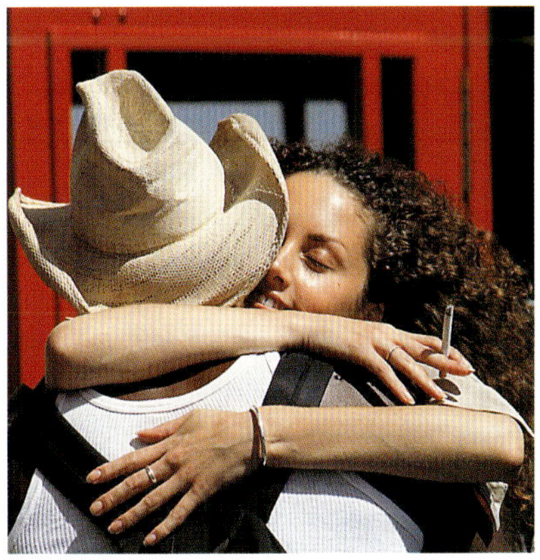

Medieval Bodies: famine and pestilence: the calamitous fourteenth century

CAMPBELL, B. M. S.,GALLOWAY, J. A., KEENE, D. and MURPHY, M. *A Medieval Capital and its Grain Supply: agrarian production and distribution in the London region c.1300*, Institute of British Geographers, Historical Geography Research Series 30, 1993

DYER, C. *Standards of Living in the Later Middle Ages*, Cambridge University Press, 1989

HAWKINS, D 'The Black Death and the new London Cemeteries of 1348', *Antiquity* 64, 637–42, 1990

JORDAN, W. C. *The Great Famine: Northern Europe in the early fourteenth century*, Princeton University Press, 1996

PLATT, C. *King Death: the Black Death and its aftermath in late-medieval England*, UCL Press, 1996

THOMAS, C., SLOANE, B. and PHILLPOTS, C. *Excavations at the Priory and Hospital of St Mary Spital,* London, Museum of London, MoLAS Monograph 1, 1997

WARWICK, R. 'Anne Mowbray: skeletal remains of a Medieval child', *London Archaeology* 5:7, 176–79, 1986

WHITE, W. J. *Skeletal Remains from the Cemetery of St Nicholas Shambles, City of London*, London Middlesex Archaeol Soc Spec Pap 9, 1988

ZIEGLER, P. *The Black Death*, Collins, 1969

Tailored Bodies: Medieval and Tudor clothing

ARNOLD, J. *Patterns of Fashion: the cut and construction of clothes for men and women c. 1560–1620*, Macmillan, 1985

ASSHELFORD, J. *A Visual History of Costume: the sixteenth century*, Batsford, 1983

CROWFOOT, E., PRITCHARD, F. and STANILAND, K. *Medieval Finds from Excavations in London: 4 Textiles and clothing c.1150–c.1450*, HMSO, 1992

CUNNINGTON, C. W. and CUNNINGTON, P. *Handbook of English Costume in the Sixteenth Century*, Faber, 1954

EGAN, G. and PRITCHARD, F. *Medieval Finds from Excavations in London: 3 Dress accessories*, HMSO, 1991

GREW, F. and DE NEERGAARD, M. *Medieval Finds from Excavations in London: 2 Shoes and pattens*, HMSO, 1988

STANILAND, K. 'Getting there, got it: archaeological textiles and tailoring in London, 1330–1580', in D. Gainster and P. Stamper (eds), *The Age of Transition: the archaeology of English culture 1400–1600*, Society for Medieval Archaeology Monograph 15, 1997

Georgian and Victorian Bodies: a London look?

ADAMS, Samuel and ADAMS, Sarah *The Complete Servant*, Southover, 1825 (reprinted 1989)

BRICKLEY, M. and STAINER, H. *The Human Bone from Redcross Way*, forthcoming

CAPLIN, R. A. *Health and Beauty or Corsets and Clothing Constructed in Accordance with the Physiological Laws of the Human Body*, London Darton & Co., 1856

CHAMPION, J. A. I., ed. *Epidemics in London*, London Centre for Metropolitan History, 1993

CHAMPION, J. A. I. *London's Dreaded Visitation, the Social Geography of the Great Plague of 1665*, Centre for Metropolitan History, 1995

CONHEENEY, J. and MILES, A. *Excavations at St Brides Lower Churchyard*, forthcoming

COX, M. *Life and Death in Spialfields 1700 to 1850*, Council for British Archaeology, York, 1996.

CUNNINGTON, C. W. and CUNNINGTON, P. *Handbook of English Costume in the 19th Century*, Faber, 1957

CUNNINGTON, C. W. and CUNNINGTON, P. *Handbook of English Costume in the 18th Century*, rev. ed., Faber, 1972

FORREST, D.W. *Francis Galton: the life and work of a Victorian genius*, Paul Elek, 1974

GALTON, Sir F. *Essays in Eugenics*, London: The Eugenics Education Society, 1909

GEORGE, M. D. *London Life in the 18th Century*, Penguin, 1976

The Habits of Good Society: a handbook of etiquette for ladies and gentlemen, London James Hogg & Sons, 1859

HOGG, J. *London as it is; being a series of observations on the health, habits and amusements of the people*, Mitcham, 1837

HUDSON, D. *Munby, Man of Two Worlds: the life and diaries of Arthur J. Munby 1828–1910*, John Murray, 1972

LANDERS, J. *Death and the Metropolis: studies in the demographic history of London 1670–1830*, Cambridge University Press, 1993

LONDON, J. *The People of the Abyss*, Macmillan, 1903

MAYHEW, H. *London Characters 1874*, London Chatto & Windus, 1881

MAYHEW, H. *London Labour and the London Poor*, 4 vols, London, 1861–2

MOLLESON, T. and COX, M. *The Spitalfields Project Vol 2 – the anthropology; the middling sort*, CBA, 1993

MORITZ, C.P. *Travels in England in 1782* (ed. Henry Morley), London: Cassell & Co., 1886

SIMON, Dr J. (later Sir John) *Reports by the City of London Medical Officer of Health 1850–60*

STEVENS, G. A. *The Adventures of a Speculist*, London: S. Bladon, 1788

Summary: London Bodies over time

Bardsley, M. and Hamm, J. *London's Health – Key facts and Figures,* Health of Londoners Project, 1995

Bardsley, M. and Morgan, D. *Deprivation and health in London – an overview of Health variations within the Capital*, Health of Londoners Project, 1996

INDEX

Page numbers in **bold** indicate illustrations.